Living History

PRINCETON ■ LONDON

www.two-canpublishing.com

Published in the United States and Canada by
Two-Can Publishing LLC
234 Nassau Street, Princeton, NJ 08542

**For information on Two-Can books and multimedia, call 1-609-921-6700, fax 1-609-921-3349,
or visit our Web site at http://www.two-canpublishing.com**

OLD JAPAN

Authors: Andrew Haslam & Clare Doran; Consultant: Heidi Potter BA; Managing Editor: Christine Morley; Editor: Jacqueline McCann; Senior Designer: Helen McDonagh; Art Director: Jill Plank; Deputy Art Director: Carole Orbell; Research: Deborah Kespert; Picture Researcher: Dipika Palmer-Jenkins ; U.S. Editor: Sharon Nowakowski; Model-makers: Corina Holzherr, Paul Holzherr, Melanie Williams; Thanks to Tim at Westpoint Studio and Peter Davies; Models: Robert Blankson, Lester Cotier, Catherine Dawes, Anteneh Elcock, Matthew Guest, Amy Kwan, Ana Ivanovic, Charlotte Walters, Miki Zoric.

ANCIENT EGYPTIANS

Authors: Andrew Haslam; Consultant: George Hart BA MPhil, The British Museum, London; Editor: Kate Graham; Assistant editor: Jacqueline McCann; Design: Helen McDonagh; Assistant model-maker: Sarah Davies; Special thanks to: Melissa Tucker, World Book Publishing

THE ROMAN EMPIRE

Author: Peter Chrisp; Consultant: Simon James BSc PhD, British Museum, London; Editor: Jacqueline McCann; Art direction and design: Helen McDonagh; Managing Editor: Christine Morley; Commissioned photography: Jon Barnes; Additional photography: John Englefield and Ray Moller; Picture Research: Lyndsey Price; Production: Joya Bart-Plange; Model-maker: Melanie Williams; Additional model-makers: Peter Griffiths, Corina Holzherr, Paul Holzherr; US editor: Melissa Tucker, World Book Publishing

NATIVE AMERICANS

Author: Andrew Haslam; Consultant: Anne Armitage BA, The American Museum in Britain; Editor: Lucy Duke; Design: Helen McDonagh; Assistant model-maker: Sarah Davies; Special thanks to: Sharon Nowakowski, World Book Publishing

J 909
LIV

Hardback ISBN 1–58728–3816
1 2 3 4 5 6 7 8 9 10 02 01

Photographic credits: Ancient Art & Architecture Collection: p6 (bl), p43, p56; Chris Uhlenbeck: p11, p19, p35, p36; Helen McDonagh: map p10; The Hulton-Deutsch Collection: p16; Japan Archive: p59; Japan National Tourist Office: p62; JICC: p30; Michael Holford: p14, p29; Robert Harding Picture Library: p6 (tr); Tony Stone Worldwide: p48; Victoria & Albert Museum: p42, p52; Werner Forman Archive: p28; Zefa Photo Library: p22, p26, p36, p40, p44, p60, p63. All other photographs on pp6–63 by Ray Moller. British Museum: p66 (tr), p74, p77, p85 (tr), p86, p90, p93, p98, p102, p103, p112 (bl), p113, p117, p120 (r); Greg Evans International: p118, p120 (tl); Griffiths Institute: p73, p76, p99 (tr), p108, p122, p123; G.S.F. Picture Library: p101 (mr); Image Bank: p67 (tr); Mel Pickering: p66 (map); Metropolitan Museum of Art: p114 (l); Rex Features: p71; Robert Harding: p85 (br) p99 (tl), p106, p112 (tl), p116, p120 (bl), RH/British Museum: p110; Science Photo Library: p101 (bl); Werner Forman Archive: p97; WFA/University College London, Petrie Museum: p72; WFA/British Museum: p67 (bl), p80, p109, WFA/E Strouhal: p100; WFA/Egyptian Museum, Turin: p104; WFA/Egyptian Museum, Cairo: p114 (r). All other photographs on pp66–123 by Jon Barnes. AKG London/Erich Lessing: p160, p173, p181; Ancient Art & Architecture Collection: p171; British Museum: p164; BM/The Bridgeman Art Library: p182; C M Dixon: p134, p147, p166; Elsevier Archive/Atlas of the Roman World: p138; Michael Holford: p141, p150, p154, p158, p162, p170; Peter Clayton: p172; Planet Earth Pictures: p126 (tr); Scala: p126 (bl), p146; Tony Stone/Jean Pragan: p182; Zefa: p168. With thanks to the models on pp126–183: Sarah Abbott, Nadine Case, Francesca Collins, Tracy Ann Francis, Sammie-Jo Gold, Matthew Harper, Aaron Haseley, Amanda Kwakye, Dean Newell, Jonathan Page, Davina Plummer, Robin Richards, Sean Richardson, James Sayle, Jamie White, Daniel Wright, Jia Jia Wang and Ali Issaq, and to Wixs Lane School, London. Eric and David Hosking: p186 (ml); Peter Newark's Western Americana: p190 (tr), p206 (tr), p227 (tl), p242 (t); Smithsonian Institution, Museum of American History: p192 (tr), p198 (tr), p209 (tr), p212 (tr), p214 (tr), p216 (tr), p225 (tr), p228 (tl), p236 (tr); Denver Art Museum: p200 (tr); Robert Harding: p243 (br); Phoebe A. Hurst Museum of Anthropology, University of California at Berkeley: p208 (bl); American Museum of Natural History, courtesy Department of Library Services: p217 (tl), p238 (bl); Range Pictures Ltd.: p186 (tr), p187 (bl, tr & br), p243 (tl); Zefa: p221 (tr); Mel Pickering: p242 (map) (bl). All other photographs on pp186–243 by Jon Barnes.

Printed in Hong Kong by Wing King Tong

Contents

Words marked in **bold** in the text can be found in the glossary.

OLD JAPAN

Studying Japan's Past

All human beings need food and shelter to survive. They also need a system of beliefs to give shape and meaning to their lives. Throughout history, people have found different ways of meeting these basic needs. By studying the people of Japan, we learn how they developed a way of life that has sustained them, physically and spiritually.

IN THIS BOOK, we look at four different periods of Japanese history, each one telling us something new about the Japanese way of life and character. We know how people lived during these times through the writings and paintings that were made then and from the work of **historians**.

Each period is represented by a symbol that is used when information refers mainly to that time. Where there is no symbol, it means that the information generally applies to all four periods.

KEY FOR SYMBOLS

🪭 (fan) Heian 790–1185

⚔ (swords) Kamakura 1185–1333

🍵 (tea bowl) Muromachi and Momoyama 1392–1600

🐸 (woodcut) Edo 1600–1868

🪭 *Studying old texts, such as* The Tale of Genji, *written in 1010, can help us understand life at that time.*

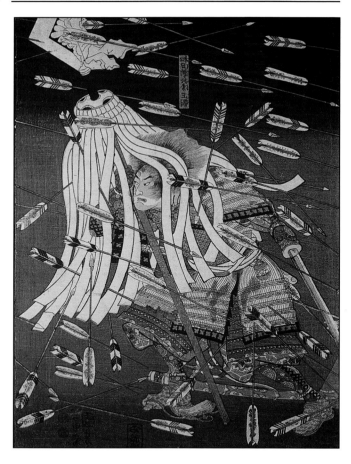

⚔ *This print,* Last Stand of the Kusunoki Clan, *shows a **samurai** warrior in battle dress.*

🪭 **THE HEIAN PERIOD** lasted from about 790 to 1185, and it is called Heian after the city where the emperor lived. This was a time when power was centered around the court. Landowners were very wealthy, but the rest of society was poor. During this time, Japanese artists and writers began to throw off the influences of China and find their own identity.

⚔ **THE KAMAKURA PERIOD** lasted from about 1185 to 1333. The court at Heian lost its power to the powerful Minamoto **clan**. The leader of the clan, Yoritomo, established himself as the ruler, or supreme **shogun**, of Japan in 1192. A military government called a ***bakufu*** was set up. Although the emperor kept his court in Kyoto, he had no real **political** power. Yoritomo chose Kamakura as his base because his supporters were mainly warriors of the eastern regions.

THE MUROMACHI AND MOMOYAMA periods lasted from 1392 to 1600. The Kamakura era had ended in confusion, with two emperors and two separate courts. For the next 30 years, the two courts were at war. Eventually, the third shogun of the Muromachi *bakufu*, Yoshimitsu, brought the two courts together and political power was centered in Kyoto. However, the *bakufu* was weak, and from 1467 there was a long period of war and unrest. Eventually, Japan was reunified under Toyotomi Hideyoshi. One of the most important cultural features of this time was the rise of **Zen Buddhism** (see page 60).

THE EDO PERIOD began in 1600 and lasted until the beginning of the modern age in 1868. It was named after the city now called Tokyo, where the supreme shogun Tokugawa Ieyasu established himself in 1603. It was a time during which Japan isolated itself from the rest of the world, banning foreigners from entering and stopping the Japanese from traveling abroad.

THE MAKE IT WORK! way of looking at history is to ask questions of the past and discover some of the answers by making replicas of the things people made. However, you do not have to make everything in the book to understand the Japanese way of life.

⏝ *This Zen "gravel" garden is like a Japanese landscape in miniature.*

Japan's isolation came about because the ruling classes feared invasion by other countries and the spread of the Christian religion, which would unsettle Japan's **class structure** (see page 12). It was a period known as "the great peace." Popular arts and crafts flourished, particularly the theater, and people were taught to read and write.

🐸 *A samurai wife wears a fashionable **kimono** of the Edo period.*

Timeline

For many centuries, Japan was made up of groups of small, independent clans whose chieftains were always at war with each other. In 660 B.C., according to legend, a chieftain called Jimmu defeated the other clans and set up his capital on Honshu island. Jimmu was believed to be a descendant of the sun goddess and became the first emperor of Japan.

IT TOOK MANY CENTURIES before Japan became anything like a unified country. In A.D. 710, the city of Nara became Japan's capital (the capital was sited wherever the ruler had his palace and was usually abandoned after his death). But it was decided that Nara had been built in an unlucky place, so the capital was moved to Heian-kyo in 794. Heian, later known as Kyoto, became the home of the Japanese emperors for over a thousand years. Today, Kyoto is still a strong center for the arts.

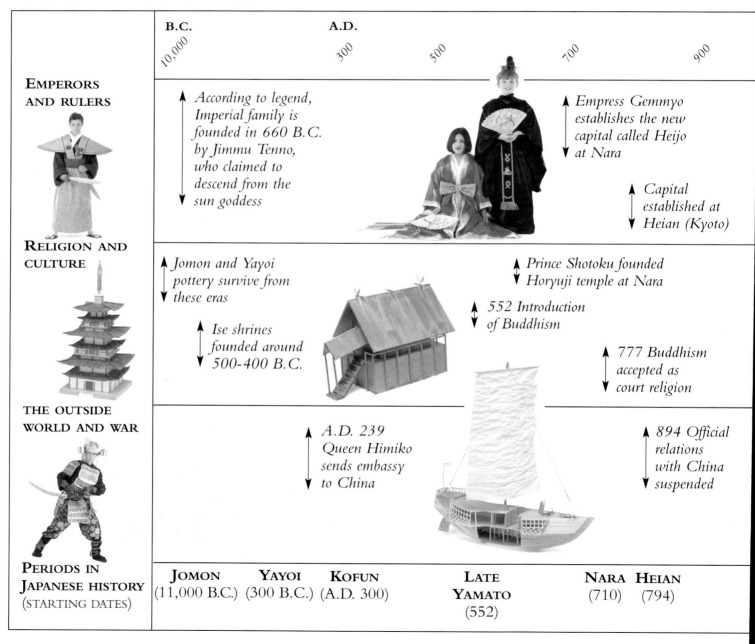

| | B.C. | A.D. | | | |
	10,000	300	500	700	900
EMPERORS AND RULERS	According to legend, Imperial family is founded in 660 B.C. by Jimmu Tenno, who claimed to descend from the sun goddess			Empress Gemmyo establishes the new capital called Heijo at Nara — Capital established at Heian (Kyoto)	
RELIGION AND CULTURE	Jomon and Yayoi pottery survive from these eras — Ise shrines founded around 500-400 B.C.		552 Introduction of Buddhism	Prince Shotoku founded Horyuji temple at Nara — 777 Buddhism accepted as court religion	
THE OUTSIDE WORLD AND WAR		A.D. 239 Queen Himiko sends embassy to China		894 Official relations with China suspended	
PERIODS IN JAPANESE HISTORY (STARTING DATES)	JOMON (11,000 B.C.)	YAYOI (300 B.C.)	KOFUN (A.D. 300)	LATE YAMATO (552)	NARA (710) HEIAN (794)

THERE WERE LONG STRETCHES of Japanese history when real power was not in the hands of the emperor. From 1190, power passed to the military rulers of Japan, known as the shoguns, and this heralded the age of the samurai warrior. Finally, after centuries of war, three warrior leaders emerged who brought peace to Japan. In 1603, Tokugawa Ieyasu was appointed shogun. His capital, Edo, was one of the largest cities in the world at that time, and his family's rule continued for 14 generations, until 1868.

MODERN TIMES in Japan date from July 1853, when four American warships asked for the right of entry to Tokyo Bay so that trading could take place between Japan and America. Until this time, Japan's rulers had turned down trading requests from foreign governments because they feared invasion and the influence of Christianity. But Japan could no longer survive alone, and entry was granted to the U.S. ships. The emperor was restored to power, and the country's first **general election** was held in 1890.

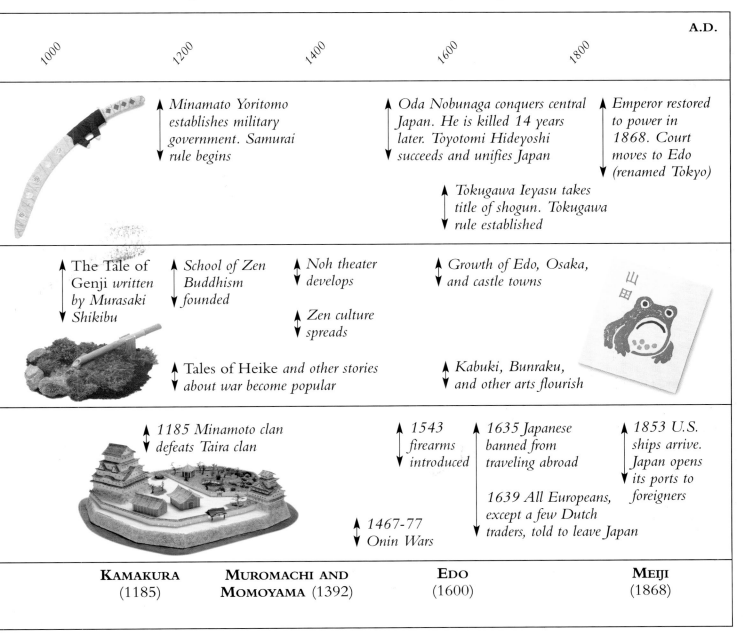

A.D.

1000   *1200*   *1400*   *1600*   *1800*

Minamato Yoritomo establishes military government. Samurai rule begins

Oda Nobunaga conquers central Japan. He is killed 14 years later. Toyotomi Hideyoshi succeeds and unifies Japan

Emperor restored to power in 1868. Court moves to Edo (renamed Tokyo)

Tokugawa Ieyasu takes title of shogun. Tokugawa rule established

The Tale of Genji *written by Murasaki Shikibu*

School of Zen Buddhism founded

Noh theater develops

Zen culture spreads

Growth of Edo, Osaka, and castle towns

Tales of Heike *and other stories about war become popular*

Kabuki, Bunraku, and other arts flourish

1185 Minamoto clan defeats Taira clan

1543 firearms introduced

1635 Japanese banned from traveling abroad

1639 All Europeans, except a few Dutch traders, told to leave Japan

1853 U.S. ships arrive. Japan opens its ports to foreigners

1467-77 Onin Wars

| **KAMAKURA** (1185) | **MUROMACHI AND MOMOYAMA** (1392) | **EDO** (1600) | **MEIJI** (1868) |

A Land of Contrasts

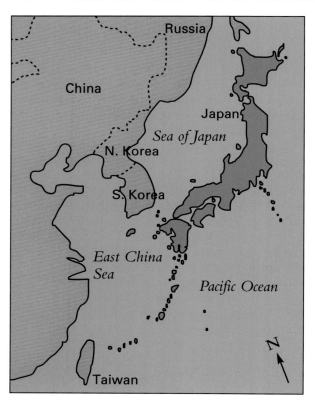

Japan is made up of around 3,900 islands that were once part of the mainland of Asia. They broke off gradually during the last ice age, about 12,000 years ago. There is **archaeological** and **anthropological** evidence that mainland peoples from China and Korea, and Pacific Islanders from the south, continued to migrate to the islands of Japan over thousands of years.

THE FOUR MAIN ISLANDS OF JAPAN – Hokkaido, Honshu, Shikoku, and Kyushu – are heavily forested, with spectacular, sometimes impassable mountains (many of them volcanic), fast-flowing rivers, and fertile plains. Isolated families, or clans, grew up in remote, sheltered valleys. Their **Shinto** religion (see page 58) sprang from their respect for the forces of nature.

◁ *Japan's islands stretch across 2,400 miles, from the cool north to the semitropical islands of Okinawa in the south. Its neighbors are North and South Korea, China, and Russia.*

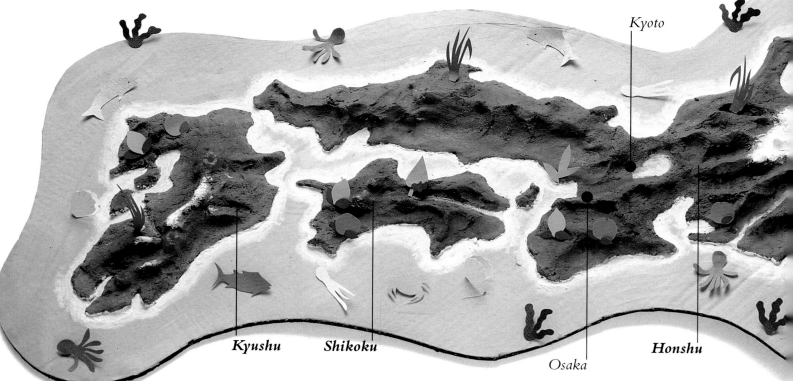

△ *This map shows a few of the crops that are grown on Japan's four main islands and the types of fish that are found in the coastal waters.*

WITH SO MANY MOUNTAINS AND FORESTS, Japan has little grazing land for animals. Rice, fish, and vegetables are the main foods.

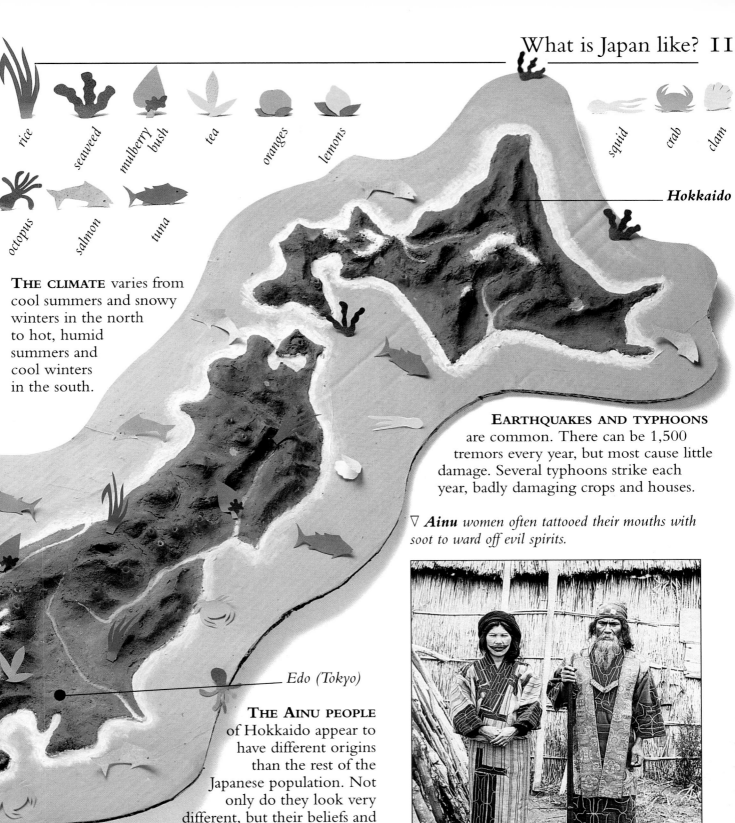

rice

seaweed

mulberry bush

tea

oranges

lemons

squid

crab

clam

octopus

salmon

tuna

Hokkaido

THE CLIMATE varies from cool summers and snowy winters in the north to hot, humid summers and cool winters in the south.

EARTHQUAKES AND TYPHOONS are common. There can be 1,500 tremors every year, but most cause little damage. Several typhoons strike each year, badly damaging crops and houses.

▽ *Ainu women often tattooed their mouths with soot to ward off evil spirits.*

Edo (Tokyo)

THE AINU PEOPLE of Hokkaido appear to have different origins than the rest of the Japanese population. Not only do they look very different, but their beliefs and language are not the same as the majority. The Ainu were driven out of Honshu, where they had settled to Hokkaido. Some experts think the Ainu may have come to Japan from Siberia thousands of years ago, but no one is sure. Very few of the Ainu remain today.

Layers of Wealth and Status

THE CLOTHES worn by Japanese people through history can tell us a lot about society at different times. For example, in the Heian period, nobles had the time and money to worry about the smallest details of their clothing. Their clothes were designed to look good – often at the expense of comfort. For people who worked outdoors, such as farmers, clothes had to be practical, inexpensive, and durable. By the Edo period, wealthy townspeople enjoyed dressing in the latest fashions. The **shogunate** authorities were worried by displays of wealth and made rules to make sure everyone dressed according to their class in **society**.

straw cloak

straw sandals

farmer's wife

farmer in winter dress

CRAFTSMEN were ranked below farmers but above merchants, because they made things that were useful, such as samurai swords or cooking pots.

headband

short kimono, called a happi coat

craftsman

FARMERS were valued in society because they paid taxes to the *daimyo* in the form of rice and, occasionally, money. Some farmers owned land and were rich, but most were poor workers. Although clothes varied from region to region, farmers usually wore short jackets and trousers made from cotton or hemp. In hot weather, they just wore loincloths – strips of material that went around their hips and between their legs. Women would keep cool by loosening their clothing a little.

🐸 **MERCHANTS** were generally despised by the authorities, because they did not actually make anything, but made money by buying and selling the work of others. However, during the Edo period, some grew increasingly wealthy and powerful, while the samurai lost their influence. The authorities tried to stop the merchants from showing off their wealth, by telling them not to wear expensive silks. The merchants got around this rule by lining their cotton robes with silk.

samurai's wife

layers of silk kimonos

wide sash, called an obi

over-jacket, or kataginu, with family crest

kimono

simple, cotton kimono

wooden shoes, called geta

divided trousers, called hakama

toe socks, called tabi

samurai

silk lining

🐸 **THE SAMURAI** were the highest class in society. They were the only people allowed to carry two swords. They had two types of dress: everyday and ceremonial, shown above.

🐸 **WIVES** of high-ranking samurai put on layers of silk kimonos, with the lighter colors worn underneath. Small, overall patterns were fashionable, as were padded hems that dragged on the floor.

merchant

THE BASIC JAPANESE garment for both men and women was a loose-fitting coat with a tie belt. It is called a kimono, a word that means "the thing worn" and can be used to describe anything from a short smock to the most elaborate gown. Kimonos probably originated in ancient China, and styles and accessories varied through the centuries, according to fashion, the sex, and marital status of the wearer. In general, ordinary people wore simple, practical clothes, increasing the layers according to the season. The ruling classes wore multilayered, fashionable robes to reflect their status in society.

IN THE HEIAN PERIOD, people wore a garment called a *kosode*, a plain T-shaped wrap with short sleeves, with a pair of wide, baggy trousers called *hakama* underneath many layers of dress. Over the years, dress became much simpler with fewer layers and eventually the *kosode* became known as the *kimono*.

△ *Ivory or wooden toggles, called netsuke, were used to anchor small items kept in the waist sash of a kimono. This ivory netsuke is a carving of Hotei, the god of luck.*

MAKE A KIMONO

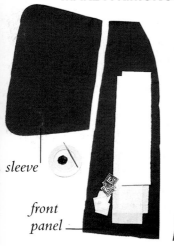

back panel

neckband

folded sleeve

sleeve

front panel

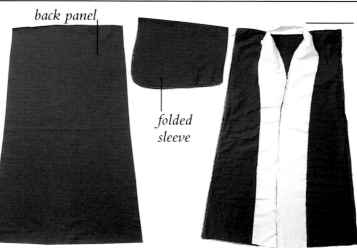

You will need: dark blue fabric, white fabric, needle, thread, glue, black fabric paint, straight pins, chalk

1 To make the back panel, lie down on the blue fabric. Ask a friend to draw a rectangle around you with the chalk. The rectangle should flare out slightly at the bottom, as shown. Cut out the shape carefully.

2 Cut out two front panels as shown. They should be the same length as the back panel and half its width. They should curve slightly at the top.

3 Lay the back of the kimono flat on the floor, right side up. Place the front panels on top, right side down, lining up the top and side edges. Sew front and back panels together along the top and the sides. Leave a gap on each side for the sleeves.

4 Cut out two large sleeve shapes as shown. Fold the sleeves in half so that the curved edges meet at the bottom. Sew the bottom edge and along the curved edge. Leave a gap for your hand to go through.

5 Cut a strip of white material for the neckband, 5 inches wide and long enough to fit along the front edges and neck of the kimono.

△ *To make a girl's waist sash, an obi, paint a plain piece of material and wrap it around your kimono twice.*

KIMONOS were carefully picked to match the season or even a particular festival. A plain, elegant style, for example, might be worn for a ceremonial occasion. Artists of the Edo period made woodblock prints showing the latest kimono designs. Ordinary people bought prints to pick up hints on what was fashionable. Kimonos could be worth a lot of money and were an important part of a woman's dowry when she married.

NOBLEWOMEN wore many layers of beautiful silks. On top of red *hakama*, they put on different-colored robes with long sleeves. When they went out in their carriages, they left one sleeve dangling outside, so that everyone who saw them would admire their good taste. For court duties and weddings, from 15 to 40 robes were worn (the larger people were, the wealthier they were thought to be). In the 1100's, the number of robes worn at one time was reduced to five.

◁ *Nobles often had their family crest embroidered on their clothes.*

family crest, called a mon

obi

kimono

6 Overlap the edge of the neckband about 1 inch with the edge of the front panels as shown above left. Pin in place, then sew, keeping your line of stitching about ³/₄ inch from the edge.

7 Turn the sleeves right side out. Slip under the front panels as shown, and sew in place, leaving a gap underneath each arm.

8 Turn the kimono right side out. Now fold over the neckband and sew to the front panels, turning the raw edge under as you go. Hem.

9 To make the family crests, called *mon*, cut squares of white material and paint on symbols. When the paint is dry, sew or glue the squares onto the kimono.

MAKEUP was also a way of showing how important people were. Both men and women whitened their faces, because it distinguished them from tanned and weatherbeaten workers and because a pale face was considered very beautiful. They patted their faces with small cotton bags filled with rice powder, moistened with perfumed water. They also used white lead, and there were many cases of people being poisoned because lead is highly toxic.

THE TYPE OF HAT, or *kammuri*, a man wore was one way to tell what rank he held. The *kammuri* was made of a silk fabric that was **lacquered** and made to look stiff. High-ranking people wore dark or pale violet *kammuri*, while ordinary nobles wore black (see page 25).

WOMEN'S HAIR was considered beautiful if it was long, thick, and shining – like the wing of a raven. Sometimes a woman wore a wig if her real hair did not match this ideal. In the Heian and Kamakura periods, women kept their hair loose, but in other eras it was fashionable to pin it up.

△ *Samurai warriors shaved the tops of their heads, then gathered the hair at the sides and back into a ponytail, which they doubled over and tied tightly.*

MEN'S HAIRSTYLES were another mark of rank. Ordinary workers wore their hair short, while noblemen wore their hair in a topknot. Up until the Edo period, nobles grew mustaches and beards, but samurai kept their faces free of hair. Monks plucked their faces and shaved their heads.

MAKE A PAIR OF JAPANESE SHOES (GETA)

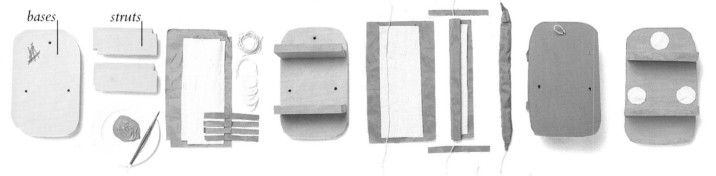

bases   *struts*

You will need: two pieces of wood, $1/2$" thick and slightly longer and wider than your foot; four blocks of wood $1/2$" thick, 2" deep, and as wide as the base; hand drill; strong nails; hammer; paintbrush; paint; string; shiny fabric; cotton fabric; glue; heavy-duty tape

1 Ask an adult to help cut the wooden base of the shoes so the corners are rounded.

2 Drill three holes in each base, as shown. Nail two struts to each base, one $1\frac{1}{2}$" from the top, the other $1\frac{1}{2}$" from bottom. Paint the shoes brown.

3 Cut two rectangles of shiny fabric as long as the shoe and 4" wide. Then cut two slightly smaller rectangles of cotton. Put the cotton on the shiny material and place string in the middle, as shown.

4 Now roll the material and the string to make two padded tubes, or thongs. Glue the edges. Then glue thin strips of material around the string at the ends of each thong.

5 Pass a string loop through the hole in the front of the shoe. Thread the thong through and knot the loop underneath. Pass the ends of the thong through the remaining holes, knot underneath, and secure with tape.

SAMURAI WARRIORS kept their hair neat and tightly tied. It could be very embarrassing if a samurai's hair came undone in battle. And it was considered a terrible disgrace if an opponent lopped off his ponytail.

If a samurai was feeling ill, he would not bother to shave his head. His hair might grow into a messy tangle, but he would be careful never to be seen in public looking like that.

▷ *Apart from haircombs and netsuke, Japanese women did not wear jewelry. Haircombs and pins were made of ivory, horn, wood, or metal and often painted.*

WOMEN reddened their lips with a spot of crushed flower-petal paste on the lower lip to make their mouths look smaller. They also plucked their eyebrows and painted black marks high on their foreheads with a paste of soot and glue. Natural eyebrows were thought to be vulgar, like "fat caterpillars" crawling on the face.

△ *Some hairstyles were very elaborate. To keep them in place, both sexes slept with their heads on padded, wooden headrests instead of pillows.*

The upper classes customarily blackened their teeth, a practice that spread to the other classes over the centuries. As the Japanese had very little calcium in their diet (no milk or cheese), adult teeth were often naturally blackened with decay. Black teeth, therefore, became a sign of maturity, and white teeth were thought to look as "naked as a skinned animal." Married women were the only people who did not blacken their teeth.

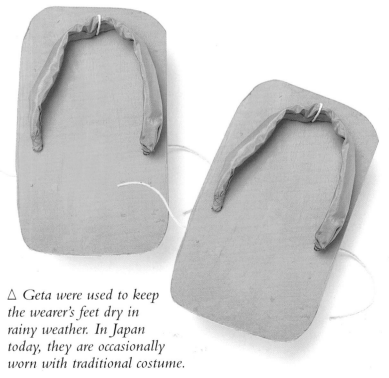

△ *Geta were used to keep the wearer's feet dry in rainy weather. In Japan today, they are occasionally worn with traditional costume.*

FOOTWEAR for ordinary people consisted of thong sandals made of straw. When it rained, they wore *geta,* simple wooden clogs, that kept their feet clear of the mud. Hunters and warriors wore shoes made of leather, and wealthy people wore lacquered wooden *geta* with high platforms and comfortably padded insides. Women who worked in the entertainment world, called **geisha**, wore *geta* so high they could not walk without the help of their servants. Sometimes two-toed, padded cotton socks, called *tabi,* were worn. The thong of the *geta* was slipped between the big toe and second toe.

Living with Nature

Whereas buildings in many parts of the world were built to provide a barrier between people and the outside world, Japanese homes were designed to blend with nature. Natural materials such as wood, bamboo, and paper were used as much for their beauty as their usefulness. Buildings were also made to be adaptable, to cope with the changing seasons.

A TYPICAL FARMHOUSE was a wooden building, one story high. The slope of the thatched roof was steep so that rain or snow would slide off it, and the eaves projected over a veranda so people could stay both cool and dry.

THE BEAMS that made up the wooden frame had interlocking joints. After a typhoon or earthquake, the owner could simply hammer any loose joints back into place.

wooden roof beam

raised living area with sunken hearth, called an irori

IN SILKMAKING DISTRICTS, farmhouses were built with a floor under the roof where silkworms were reared on beds of mulberry leaves. Although farmers made the silk, they were not allowed to use it. It was a fabric reserved for the nobility.

shoes

thatched straw roof

wooden ladder for roof repairs

△ *The kitchen was usually situated at ground level. It was full of utensils for cleaning, chopping, and cooking food.*

BEFORE MOVING INTO their new house, a family fixed charms to the roof to frighten away demons. Then, a sign with the owner's name on it was hung above the door to show that the family had moved in.

ALL THE VILLAGERS helped each other to build and repair their houses, under the guidance of the village carpenter. The main pillars were set in place (one **ken** apart, about the length of a man lying down) followed by the roof beams. The floorboards were laid on a raised framework, then the sunken hearth, or *irori*, was built. Once the roof was thatched and the outer walls filled in, the house was finished. The villagers held a celebratory feast, with the carpenter as guest of honor.

INTERIORS were very simple. People were more concerned with cleanliness than comfort. They removed their outdoor shoes before stepping onto the raised platform that was the living, eating, and sleeping area. A bucket or tub was conveniently placed at the entrance to wash muddy feet. For preparing food, people kept clean water in a wooden trough at the back of the house.

bucket filled with fresh water

frame for carrying loads

JAPANESE HOMES were designed to adapt to the seasons. In winter, blinds were kept shut and screens, paper walls, and wooden shutters helped to keep the cold out. In summer, these things were moved aside to allow in cooling breezes.

TOWN HOUSES for the merchant class were built close together in rows along the streets, with small gardens at the rear. The houses had features similar to the farmhouses, such as small rooms separated by sliding doors.

MOST ROOMS were used for most purposes. Screens and sliding paper walls could easily be moved and put somewhere else. If the family decided to have a party, for example, they could remove a paper wall to make the room larger.

SCREENS were used to block drafts and for privacy. Most people used screens made of wicker. But in a wealthy home, there might be several decorated screens of lacquered bamboo, sometimes framed with gold and encrusted with gems.

MAKE A PAPER SCREEN (SHOJI)

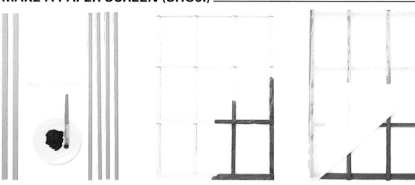

You will need: 24 cardboard strips, 23½" x ½"; 12 cardboard strips, 15¾" x ½"; strong tape; black paint; paintbrush; string; glue; scissors; white tissue paper, 24" x 16"

1 Tape each long strip to another strip of the same length to make 12 extra-thick strips. The screen is made of three panels. To make one panel, tape four short strips horizontally to four long vertical strips, as shown above.

2 Paint the panel black. When the paint is dry, spread glue on one side of the panel and lay the tissue paper over it, keeping it flat and smooth. When the glue is dry, trim the excess paper.

3 Make two more panels in this way. To join the panels, make a hole through the frame and paper at the top and bottom of the screens. Thread string through and tie the panels together, as shown below. Keep the strings loose, so the panels can be folded.

▽ *Interior of a late-Edo town house*

hanging scroll

alcove, called a tokonoma

THE BEST ROOM IN THE HOUSE had an alcove with a raised floor, called a *tokonoma*. This was used to display a piece of pottery or a flower arrangement. On the walls hung a picture or some calligraphy. Originally, a *tokonoma* was reserved for the samurai class, but by the Edo period, it was used by most people.

TATAMI are straw and rush mats made to standard sizes of one *ken* long and half a *ken* wide. Two *tatami* side by side form a square. This was used to calculate the size of a room.

COOKING EQUIPMENT included oil jars, cauldrons, trays, buckets, bowls, baskets, and boxes, as well as cleavers, a variety of sharp knives, mortars, and pestles. These were all stowed away neatly in wooden chests.

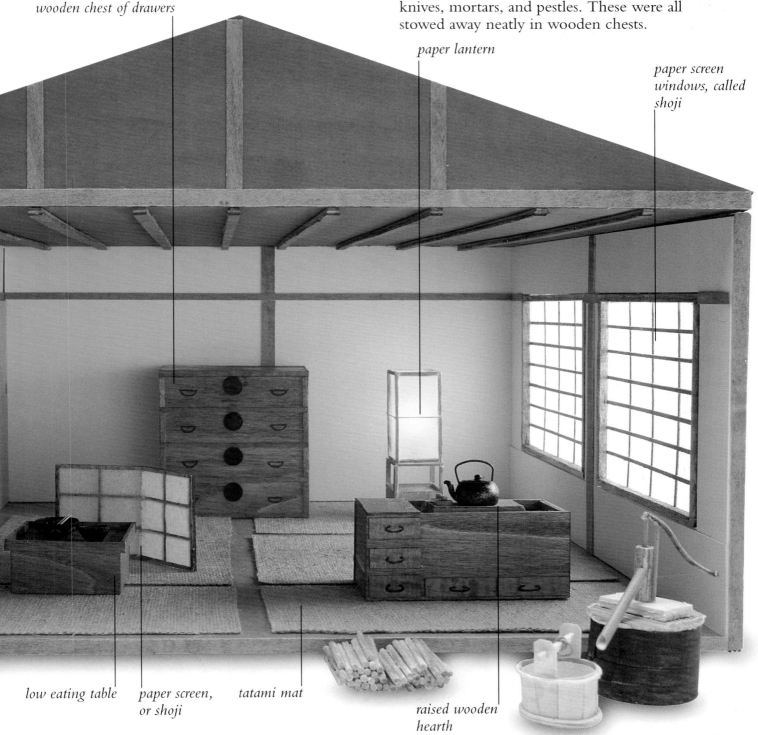

wooden chest of drawers

paper lantern

paper screen windows, called shoji

low eating table

paper screen, or shoji

tatami mat

raised wooden hearth

△ Within the castle walls, the daimyo created peaceful gardens where he could contemplate the beauty of nature.

⟩ **THE WALLS** that surrounded the castle and formed the foundations of the keep were built of stones carefully piled on top of each other. The base of the walls curved outward for stability, then rose smoothly and vertically, which made the walls very difficult to climb. Defense ditches and moats meant that the only way into the castle was over a series of portable bridges, which could be removed in case of attack.

▽ Castles were usually built on raised mounds, to command and defend the surrounding rice paddies from which the shogun obtained his income.

⟩ **IN THE 1500'S**, guns and cannons were introduced to Japan. The flimsy wooden military fortresses, built by the shogun and samurai to keep order in the land, became vulnerable. The shogun had to build permanent castle compounds with strong stone walls to withstand gunshot and cannonballs.

small keep

windows for throwing stones or boiling water onto the enemy

gaps for firing guns and arrows

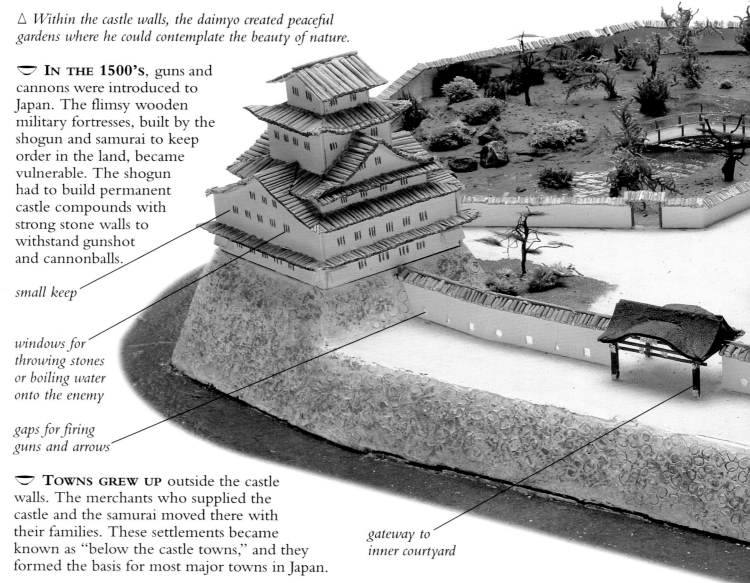

gateway to inner courtyard

⟩ **TOWNS GREW UP** outside the castle walls. The merchants who supplied the castle and the samurai moved there with their families. These settlements became known as "below the castle towns," and they formed the basis for most major towns in Japan.

⌣ **NEAR THE SHOGUN'S QUARTERS** there were further defense systems. Guards hid in secret chambers, ready to leap out and attack intruders. The floor of the corridor leading to the shogun's rooms was specially made with planks that squeaked. It was known as a "nightingale" corridor because it "sang" if someone tried to creep silently along it.

⌣ **AT THE HEART** of every castle compound was the keep, or *tenshu*. The main keep was usually made up of seven interlinking stories. The doors and screens of the rooms within were decorated by the best artists in the land.

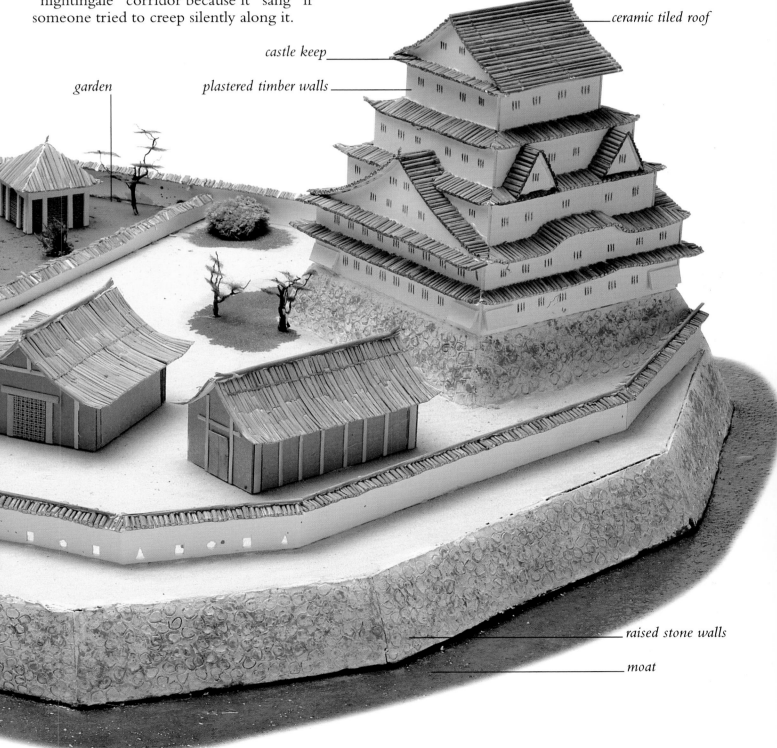

ceramic tiled roof

castle keep

plastered timber walls

garden

raised stone walls

moat

Life at Court

In 794, Emperor Kammu moved his court to a place he called *Heian-kyo*, meaning "capital of peace and tranquility" (now Kyoto). For four centuries, court life flourished there. In the early part of this period, courtiers copied the ways of their sophisticated neighbors, the Chinese, but by the year 1000, a distinctly Japanese culture began to appear.

STYLE AND MANNERS were very important in the Heian court. Noblewomen, for instance, wore at least 12 different colored silk robes and spent many hours choosing the colors and deciding in which order to wear them. Getting dressed was a form of art. Paintings from this time often show women elegantly collapsed in a billow of clothing, most likely staggering under the weight of their garments.

MAKE A FAN

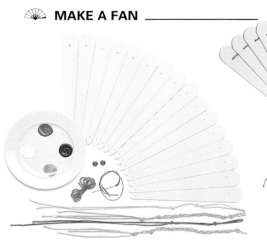

You will need: cream-colored posterboard; paints; paintbrush; 2 buttons; needle; scissors; drawing compass; colored thread

1 Cut posterboard into 16 tapering strips, 9" long x 1¼" wide at the top. Round off the top of each strip, as shown. Use the compass to make a hole in each strip's center at top and bottom, as shown above.

2 Lay the strips on top of one another, and pull the thread through the holes at the narrow end. Secure the bundle of strips by tying one button to the front and another to the back.

3 Spread the fan out and sew a length of thick thread, or several pieces of thin thread, through the holes in the top of the fan. Knot the thread at both ends.

4 Paint the open fan with a design of a cherry tree in full blossom. When fan is dry, decorate with lengths of braided threads tied to the sides of the fan.

THE MAIN DISTRACTIONS at court were love affairs and religious occasions. People dressed in colorful costumes and sang and danced at the many religious ceremonies. Trips to the countryside became ritualized. Courtiers would travel to see flowers in bloom or to enjoy the smells of different incense woods.

△ *It was the custom for noblewomen to hide their faces from men, so they used beautifully decorated fans as a screen.*

ARISTOCRATIC FAMILIES lived in mansions consisting of a main hall connected to various pavilions by galleries. Their houses were set in landscaped gardens with lakes and little islands and were surrounded by a wall. Like the homes of most people, the pavilions were simply furnished and icy cold in winter. Families ate two main meals, at about 10 A.M. and 4 P.M. Dishes included rice, seaweed, fruit, and vegetables.

LITERARY AND CALLIGRAPHY SKILLS were held in high regard by both sexes. Most nobles wrote poetry, which was especially important for conducting love affairs. Women of the period were known for their elegant novels, diaries, love letters, and poetry. In fact, Japan's earliest and most famous novel, a 1,000-page epic called *The Tale of Genji*, was written by a Heian lady of the court named Murasaki Shikibu. It tells of the life and many loves of a prince.

MARRIAGES between noblemen and women were arranged for the benefit of their families. It was common practice for a wife and her children to remain at home with her family and be visited there by her husband.

▷ *This nobleman and woman show their high rank by wearing costly silks. The man also wears a kammuri, a hat reserved for court members.*

Daily Life in Town

The city of Edo was for a long time the largest and one of the most sophisticated cities in the world. It was a major center for trade and all the main highways converged there. The *daimyo* all had large houses in Edo, and there were temples, shrines, several theaters, a pleasure district, and shops of every kind.

CHILDREN were prepared for their future lives at home. Girls learned how to sew, cook, and wash, while boys learned their father's trade or were sent off to learn the trade of one of his friends. In the spring and summer, children played games outside or went hunting for crickets and fireflies. During the winter months, families spent their evenings together, reading, talking, or playing board games such as **Go**, a game that is still popular in Japan today.

△ *A bathhouse was the perfect place for townspeople to relax. The one above is fed by hot spring water.*

BOYS AND GIRLS were taught to read, write, and do arithmetic in schools that were often attached to temples. Sons of military families were often sent away to be taught by monks or to the homes of even richer families, where they were educated in return for their services as **pages**. Merchants also made sure their daughters were educated, so they could help them run their businesses.

▷ *At New Year, children played with spinning tops made of bamboo and paper.*

MEN were the providers, although women were usually in charge of the family finances. Men were sometimes accused by their wives of wasting the family's money in the city's theaters, restaurants, and bars. However, as heads of the household, men felt they had the freedom to behave as they pleased, whatever their wives said.

WOMEN were expected to do all the housework and cooking, with the help of servants if the family could afford them. Wives served their husbands at mealtimes, but did not eat with them. Among the merchant class, some women owned property and ran businesses and shops. Women were usually very busy with household duties, but occasionally they went on pilgrimages or visited the theater. Many women looked forward to the day when they would have a daughter-in-law to take over the housework.

MOST TOWN HOUSES did not have baths, so public baths were very popular. These were places where men and women could relax, gossip, and get clean. Because soap was expensive, people used rice bran to wash with instead.

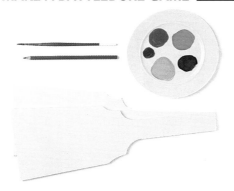

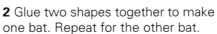

You will need: four pieces of balsa wood, pencil, paintbrush and paints, a shuttlecock, craft knife

1 Ask an adult to help you cut out four pieces of balsa wood in the shape shown left. They should be 15″ long x 5″ wide at the top.

2 Glue two shapes together to make one bat. Repeat for the other bat.

3 Copy or trace a design onto the bats.

4 Paint the handle and the middle section to look like wood. Then color in your design. Finally, paint the shuttlecock gold, red, and orange.

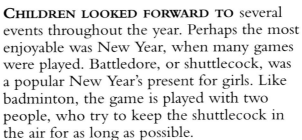

△ *Originally, battledore was played with a soybean instead of a shuttlecock. Beans were believed to ward off evil and disease.*

CHILDREN LOOKED FORWARD TO several events throughout the year. Perhaps the most enjoyable was New Year, when many games were played. Battledore, or shuttlecock, was a popular New Year's present for girls. Like badminton, the game is played with two people, who try to keep the shuttlecock in the air for as long as possible.

The Warrior Class

During the end of the Heian period, many wars raged throughout Japan. This led to the rise of a group of warrior noblemen called *bushi* (fighting men), or samurai. The samurai had an important influence on Japanese society until the 1800's.

⚔ **A WARRIOR GOVERNMENT** seized power from the emperor in the 1100's. Although the emperor and his court continued to live in the capital Kyoto, real power was held by the military ruler, known as the shogun, in the city of Kamakura. The shogun was served by a loyal band of samurai.

▷ *This samurai dolphin helmet, made from leather, lacquer, and gilt, was meant to make the samurai look impressive, so that he could intimidate the enemy.*

⚔ **MAKE A SAMURAI SWORD**

hilt

hilt

You will need: cardboard, paper, glue, paintbrush and paints, black and white lightweight fabric strips, craft knife

1 With an adult's help, cut a curved knife shape 2″ x 27″ and cut a round hilt, with a slit, from cardboard.

2 Slide the hilt onto the sword so that it sits above the blade.

3 Spread glue onto both sides of the sword and wrap strips of white fabric around the sword and the hilt as shown above.

4 Paint the sword gold. For the grip, cut two pieces of cardboard. Glue as shown. Wrap with black cotton. Decorate your sword.

🐸 **THE SAMURAI** were fearless fighters who trained for years to learn the skills of swordmanship and archery. The training was very demanding. As well as learning how to fight, the samurai had to go for long periods without food to test their endurance. They were also taught to think and behave in a special way called the *bushido*, the "way of the warrior." By learning the *bushido*, a samurai warrior developed an almost religious devotion to carrying out his duties. He was also prepared to die for the shogun, if necessary.

THE SWORD was the samurai's most valuable possession and was handed down from father to son. Those who made swords were highly respected. They even dressed in the white robes of a Shinto priest. Sword blades were made of a combination of hard and soft metal. They were so sharp that they could behead an enemy with a single blow. Sword guards, called *tsubas*, were beautifully decorated to reflect the skill needed to make the blade.

▷ *The samurai wore light and loose-fitting clothes, so they could move quickly in battle. Armor was worn over the top for protection.*

SAMURAI ARMOR was made of hundreds of scales of lacquered iron. These scales were tied together in rows with silk cord. The way they were linked together made the armor very strong, giving the samurai the protection they needed.

WHEN FACING THE ENEMY, the samurai performed a number of rituals. Each warrior announced his name, family background, and a list of brave deeds he had done. Then the battle would begin. The victor praised his enemy before cutting off his head. In case his life should end in the same way, a samurai always burned incense in his helmet, so that if his head was cut off in battle, it would still smell sweet!

FOR HUNDREDS OF YEARS, the samurai were valued for their skill at warfare. During the Edo period, peace spread throughout Japan, and the samurai became more involved with administrative duties and matters of ceremony than with fighting.

helmet with horns to frighten the enemy

neck shields

△ *This Japanese sword guard shows three holy men,* **Confucius**, **Buddha**, *and Lao-Tse, tasting rice wine beneath a pine tree.*

breastplate

sword hangs from the waist

iron-scale armor

boots made of leather or bearskin with studded soles

Seasons and Celebrations _____

Life for the Japanese followed the rhythms of nature strictly. Different foods were eaten according to the season, and homes were rearranged to cope with the changing weather. Even the Japanese calendar of celebrations and festivals was based on ancient ceremonies to mark the yearly planting, growing, and harvesting cycles.

MAKE A CARP STREAMER _____

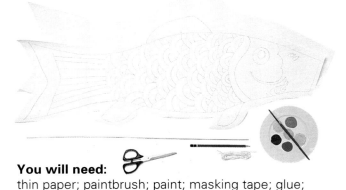

You will need:
thin paper; paintbrush; paint; masking tape; glue; scissors; string; thin, flexible cane

1 Lay two sheets of thin paper on top of each other. Draw a fish shape, including fins and tail, as above.

2 Cut out the shape and paint the fish on the outer sides of the pieces of paper. Gluing the edges only, stick the two plain sides of the fish together. Leave the mouth and tail unglued.

3 Tape the cane into a circle and place it inside the fish's mouth. Fold the fish's lips over it and tape in place. Tie string to the hoop to hang or fly your carp.

△ *During the Doll Festival, girls give parties for their friends and enjoy special candies and drinks.*

SPRING begins in the cold of early February, when the plum trees bloom. It ends with Boys' Day on May 5.

▷ *Families with sons hung carp streamers from poles outside their homes on Boys' Day.*

BOYS' DAY was originally a festival to prepare farm laborers for the hard work of transplanting rice seedlings. In Heian times, it was known as the sweet flag festival (named after a type of plant), and people hung out branches of sweet flag to keep evil away from their homes. Because the stem of sweet flag looks like a sword, the ceremony gradually became a celebration of martial arts. By the Edo period, the festival was associated with symbols of manliness and courage. The paper carp that hang from flagpoles today on Boys' Day are symbols of courage and ambition, in recognition of an age-old tale of a carp that once swam all the way to heaven to become a dragon. Displays of dolls are also common today, with models of folk heroes, warriors, and emperors.

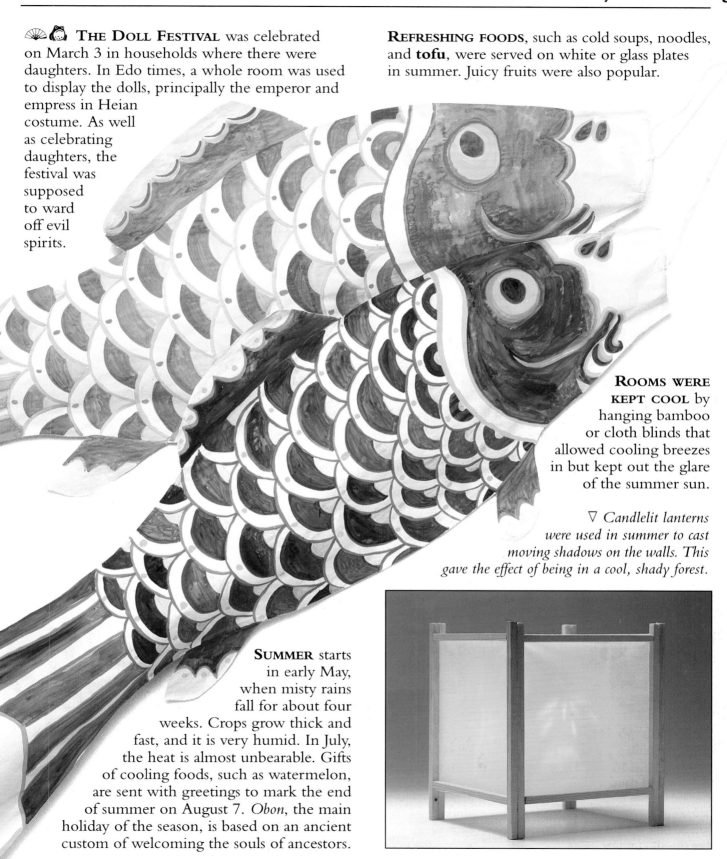

THE DOLL FESTIVAL was celebrated on March 3 in households where there were daughters. In Edo times, a whole room was used to display the dolls, principally the emperor and empress in Heian costume. As well as celebrating daughters, the festival was supposed to ward off evil spirits.

REFRESHING FOODS, such as cold soups, noodles, and **tofu**, were served on white or glass plates in summer. Juicy fruits were also popular.

ROOMS WERE KEPT COOL by hanging bamboo or cloth blinds that allowed cooling breezes in but kept out the glare of the summer sun.

▽ *Candlelit lanterns were used in summer to cast moving shadows on the walls. This gave the effect of being in a cool, shady forest.*

SUMMER starts in early May, when misty rains fall for about four weeks. Crops grow thick and fast, and it is very humid. In July, the heat is almost unbearable. Gifts of cooling foods, such as watermelon, are sent with greetings to mark the end of summer on August 7. *Obon*, the main holiday of the season, is based on an ancient custom of welcoming the souls of ancestors.

Rice, Fish, and Vegetables

Japan is a country of steep mountains, which makes growing crops very difficult. It also means that there is only a small amount of land available for farming. Despite the problems, rice was introduced in the first century and has remained the staple food of the Japanese ever since.

PLANTING, GROWING, AND HARVESTING RICE is hard and time-consuming work. All the people in a village gathered together to help plant and harvest this vital crop.

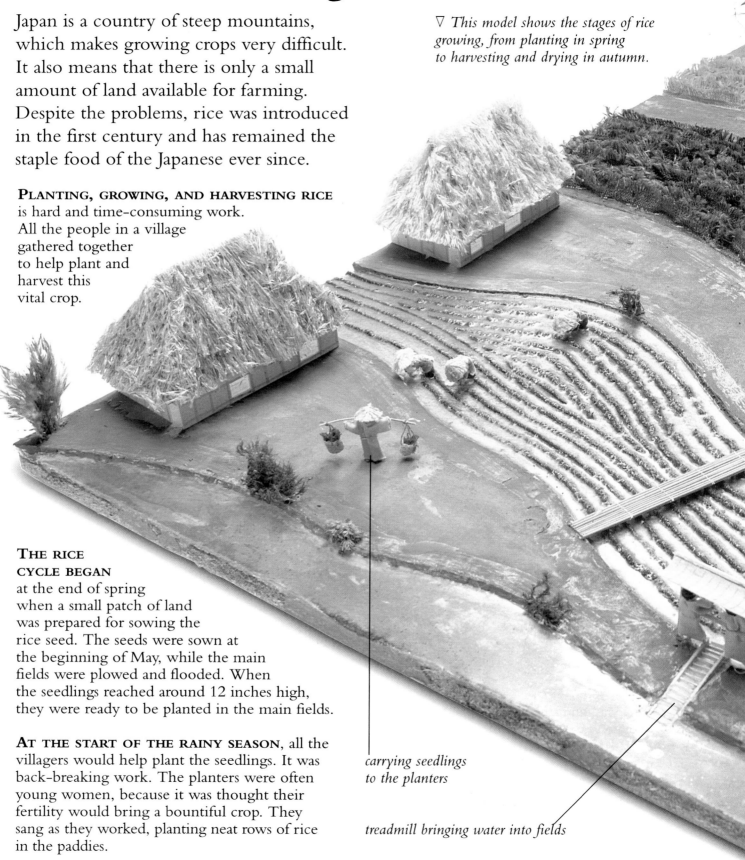

▽ *This model shows the stages of rice growing, from planting in spring to harvesting and drying in autumn.*

carrying seedlings to the planters

treadmill bringing water into fields

THE RICE CYCLE BEGAN at the end of spring when a small patch of land was prepared for sowing the rice seed. The seeds were sown at the beginning of May, while the main fields were plowed and flooded. When the seedlings reached around 12 inches high, they were ready to be planted in the main fields.

AT THE START OF THE RAINY SEASON, all the villagers would help plant the seedlings. It was back-breaking work. The planters were often young women, because it was thought their fertility would bring a bountiful crop. They sang as they worked, planting neat rows of rice in the paddies.

young rice plants

raised bank or dike separating the paddy fields

rice seedlings planted in flooded paddy field

🐼 **DIFFERENT METHODS** were used to keep the precious rice crop healthy. Some, such as spraying the fields with a mixture of whale oil and vinegar, were quite effective against hungry pests. Other methods included magic rituals or offering prayers to the gods to bring rain.

stripping, or heckling, the harvested rice

AS THE PLANTS GREW, they had to be kept clear of weeds and the water level had to be checked constantly. If water was scarce, the farmers would argue over their share. Some might even divert water away from a neighbor's fields into their own.

harvesting the rice using sickles

HARVESTING took place around October or November. The water was allowed to drain away from the field, and then sickles were used to cut down the rice. The long sheaves of rice were gathered into bundles or circular stacks and left to dry in the sun. Then the grain was stripped, or heckled, by pulling the plant between two sticks or hitting the plant against a large, open barrel. The remaining grain was winnowed, or separated, by being thrown up into the air. The farmer was left with brown, or unpolished, rice still covered in its outer husk. Once the harvest was complete, the tax collector visited each farm to calculate the *daiymo*'s share of the rice.

△ *Over the centuries, farmers developed several ingenious methods of irrigation, such as the waterwheel shown above.*

Japan is surrounded by sea and has many lakes and rivers, so fish has always been an important part of the Japanese diet. Fish has provided much-needed protein. Sea and river fish, shellfish, and even seaweed were collected and eaten. Fish was sometimes cooked, but it was also sliced and eaten raw.

FISHERMEN worked either part-time or full-time. Those who worked part-time spent most of the year farming and only fished during the season. Full-time fishermen spent every day, weather permitting, going out to sea or along the rivers and mending their nets and boats. Their wives would often help to support the family by growing some rice and vegetables.

LARGE FLEETS OF FISHING VESSELS set sail from the coasts around Edo. They were financed by the merchants and brought back daily catches that were sold as soon as they were unloaded. Ordinary people often fished in local lakes and rivers to supplement their basic diet.

▽ *Women gathered different types of seaweed and shellfish from the seashore to eat or sell at the market.*

△ *Cormorant fishermen suspended small fires in buckets from the bow of their boats to attract fish.*

mooring pole

ON SOME RIVERS, cormorants were trained to dive in the water and snap up the fish. A metal or rope ring around a bird's neck stopped it from swallowing, so the fishermen could retrieve the catch from its mouth.

thwart

bow

straw matting used for grip

scoop net

△ *On this boat, the fishing net was attached to the boat and carefully lowered into the water. After a while, the fishermen raised the net and scooped out any fish caught in the net.*

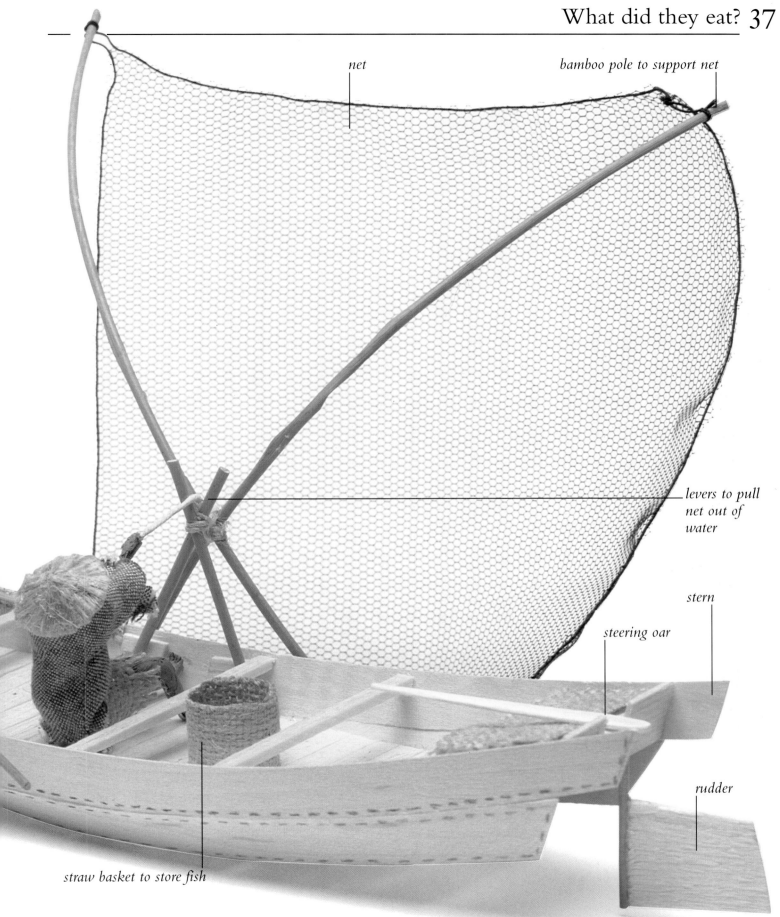

net

bamboo pole to support net

levers to pull
net out of
water

stern

steering oar

rudder

straw basket to store fish

THERE WERE MANY RITUALS attached to eating and drinking in Japan. Much care was taken with the preparation of food and drink. A lot of time and imagination went into making food look as attractive as possible, by choosing different colors and textures of food and arranging the food on beautiful plates and in small bowls.

FISH, rather than meat, was the main source of protein for most people. It could be eaten in many different ways: boiled, grilled, or cut into thin slices and dipped in **soy sauce** and eaten raw. Another popular dish was *sushi*: raw fish rolled in **vinegared rice** and then wrapped in a sheet of seaweed.

TEA ARRIVED from China in the 800's. At first it was used as a medicine, but by the 1300's nobles and samurai drank it at social gatherings. It was not until a century later that tea became a popular drink for everyone. Then, it was sipped at the end of a meal to wash down the last few grains of rice.

DRINKING RICE WINE, called *sake*, was enjoyed by men and women, and there were several customs associated with drinking it. Sake was served only during the first part of the meal. It was considered very rude to pour your own, so people took turns pouring sake for one another.

MAKE SUSHI

You will need: vinegared rice; tofu; chopped, cooked mushrooms; crab sticks; cucumber; avocado; smoked salmon; a sheet of seaweed (*nori*) or steamed cabbage leaves; soy sauce; thin cane table mat

1 Place the seaweed on the cane mat. Cover all of the seaweed with rice, except one edge. Lay the other ingredients in strips across the rice.

2 Use the mat to roll the seaweed into a tube. The rice should be wrapped around the other ingredients.

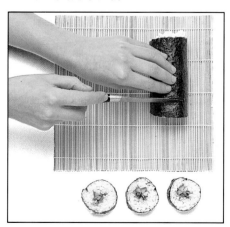

3 Unroll the mat. Slice the seaweed roll into pieces 1½" across. Now dip your sushi into the soy sauce and eat it.

CHOPSTICKS, or *hashi*, have been used in Japan for over a thousand years. They were usually made of wood, but they could also be made of ivory, bone, silver, or gold. Extra long chopsticks were used for cooking and serving food. In Japan, chopsticks are pointed at one end, but in China they are blunt.

1 Hold the first chopstick between your thumb and first finger. Rest it lightly against your middle and third finger.

2 Hold the second chopstick between your thumb and first finger, resting it against your first and middle fingers.

3 Try to keep the first chopstick still and move the second chopstick up and down, so that the pointed ends touch each other.

◁ *The type of hand-rolled sushi shown here was first eaten toward the end of the Edo period. But raw fish dipped in soy sauce and called sashimi dates back even further.*

Getting Around

Traveling in Japan before the Edo period was difficult. Steep mountains and rivers and heavy rains and typhoons made traveling hazardous. A few determined people traveled on official business or made pilgrimages to holy shrines. It was not until the Edo period that highways provided safer and more convenient links between towns and cities. Travel became easier for more people.

DURING THE HEIAN PERIOD, there were very few good roads, and bands of robbers made them unsafe to travel. However, nobles from the capital still ventured out on trips, either to see the cherry blossoms or to visit a local shrine.

△ The palanquin was a type of bamboo box suspended from two poles. It was supported by men who were paid to carry passengers.

THE MAIN FORMS OF TRANSPORTATION were the palanquin and the slow and uncomfortable ox-drawn carriage. Carriages were a status symbol, and there were many rules about the kind of carriages that low- or high-ranking nobles could travel in. Nobles competed with each other by showing off their beautiful carriages. The imperial family traveled in the most elaborate carriage, which had a green gabled roof and was so high that a ladder was needed to climb into the seat.

▷ This type of carriage was used mainly by the nobility at the time of the Heian court.

△ Due to the rough conditions of the highways, and the many mountains and rivers, most people traveled on foot.

TRAVEL BECAME EASIER during the Edo period, as more roads were built connecting major centers. Ordinary people traveled for business as well as pleasure. Nevertheless, people could not travel wherever and whenever they wanted. They needed special papers from the authorities, which were checked by officials at certain intervals on the main routes.

THE TOKAIDO, or eastern sea road, was one of the most important highways at this time. It stretched from the city of Edo to Kyoto, providing a vital communication link between the cities. Messengers ran along the highway in relay teams, carrying important letters or money from one city to another. Those running on business for the authorities carried lanterns marked "official business" and were given special treatment at checkpoints and ferries.

DAIMYO and their servants frequently traveled in processions from their estates to the capital, Edo. As the processions passed along the highways, ordinary people had to show their respect by moving to the side of the road and dropping to their knees. Post-stations, where the nobles could hire horses and porters, were placed at regular intervals along the highway.

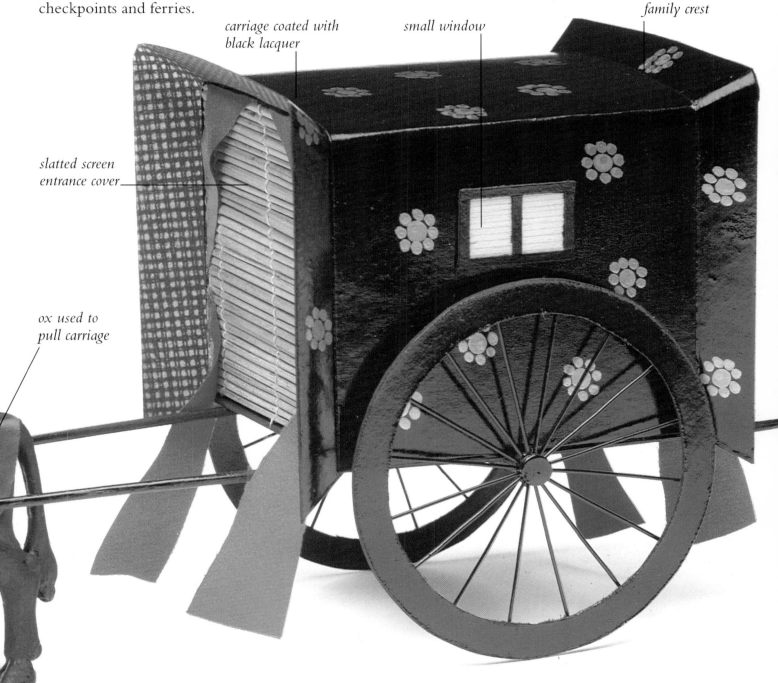

carriage coated with black lacquer

small window

family crest

slatted screen entrance cover

ox used to pull carriage

Transportation and Trade

With the growth of towns and large cities like Edo, and Osaka to the southwest, trade flourished. Improved methods of transportation by road and sea meant that merchants were able to move their goods more easily around the country. Despite the authorities' attempts to stop the growing power of the merchant class, many merchants became very wealthy.

△ *Ferry boats were used to carry travelers across rivers. If there were no ferry boats, a porter would wade across the river, carrying travelers and their belongings for a small fee.*

🐼 **TRADE INCREASED** inside Japan, both by road and sea. Waterways in particular were very important in the city of Edo. A system of canals was used not only to move people from place to place, but also to move goods by barges from warehouses to different parts of the city. As the city grew larger, more bridges were built. The most famous bridge was called Nihonbashi.

△ *Nihonbashi, "the bridge of Japan," was the meeting place of the five main highways in the city of Edo.*

🐼 **DURING THE EDO PERIOD,** trade with the rest of the world was very restricted. Japanese ships did not sail to other countries, and in 1635, the Japanese were forbidden to go abroad. A few Chinese and Dutch traders were allowed to live on a small island off Kyushu. As these were the only foreigners allowed inside Japan, the Japanese were naturally very curious about them. The Dutch traders were known as "red hairs" because of their light-colored hair. Some Japanese people even thought that they had hoofs instead of feet.

SMALL JUNKS OR COASTAL SHIPS transported goods around the country, moving cargo from harbor to harbor. One of the most important trade routes was between the cities of Osaka and Edo. Large cargoes of rice, sake, and soy sauce were ferried back and forth.

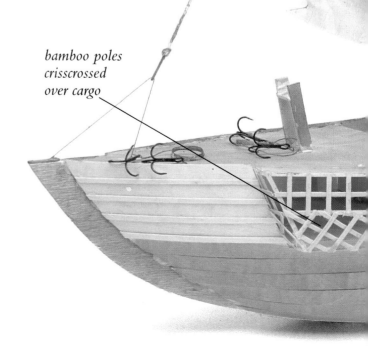

bamboo poles crisscrossed over cargo

large sail made of hemp

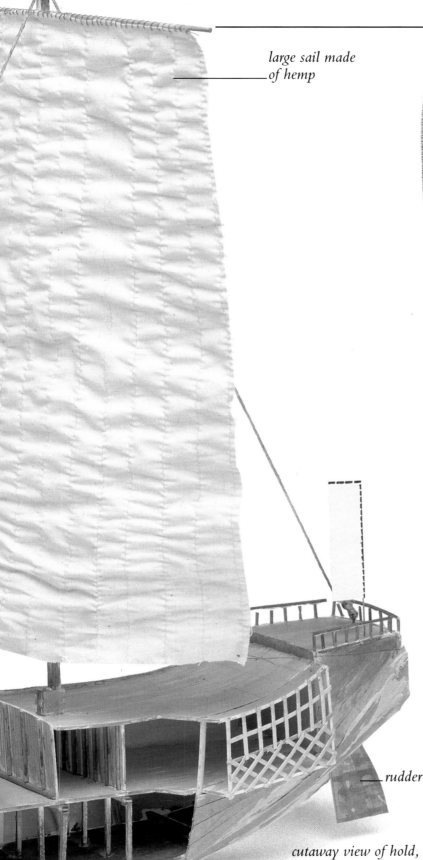

◁ *The oban was a large, gold coin that was used mainly by samurai or wealthy merchants or at special ceremonies.*

MERCHANTS grew increasingly important as Edo and Osaka became much more commercial. As well as opening shops in the cities, merchants acted as money-lenders to the samurai and made profits on the loans. They also played important roles as money changers, converting rice into money and even lending money to the *daimyo* against delivery of rice crops. A result of all this trade was that the merchants became very powerful economically.

MONEY was hardly ever used by the majority of people. Instead, people relied on trade. They would trade goods for rice, or sometimes swap valuable objects, such as musical instruments or clothes, for the things or services they needed.

Using money was complicated, because gold, silver, copper, and iron were all used for making coins in different parts of the country. For example, gold was used in the city of Edo, but in Osaka and Kyoto, silver coins were common. For everyday purchases in shops, most people used small copper coins that they kept tucked into the folds of their kimonos.

rudder

cutaway view of hold, which stored cargo of soybeans or sake

◁ *One of the main shipping lines was the Higaki, or "diamond line," so called because of the diamond-shaped pattern on the ship. The pattern was made by bamboo poles that were crossed over the cargo to stop it from falling overboard.*

A Rich Cultural Life

In early Japanese history, music and dance were more often associated with religious ceremonies. Gradually, music and dance became accepted forms of entertainment. In the Heian period, music from Korea, China, and India was also popular in court.

IN THE HEIAN COURT, music and dance were very important to the nobles. They were an essential part of court rituals and everyday life. An educated person was expected to know how to dance or play a musical instrument. It was also believed that if people danced, played, or sang well, they would reveal their true characters.

MAKE A DECORATIVE SHAMISEN

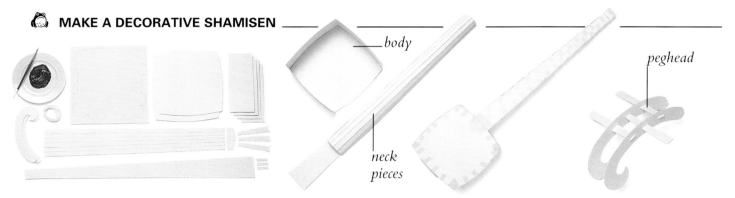

body

neck
pieces

peghead

You will need: tape, string, yellow and brown paints, paintbrush, cream paper, pencil, scissors, glue, cardboard

1 For the body, cut two 7³/₄"rounded cardboard squares. Cut four cardboard rectangles 7³/₄" x 2¹/₂". Tape three to one square, making an open box.

2 For the neck, cut two lengths of cardboard: one 28¹/₂"x 1¹/₂" at one end and 3¹/₄" at the other end; the other 23¹/₂" x 3¹/₄" at one end and 6¹/₂" at the other end. Draw five lines along the short length. Score using scissors and bend to shape. Tape neck pieces together and fix to body.

3 Add last rectangle and square to close up body. For the peg head, cut two shapes from cardboard as shown above. Make three slits in each. For tuning pegs, cut three cardboard strips. Pass through slits and glue in place. For the fret, cut a thick piece of cardboard 1¹/₂" long. Glue across top of neck.

MUSIC AND DANCE played an important part in village festivals. A whole village would gather to sing folk songs and dance. Often the songs and dances were special to that region of Japan. Some of the men and women would dance in circles, while other members of the village played flutes and drums or sometimes the **shamisen**.

FOLK SONGS have a long history in Japanese music. From the **Kamakura period**, groups of blind minstrels would wander the country singing tales of famous battles. The *Tales of Heike* was famous and told the story of two powerful families, the Taira and the Minamoto clans, who fought during the 1100's. Minstrels played a type of lute called a *biwa* while singing these tales to their audience.

◁ *Drums of all sizes are used to accompany traditional music at festivals throughout Japan.*

THE SHAMISEN came to Japan from Okinawa in the late 1500's. At first the *shamisen* was played by blind lute players, but it quickly became a favorite instrument in the entertainment districts of cities. It was widely used in **Kabuki** theater and by female entertainers called *geisha* and was also popular with ordinary townspeople.

GEISHA were women trained from an early age to entertain by singing, dancing, playing the *shamisen,* and talking in a witty and elegant manner. Famous *geisha* were like movie stars, and their skills at music and dance were greatly appreciated. They often had several maids who might also be training to become *geisha*.

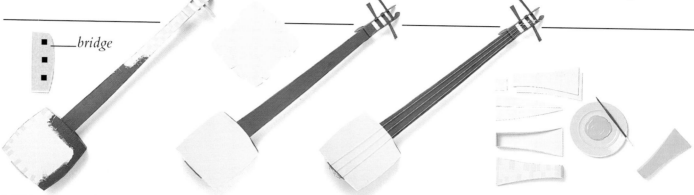

4 Slide the peg head over the end of the neck and glue in position.

6 Cut a large square of cream paper and glue over the body.

8 To make the plectrum, cut shapes out of the white cardboard as shown above. Tape the pieces together and paint yellow.

5 For the bridge, cut an arched rectangle of cardboard, 3¼"x 1½", as above. Make three holes in the top of the arch. Now glue to end of the body. Paint the *shamisen* brown.

7 Tie three strings to the tuning pegs. Pass the strings over the fret and tie to the bridge at the end of the *shamisen* body.

◁ The shamisen has three strings, which are strummed. It is used to accompany people who sing or chant in a type of puppet theater known as **Bunraku**.

NOH THEATER has its origins in rituals that were connected with the rice harvest and with entertainment in Buddhist temples.

In a NOH performance, the actor moves in a slow, elegant fashion across an almost bare stage. Four musicians sit at the back of the stage and accompany a group of people who chant a story in a solemn way. This chant tells a story as the performance unfolds. The main character often wears a mask that represents a certain type of person, perhaps a young man or maybe a ghost. The expression on the mask tells the audience if the character is sad, jealous, or angry.

Originally, Noh theater was not intended for ordinary people, but was only for the nobles and samurai. It became so popular among some high-ranking lords that they would invite Noh actors to their homes to perform and would even take part in the performance themselves.

◁ Noh masks are thought to have a religious significance. This is the mask of Okina, the holy sage. The Okina mask is worn in a special dance in which prayers for peace and fertility are offered.

MAKE A NOH MASK

  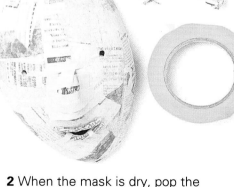

You will need: paint, paintbrush, sandpaper, strips of newspaper, wallpaper paste, string, wool, masking tape, balloon

1 Blow up the balloon. Cover one half with several layers of newspaper strips soaked in the paste. Use paper, paste, and tape to form a nose.

2 When the mask is dry, pop the balloon and smooth any rough edges with sandpaper. Cut out two holes for the eyes halfway up the mask.

BUNRAKU was a form of theater popular during the Edo period. The stars of Bunraku were not actors, but puppets that were half the size of a real person. While the puppets provided all the movements on stage, someone offstage sang in a chantlike way, telling the story and providing the voices of the puppets.

TWO OR THREE PUPPET MASTERS, dressed in black, controlled the movements of the puppets. The puppets made all kinds of happy and sad expressions, as even their eyeballs and eyebrows could be moved. A musician would play the *shamisen* to accompany the voices of the chanters.

KABUKI THEATER began in 1586 when, according to legend, a woman called Okuni danced in a dry river bed in Kyoto. Before long, Kabuki performances became very popular and drew huge crowds. The authorities were afraid of trouble breaking out among the audience, so they passed various laws banning young boys and women from taking part in Kabuki. They thought that this would put a stop to the performances. But adult male actors took on the women's roles. Soon they became so skilled that their beautiful appearance and costumes often set the style for fashion in the cities.

Kabuki performances were very lively and colorful, recounting tales from Japanese history, adventures of superhuman heroes, and love stories. During the play, members of the audience would shout out words of praise or even rude comments to the actors.

▷ *Kabuki actors start their training at a very early age. They have to learn all the roles and every aspect of Kabuki movement, makeup, and costume.*

3 Paint the mask with several coats of white paint. When the paint has dried, draw the outline of the eyes and nose in black and the lips in red.

4 To make the Okina mask, add tufts of yarn for eyebrows and pieces of string to make a beard.

THE ENTRANCES AND EXITS of a Kabuki actor were very exciting. The actors were famous for striking dramatic poses, flinging their head and arms around, and stamping their feet. Some costumes were designed to look oversized and colorful, to give the actor a larger-than-life presence on stage.

THE SHOGUNATE AUTHORITIES thought that the plays and actors set a bad example for ordinary people. They passed laws that treated the actors and other entertainers almost like criminals. Samurai were discouraged from attending Kabuki plays, but sometimes they would disguise themselves and sneak into the theater.

THE NOBLES had a great deal of free time during the Heian period. Games and sports were an important way for them to amuse themselves, although some games and sports were more than just entertainment. **Sumo** wrestling contained important rituals that were part of Shinto belief; the referee even wore the costume of a Shinto priest. Other sports were practiced for very practical reasons. **Martial arts,** such as **karate, kendo,** and **judo,** were developed to help a warrior improve the skills he needed in battle. All of the martial arts required strong concentration and mental discipline.

KENDO, which means "the way of the sword," was developed so that the samurai could keep up with sword practice. By the 1300's, there were several schools teaching kendo. The spontaneous moves and rituals of kendo went hand in hand with the Zen Buddhist idea of *mushin,* or "no mind." Rivals moved so quickly that they did not have time to think. They had to rely on their reflexes.

✄ MAKE A DECORATIVE KENDO MASK

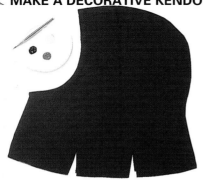

You will need: cardboard, glue, black felt, paint (red, gold, and black), brush, needle and thread, scissors

1 Cut two or three long strips of cardboard, 1″ wide, and glue together.

2 Curve the strip into an oval large enough to fit over your face.

3 Cut another strip, 1″ wide, and glue it lengthwise along the oval, making it curve outward.

4 Glue short strips across the oval, curving them outward, as shown.

5 Paint the oval shape red and the other strips black. When dry, paint a gold line on top of each black strip.

SUMO WRESTLING is the most ancient sport in Japan. Originally, wrestlers fought in a small ring in Shinto shrines during festivals. The object was to make the opponent touch the ground with a part of his body other than his feet or fall out of the ring. From about 1780, meetings were held over 10 days, and wrestlers were ranked according to their ability. Eventually, sumo stadiums were built, and popular wrestlers were as famous as the great Kabuki actors.

◁ *Shinto rituals play an important part in sumo. A wrestler must wear his hair and belt in a precise way.*

△ *Opponents sit in this crouching position before and after combat.*

◁ *This position is good for both attack and defense.*

IN KENDO TODAY, instead of using a sword, a long bamboo pole called a shinai is used. Those who practice kendo are known as kendo-ka. Action is so swift that it is impossible to prepare moves in advance.

◁ *The "cut" is a position of attack.*

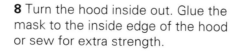

6 For the hood, place two pieces of black felt together. Cut out the shape shown above. Place the mask on the felt and cut around it to make the correct size gap for your face.

7 Sew both pieces of felt together along the back of the hood.

8 Turn the hood inside out. Glue the mask to the inside edge of the hood or sew for extra strength.

△ *It is important to hold the shinai with a firm grip.*

🐸 **JUDO**, "the way of gentleness," comes from a martial art called *ju-jitsu,* which involves opponents trying to wrestle each other to the ground. It started as a form of unarmed self-defense and was popular in the late Edo period. By 1911, it was widely taught in schools all over Japan.

KARATE did not actually reach mainland Japan until the 1920's. Originating in China, the word *karate* means "empty hand." The fists and feet are used for fighting instead of weapons.

◁ ▷ *While sparring, oponents keep their eyes constantly trained on one another.*

A Living Language

Nobody is very sure where the Japanese language comes from. One theory is that it is related to Korean; another is that it originates from a group of languages that come from central Asia. The way Japanese was spoken varied from region to region. In northern Japan, the **Ainu** people spoke a language that was totally different from Japanese.

UNTIL THE 600's, the Japanese had no way of writing their own language. During the Heian period, they looked to China in order to develop a writing system. By using Chinese characters, the Japanese were able to enrich their own language and record their ideas.

HANKO, or seals, were used as signatures. They were tubes of carved ivory or jade, with the character of the owner inscribed at one end. **Hanko** were used by officials to sign important documents.

MAKE A HANKO

You will need: orange paint, paper, felt-tip pen, sharp knife, potato

1 Ask an adult to cut the potato in half. Draw one of the characters shown above on each half.

2 Ask an adult to help you cut around the character. Remove the unmarked bits of potato, so that the character stands out.

3 Paint the top of the character and press it firmly onto a piece of ordinary paper, or special Japanese paper, to make a print.

▷ *These two characters read "Yamada," a fairly common name in Japan. Today, words of Chinese origin still make up more than half of all Japanese words.*

CALLIGRAPHY, the art of handwriting, has been popular in Japan since the Heian period. At first, **calligraphy** was used to record Buddhist prayers and famous Chinese sayings and poems. The style and technique used to produce beautiful texts were greatly appreciated, in the same way that a painting might be admired. Special brushes were dipped in black ink, and a poem, or another piece of writing, was copied onto delicately colored sheets of paper. The way the words looked on the paper was just as important as what they said.

◁ *This girl is using calligraphy brushes to write a letter.*

FOR MANY CENTURIES, scholars and officials used the Chinese language for writing. However, the Japanese language, when spoken, sounded very different from Chinese, and Chinese characters were complicated and took a long time to write. A new system of writing was needed to record Japanese sounds and to simplify Chinese characters. A set of syllables called *kana*, which were originally based on Chinese, gradually evolved. Each *kana* syllable could be used to represent a Japanese sound. Over time, two sets of *kana* came into being, one called *hiragana*, and the other called *katakana*. So, along with Chinese characters, there were three ways of writing. Sometimes all three can be found within one sentence.

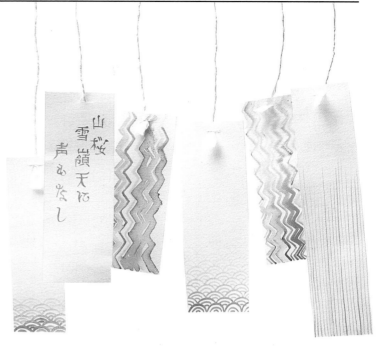

△ *Prayers written on strips of paper are often hung around Shinto shrines for good luck.*

yama

da

🐸 BY THE END OF THE 1600's, many people were able to enjoy reading plays, stories, and poetry. This was due to more advanced methods of printing and to people being able to borrow books from libraries.

JAPANESE LITERATURE began to emerge shortly after the writing system was introduced. The earliest recorded piece of writing is called *The Kojiki*, which means "record of ancient matters." It describes the birth of Emperor Jimmu and how the Japanese islands were created.

🪭 The first Japanese poems date from the end of the 700's. The *Man'yoshu* is a collection of about 4,500 poems divided into 20 books. One of the themes running through the poems is a warning that life is very short and soon over.

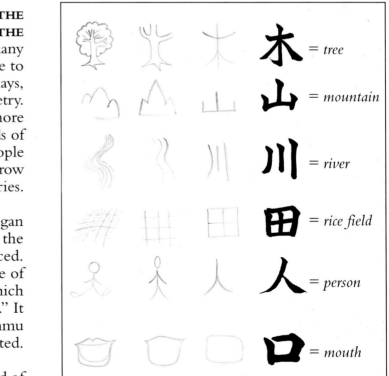

木 = tree
山 = mountain
川 = river
田 = rice field
人 = person
口 = mouth

△ *Chinese characters developed from simple drawings. Gradually the drawings developed and became the characters that are used today.*

Arts and Crafts

Although China was a major influence on arts and crafts in Japan, the Japanese created their own sense of style. They made many beautiful paintings and **ceramics** that reflected Japanese history and culture. It was also important that even everyday objects, although simple, were beautiful.

THE ART OF PAPERMAKING arrived in Japan from Korea in the 600's. The Japanese soon found many ways to put paper to good use. Not only was it used as a writing material, but its lightness and strength made it a practical, and often beautiful, building material. It was also used for religious purposes, for writing prayers and marking sacred places with prayers written on paper strips.

PAPERMAKING

You will need: wood strips, four 7" x ¹/₂" and four 9" x ¹/₂"; staple gun; hammer; muslin; hacksaw; large, shallow baking tray; food blender; nails; strips of white paper; flower petals; grass; pieces of cloth; glue

1 Glue or carefully nail the pieces of wood together to make two rectangular frames the same size.

2 Stretch a piece of muslin over one of the frames and staple it to the edge of the frame.

3 To make the pulp, tear the paper into small squares and soak in water overnight. Later, add more water and puree in blender.

4 For color, add some shredded flower petals and grass to the pulp.

△ *This hand-painted screen is made of paper.*

DURING THE EDO PERIOD, the wives of fishermen and farmers made work clothes out of paper. They used a special type of paper called *shifu,* which was made from twisted paper woven into strips. A finer version of *shifu* was also used to make tablecloths, handkerchiefs, and even mosquito netting.

PAPER PRODUCTION became a big industry during this time. Different regions specialized in producing paper for specific purposes. Paper was needed for writing letters, printing books, and making woodblock prints. It was also used for everyday things: sliding screens inside houses were made of paper, as were windows, lanterns, and fans. Some clothes were made of paper, such as the *kamiko* worn by Buddhist priests. Parasols were made of oiled paper that was waterproof. They gave good protection against the sun and rain. Before the Heian period, parasols were carried by warriors, priests, and nobles.

THE TEXTURE, COLOR, AND DESIGN of paper were all very important points to consider when writing a letter or creating a piece of calligraphy. During this period, paper designs became very intricate. Paper was dyed with blue, white, violet, indigo, and brown inks that were blended to form interesting shapes. Gold or silver patterns were sometimes printed on it, and even fine metal flakes were mixed into the paper.

THE PERSONALITY OF A WRITER was judged not only by the content of the letter, but also by the kind of paper he or she used. Therefore, anyone sending a letter would spend a long time carefully choosing the type and color of the paper and practicing calligraphy. Whoever received the letter could tell whether the writer had good taste or not.

5 Pour the pulp into the baking tray. Hold the frames together, with the muslin screen in the middle.

6 Dip the frames into the pulp, covering them completely. Take the frames out without tilting them. As the water drains into the tray, gently shake the frames from side to side, so that the pulp spreads evenly.

◁ *To make colored or patterned paper, add blades of grass, flower petals, or torn pieces of colored paper.*

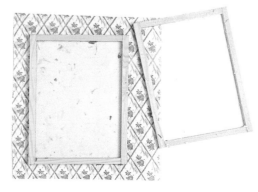

7 To dry the paper, remove the frames, as shown above. Lay the muslin screen with the layer of pulp on it face down on a damp cloth. Use another cloth to mop up excess water on the muslin. The pulp should stick to the damp cloth; then you can gently peel the pulp and cloth away from the muslin screen.

8 Pin the cloth and layer of pulp up to dry, or leave it in a dry place. When dry, lay the cloth face down and peel it away from the sheet of paper.

THE ART OF WRAPPING PRESENTS has always been very important in Japan. Before paper was commonly used, gifts were wrapped in fine cloth. There are still many special rules about how gifts should be wrapped; it is considered very poor taste not to wrap a present correctly.

LACQUER is a type of resin that comes from the lacquer tree found in the northern parts of Japan. It was used on all kinds of objects, from tables to writing boxes and vases to hair ornaments, to give them a hard, glossy appearance. Gold lacquerware was also used at banquets.

TO LACQUER AN OBJECT, it was first coated with lac, the sap collected from the lacquer tree. A piece of linen was placed on top of the layer of lac, and several more coats were brushed on. When the layers were dry, the surface was polished many times to give a shiny, black appearance.

MAKE A LACQUERED BENTO (LUNCH) BOX

You will need: scissors, cardboard, masking tape, glue, paints, brush, varnish

1 Cut three squares from cardboard: base: 6³/₄", lid: 7", inside lid: 6¹/₂". For the side panels, cut eight rectangles: four measuring 6³/₄" x 2¹/₂" and four 6¹/₂" x 2¹/₂".

2 Glue matching side panels together for extra strength.

3 Tape all the pieces together, as shown above, to make a box. For the lid, glue the smaller square to the underside of the larger one.

4 Paint the outside of both the lid and the box black. Let dry.

5 Now paint the inside of the box and lid red, then let dry.

WOODBLOCKS were used for printing in Japan as long ago as the 700's. The use of woodblock printing probably came from China and was first introduced by Buddhists, who used the blocks to print prayers and charms.

WOODBLOCK PRINTS in the 1600's showed the glamorous lives of *geisha*, actors, and sumo wrestlers. The world in which these famous people lived was so different from everyday life that it was called *ukiyo*, or "floating world."

MAKE A BLOCK PRINT

You will need: craft knife, pencil, 4 polystyrene tiles, tracing paper, felt-tip pen, paint, brush, paper, glue

1 Glue all four tiles together.

2 Draw the frog on the tracing paper. Place the tracing on the tiles. Go over the tracing with a pencil to leave an impression on the tiles. Trace the impression with a felt-tip pen.

3 Ask an adult to help you cut out the frog using a craft knife. Cut through the top two layers of the tiles so that your design stands out in relief.

AT THE END OF THE HEIAN PERIOD, new techniques in lacquerware were created. In one particular technique, tiny pieces of real gold and silver were sprinkled onto the lacquer while it was still wet.

6 Use gold paint to decorate the box. When the paint is dry, varnish the box to give it a laquered look.

AN ARTIST, ENGRAVER, AND PRINTER were needed to make woodblock prints. The artist made the original drawing, an engraver carved the drawing into the wood, and the printer applied the inks to the blocks and printed the image on paper.

4 Paint the raised surfaces with different colored paints. While the paint is still wet, turn the tile over and press it onto the paper to make a print.

DURING THE 1600's, trade in porcelain and lacquerware became very important between Japan and Europe. Thousands of bowls, chests, and objects of art coated in lacquer or decorated with mother-of-pearl or ivory were shipped to Europe.

LACQUERED WRITING BOXES decorated with mother-of-pearl or gold were highly prized possessions for the Heian nobility. But, by the Edo period, these objects of art belonged not just to the privileged nobles and samurai. Ordinary people, who had perhaps become wealthy through trade, also wanted to buy beautiful objects to keep in their homes. Many people started to buy woodblock prints, which were almost as cheap as a bowl of noodles.

▽ This woodblock print is copied from an 18th-century design called "Frog," by Matsumoto Hoji. You could use your hanko to sign your print.

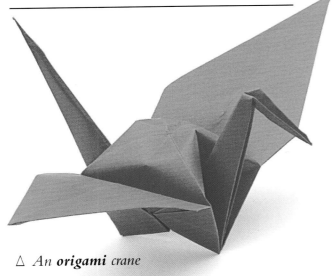

△ An **origami** crane

ORIGAMI, or paper folding, originated with the Shinto religion at the end of the Heian period. Figures of Shinto gods were made from paper and hung around shrines. It is thought that the first piece of origami was made by Fujiwara no Kiyosuke, a man who folded paper into the shape of a frog.

IN THE KAMAKURA PERIOD, nobles would attach a piece of origami to their swords to bring them luck in battle. Later, in the Muromachi period, special schools were opened to teach people the art of origami. As paper became more readily available, the art of paper-folding became a popular pastime for many people.

ORIGAMI FLAPPING BIRD

a	b	c	d	e	f

You will need: square piece of paper

1 Fold the paper in half along the two diagonals. Unfold, turn the paper over, and fold in half horizontally, then vertically. Make the creases very sharp. Unfold the paper as in *a*.

2 Fold the paper in half horizontally.

3 Hold both sets of corners and push all four corners inward as in *b*, to make a star shape.

4 Lay flat in a square shape, *c*, with the opening at the bottom.

5 Fold the edges of the top layer in toward the center crease, *d*.

6 Fold the top triangle down over the two triangles at the front, *e*.

7 Pull out the two folded triangles again, as in *f*.

8 Now, take hold of the bottom point and lift up the top layer of paper. Pull it up and back as in *g*.

△ This porcelain dish was made in the town of Arita, where the first Japanese porcelain was made.

POTTERY was used in Japan as early as 800–300 B.C. Early pottery was made of clay that was shaped into basic pots for storing food. In the 1500's, Korean potters who came to Japan changed the style of Japanese ceramics. They set up kilns on the island of Kyushu and helped to create styles that later influenced the production of porcelain in Arita.

FROM THE 1500's, tea bowls that were designed for use in the tea ceremony were considered valuable possessions. Some bowls were made to look old. A famous teacher of the tea ceremony, Sen no Rikyu, asked a tile maker to design a simple tea bowl. He made a plain bowl, such as a peasant might use. This simple style of pottery became known as *raku*.

IKEBANA, or flower arranging, has its roots in both the Shinto and Buddhist religions, where flowers were presented as offerings to gods. In the 1400's, a style of *ikebana* called *rikka* was introduced. Trees, shrubs, and flowers were arranged in a way that reflected a scene from the natural landscape. In the home, people used more simple arrangements with only one type of plant or flower. The longest flower represented heaven and the future, the second represented humans and the present, while the third represented the earth and the past.

▷ *Some flowers have special meanings. Japan's national flower is the chrysanthemum and represents the emperor.*

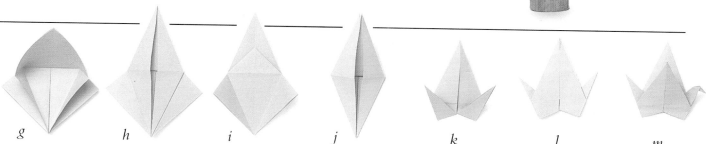

g   h   i   j   k   l   m

9 Pull the corner up and flatten out the diamond shape as in *h*.

10 Turn the whole shape over, *i*.

11 Repeat steps five to nine on this side. This will give you a long thin diamond shape with a smaller triangle hidden in the middle, *j*.

11 Fold the bottom triangles up and outward, below the center crease, *k*.

12 Fold the triangles back down. Open the sides of the diamond, and tuck each triangle up the middle, of its outside pocket as in *l*.

13 For the head, turn the tip of one of the triangles over as in *m*.

14 Pull the upper parts of the triangle apart and fold downward to form the wings.

15 Hold the flaps underneath your bird and pull them gently back and forth.

MANY DIFFERENT SHAPES AND STYLES can be made in origami, from simple cubes to animals such as monkeys or rabbits. A very popular shape to make is the crane, which is the symbol of long life and good fortune. When people wish for something special, they sometimes fold hundreds, or even thousands, of cranes and thread them on long lengths of string. Then they hang the cranes outside Shinto shrines as offerings to the spirits.

▷ *The most important aspect of origami is that the paper is always folded — it is never glued or cut. Some of the best designs are also the most simple.*

Nature's Law

Different religious beliefs have existed side by side in Japan throughout history. Families were happy to combine them in their daily lives, depending on their needs. The Shinto religion was used for births and marriages. But for matters concerning death, for example, when remembering or praying for dead members of the family, people followed Buddhist teachings. Confucianism, which originally came from China, provided strict guidelines for behavior within society. It stressed, in particular, the importance of treating elders with respect.

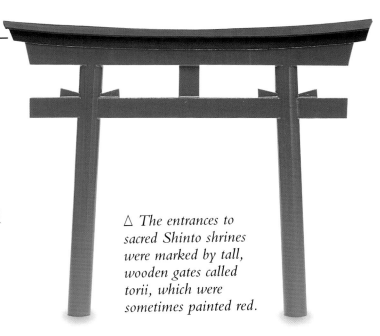

△ *The entrances to sacred Shinto shrines were marked by tall, wooden gates called torii, which were sometimes painted red.*

SHINTO means "the way of the gods" and is the oldest form of religion in Japan. Shinto followers believe in the worship of spirits called **kami**. These spirits are thought to live in the sky, islands, waterfalls, mountains, and tall trees. Mount Fuji, the highest mountain in Japan, is believed to be sacred. Some animals are sacred because they are thought to be the messengers of the *kami*.

THE SHINTO RELIGION has no sacred scriptures or set of rules. It developed from a mixture of folk tales and legends from the earliest days of Japanese history. A respect for nature has always been very important in Shinto. People tried to keep the local *kami* happy with offerings of food and drink in order to ensure a successful harvest and to protect themselves from bad luck.

MAKE A SHINTO SHRINE

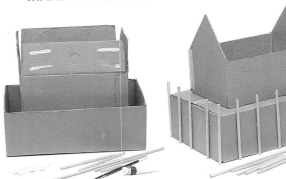
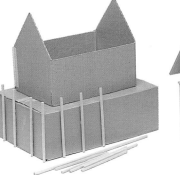

You will need: a large and a small cardboard box, large pieces of cardboard, thin doweling, four craft sticks, brown paint, paintbrush, masking tape, strong glue, craft knife

1 Close the larger cardboard box and tape the lid. With the help of an adult, cut the smaller box into a house shape. Glue to the top of the larger box, as shown. Carefully cut 20 lengths of dowel and glue around base of shrine as shown.

2 For the rail, carefully cut three long and two short pieces of dowel to rest on top of the upright dowels. Leave a space for the stairs. Glue in place.

3 For the roof, ask an adult to help you cut two large sections of cardboard and glue them in place.

4 Cut a length of dowel the same length as the roof and glue along the ridge of the roof.

5 To make stairs, cut a long strip of cardboard. Glue at an angle to the first floor. Cut another strip the same length as the slanted part. Peel off top layer. Glue in place with bump side up.

6 Cut two cardboard rectangles. Glue together to form a roof. Glue 2 dowels to the base of the stairs. Glue the roof to the top of the posts and shrine wall. Glue a dowel along the ridge of this roof.

THROUGHOUT MOST OF THE HEIAN PERIOD, Shinto was the main religion practiced, particularly in the countryside and at the Heian court. People were very superstitious; anything to do with death, illness, or blood was to be avoided at all costs. If someone fell ill or died, bits of willow wood were hung from houses as a warning to keep away.

THE SHINTO SHRINES AT ISE are the most sacred shrines in Japan and date back to the 300's or 400's. Until the 1400's, they were visited only by members of the imperial family, but later they became a popular place of pilgrimage for many Japanese. One of the shrines is dedicated to the sun goddess Amaterasu. According to Shinto belief, the rulers of Japan are supposed to be descended from this goddess.

DURING THE EDO PERIOD, pilgrimages to famous shrines and temples became very popular. Some people saw them as a good excuse to travel with friends. Others went on pilgrimages to ask for special favors or to thank the *kami* if their family had received good fortune.

△ *Daikoku, on the left, is a Shinto god of luck. He carries a mallet for grinding rice and is associated with the rice harvest. Inari (the fox), on the right, is one of the most popular kami in Japan today. The red cloth is a sign that the kami is being taken care of. People make offerings of food and drink to the kami to keep them happy.*

7 To make the roof decoration, cut two craft sticks in half and glue into cross shapes. Glue a cross to the front and back of the roof ridge. Glue three short pieces of dowel across the ridge as shown. Paint your shrine brown.

BUDDHISM is a religion that spread to Japan from China and Korea in the 500's. It began in India with the teachings of Buddha, a man who lived from 563 to 483 B.C. He achieved **enlightenment**, a perfect mental and physical state, and spent the rest of his life teaching his disciples.

▷ *As Buddhism spread throughout Japan, many new temples were built with pagodas. Underneath the pagoda, relics of Buddha, such as pieces of clothing that he may have worn, were buried.*

Most Japanese pagodas are made of wood.

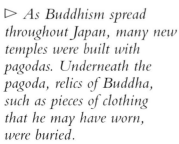

upper stories used to view surrounding area

△ *The Great Buddha at Kamakura was built in 1252. The statue is made of bronze and stands 38 feet high.*

DURING THE 500'S, Prince Shotoku encouraged the growth of Buddhism in Japan. The rulers of Japan were attracted to Buddhism because they thought that the whole country would be protected from danger if they followed this religion. Many temples were built throughout the country so that monks and nuns could study and teach.

IN THE HEIAN PERIOD, BUDDHISM became increasingly popular. The nobles at court found the complex beliefs even more challenging than Shinto. By the late 1100's, Buddhism had reached ordinary people. They were comforted by the belief that anyone could reach paradise by calling out to the Buddha to save them.

ZEN BUDDHISM was introduced to Japan in the late 1100's and 1200's by a monk called Eisai, who had studied in China. Zen had some very strict practices. Monks would **meditate** for many hours, sometimes receiving sharp blows with sticks to help them concentrate more fully. It was also believed that you could meditate while doing normal jobs, such as cleaning or even eating.

⚔ **THE STRICT DISCIPLINE** that was needed to follow Zen Buddhism made the religion popular among the samurai. They were attracted by the calmness of the religion, the strict meditation routines, and the possibility of enlightenment. The samurai used many of these ideas to help them become fearless fighters, unafraid of death.

Zen ideas also had a strong influence on art and culture. In times of unrest, artists and scholars took refuge in temples and monasteries. As a result, Zen arts, such as gardening, calligraphy, ink painting, and the tea ceremony, flourished in these centers.

⚔ ▽ **THE TEA CEREMONY** was practiced by Zen monks who drank tea to help them stay alert when they meditated. To help them concentrate, it was important to pay attention to every detail of tea making, from boiling the water to the way the tea master whisked the green frothy tea in the tea bowl. The atmosphere was very quiet so that people could relax, meditate, and forget their normal lives. The same ideas also lay behind the design of a Zen garden.

△ *Water is incorporated into many Zen gardens to suggest a waterfall, ocean, or fast-flowing river. Or else it may simply provide a soothing sound as it drips into a stone basin.*

⚔ ▽ **ZEN GARDENS** were designed with Zen beliefs in mind. Sometimes water or flowers were used, or dry landscapes were created using moss, stones, gravel, and sand. Often the gravel was carefully raked into swirling patterns. An onlooker was supposed to imagine what all the different shapes in the garden might be. For example, rocks might represent mountains, or raked gravel could be a whirlpool or waves on the sea or a river.

⚔ MAKE A ZEN GARDEN

4 Add the stones and moss to complete your miniature Zen garden.

You will need: shallow cardboard box, thin doweling, plastic comb, small rocks, moss (from a florist's shop), sand, craft knife, glue

1 Cut down the sides of the cardboard box, if necessary, to make a shallow tray, as shown.

2 Ask an adult to cut a section of comb. Glue the comb to one end of the dowel. Pour a layer of sand in the tray and shake gently until smooth.

3 Rake curved patterns in the sand, as shown.

Japan in the Modern Age

Japan is now home to over 123 million people. It has the seventh largest population in the world. Most of the country is mountainous, so flatter areas are very densely populated. Japanese cities today have a modern feel to them, with skyscrapers and swift public transportation. As one of the most technologically advanced countries in the world, Japan has an enormous influence on world economy. However, tradition still plays an important role in Japanese society.

FESTIVALS are an important part of the Japanese year. People still gather to see the cherry blossoms and have picnics under the trees, just as the Heian nobles did. Carp streamers and dolls are put on display for Boys' Day in May and for the Doll Festival in March.

▽ *The tea ceremony is an important ritual in Japan today.*

△ *This park in Tokyo is crowded with people enjoying the cherry blossoms.*

TRADITIONAL JAPANESE ARTS are studied at special schools. Many women at some time or other study an ancient art, such as *ikebana* or the tea ceremony. Although most Japanese wear Western-style clothes, at weddings and other formal occasions, they often swap their suits or jeans and T-shirts for kimonos.

OLD SKILLS often go hand in hand with new ones. At school, children learn subjects such as science and foreign languages, which will serve them in the modern age. The ancient skill of calligraphy is still vital. Young people have to learn to write up to 2,000 characters before they leave school.

△ *Inside a modern home in Kyoto*

BECAUSE USABLE LAND IS SCARCE, houses are often expensive and fairly small, especially in the cities. Some aspects of Japanese architecture have not changed since early times: a modern apartment may have one traditional Japanese room, with a *tokonoma*, *tatami*, and sliding paper doors. But the other rooms are more likely to be furnished in Western style.

△ *The Shinkansen, or bullet train, links Tokyo with Kyoto and Osaka, passing Mount Fuji on the way.*

JAPAN IS A LEADER in the manufacture of cars, rail technology, and the electronics industry. Some Japanese companies are among the largest in the world, and many more are well known outside Japan. For over a century, Japan has been trading openly with other countries — mainly with its Asian neighbors, the United States, and Europe.

THE SAMURAI warrior has faded into history, but his legend lives on through comics, movies, and television. Although the samurai and shoguns no longer exist, Japan still has an emperor who lives in Tokyo, the modern name of Edo. He symbolizes the state and the unity of the people, although he has no real political power.

OVER THE LAST CENTURY, Japan has changed from being an isolated, inward-looking country to one that plays an active and successful part in today's world. Although it has adopted many modern practices and Western influences — from hamburgers to rock music — it has a strong cultural identity that is firmly rooted in its fascinating past.

▽ *Although many Japanese now play baseball and basketball, martial arts have gained in popularity — not only within Japan, but throughout the world.*

ANCIENT
EGYPTIANS

Studying Egyptian Life

All human beings need food and shelter to survive. They also need things to look forward to that give their lives hope and meaning. Throughout history, different groups of people around the world have come up with their own ways of meeting these basic needs. Studying past **civilizations** can tell us how people used the resources around them to build shelters, how they farmed or found food, and how they met their spiritual needs and hopes for a better future.

△ *Simple farming methods involving oxen trampling grain were used by the Egyptians.*

▽ *This map shows modern-day Egypt and its neighbors, some of which were of major importance to ancient Egypt.*

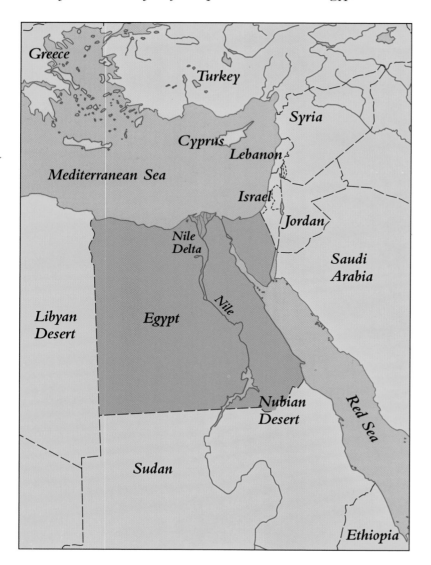

IN THE COURSE OF HISTORY civilizations have risen and eventually fallen because of internal troubles or pressures from outside. The story of the ancient Egyptian civilization is a very long one. It lasted for over 2,000 years. The Roman Empire rose and fell in half that time, and the ancient Greek civilization lasted less than 1,000 years.

TO HELP people make sense of this vast stretch of time, the greatest period of Egyptian history is usually divided into three periods, or kingdoms. In this book we have given each kingdom a symbol, which is used purely as a guide, when information relates to that time.

KEY FOR SYMBOLS

- Old Kingdom 2686 B.C. – 2181 B.C.
- Middle Kingdom 2055 B.C. – 1650 B.C.
- New Kingdom 1550 B.C. – 1069 B.C.

EGYPT'S GEOGRAPHICAL LOCATION plays a vital part in understanding its development as a civilization. During the period covered in this book, foreign trade and travel grew with the discovery of valuable raw materials from abroad.

THE EGYPTIANS traveled to nearby countries by sea or over land. As the wealthiest country of the ancient world, Egypt had much to offer its neighbors, such as gold from the Eastern Desert, in exchange for what it lacked. This made for good trading relations at first, but later led to invasion by foreign countries eager to exploit Egypt's fine natural resources.

EGYPT'S LEGACY to the world lies in the most spectacular monuments ever built. The **pyramids** at Giza, the Great Sphinx, and magnificent temples are all wonderful technological achievements. In fact, experts are still trying to understand how the Egyptians were able to build such massive constructions with very simple tools.

△ The magnificent temple at Abu Simbel was carved out of sandstone cliffs in the Nubian Desert on the orders of Ramses II.

ARCHAEOLOGISTS AND ANTHROPOLOGISTS have, however, been able to explain a lot about the daily life of the ancient Egyptians by the wall paintings, documents, treasures, personal possessions, and household items that have been discovered in the remains of tombs and temples.

THESE FINDINGS also reveal much about the Egyptians' religious faith and their views on death and what followed. Experts have been able to work out a lot about their belief in the **afterlife** from the discovery of tomb models buried with the dead, coffins covered with written spells to protect against danger, and **mummies**— perfectly preserved bodies for burial.

◁ This wall painting shows the type of boats the ancient Egyptians used, the birds found on the banks of the Nile, and the tools that noblemen used for hunting.

THE MAKE IT WORK! way of looking at history is to ask questions about the past and to find the answers by making the things people made as close as possible to the way they made them. You do not have to make everything in the book to understand the ancient Egyptians' way of life—in fact, just by looking at the step-by-step instructions, you will be able to see how they put things together and made them work efficiently.

Timeline

In this book we look at history by finding out how ancient Egyptians lived. Another way to look at history is to study the events and political changes that occurred over time. You can see from this chart, for instance, which dynasty of **pharaohs**, or kings, was on the throne, when Egypt started trading with other countries and when foreign invaders arrived.

EGYPTIANS WERE RULED by pharaohs and the throne was passed down through the family from generation to generation. A dynasty, or family line, continued until the male line died out and an outsider, possibly with the support of the army or court, married the queen or heiress. There was rarely a struggle. Each dynasty had its own traditions and character. Some built monuments, some encouraged the arts, some were weak and lazy, and others financed powerful armies which carried out impressive military campaigns.

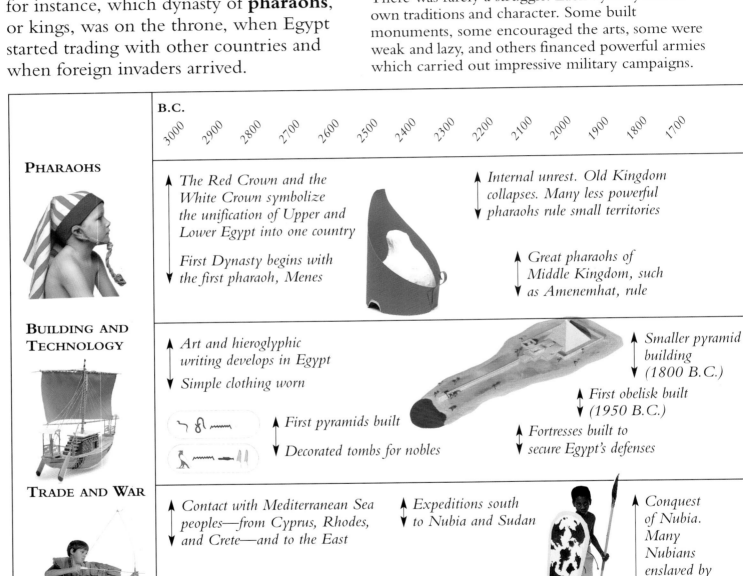

B.C.

3000 2900 2800 2700 2600 2500 2400 2300 2200 2100 2000 1900 1800 1700

PHARAOHS

The Red Crown and the White Crown symbolize the unification of Upper and Lower Egypt into one country

First Dynasty begins with the first pharaoh, Menes

Internal unrest. Old Kingdom collapses. Many less powerful pharaohs rule small territories

Great pharaohs of Middle Kingdom, such as Amenemhat, rule

BUILDING AND TECHNOLOGY

Art and hieroglyphic writing develops in Egypt

Simple clothing worn

First pyramids built

Decorated tombs for nobles

Smaller pyramid building (1800 B.C.)

First obelisk built (1950 B.C.)

Fortresses built to secure Egypt's defenses

TRADE AND WAR

Contact with Mediterranean Sea peoples—from Cyprus, Rhodes, and Crete—and to the East

Expeditions south to Nubia and Sudan

Conquest of Nubia. Many Nubians enslaved by the Egyptians

Trading for jewels and cedar trees begins with Lebanon, Byblos, and Somalia

OLD KINGDOM
(2686 B.C.–2181 B.C.)

INTERMEDIATE PERIOD

MIDDLE KINGDOM
(2055 B.C.–1650 B.C.)

EACH KINGDOM—Old, Middle, and New— witnessed a succession of ruling dynasties. Between the kingdoms themselves there were periods of chaos and conflict. This was because of political unrest within Egypt, with a number of different rulers fighting for control of the country, and foreign invasion. After the New Kingdom ended, there were only brief periods of calm and prosperity as repeated raids from Sudan, Persia, and Macedonia became increasingly threatening and disruptive.

EGYPT FINALLY FELL to the Greeks in 332 B.C. For the next 300 years the Ptolemy family ruled the country, and important people adopted Greek **culture** and learned to speak Greek. By 30 B.C., Egypt had become a province of Rome. Over the next several hundred years the gradual erosion of Egyptian culture and religion continued. An Arab invasion of A.D. 7 saw the arrival of Islam and in A.D. 324, Egypt officially turned to Christianity replacing all the country's temples with **Coptic** churches and monasteries.

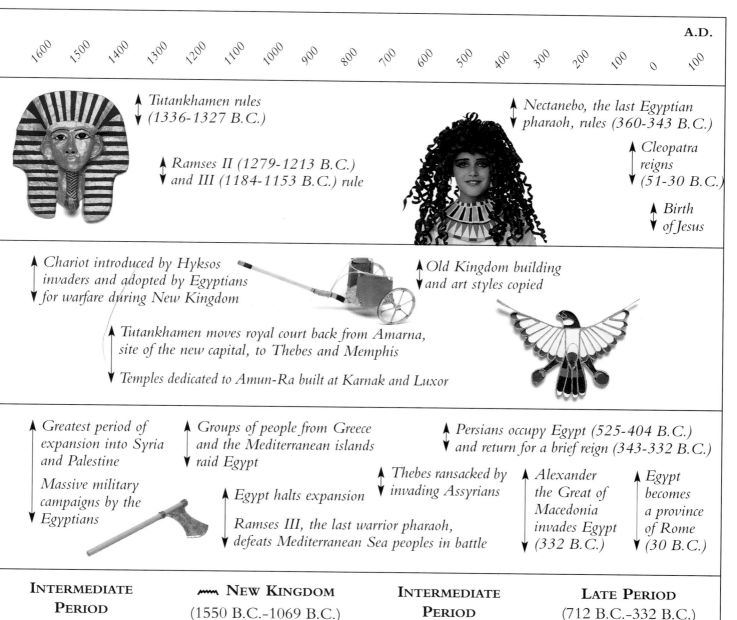

A.D.

1600 1500 1400 1300 1200 1100 1000 900 800 700 600 500 400 300 200 100 0 100

Tutankhamen rules (1336-1327 B.C.)

Nectanebo, the last Egyptian pharaoh, rules (360-343 B.C.)

Ramses II (1279-1213 B.C.) and III (1184-1153 B.C.) rule

Cleopatra reigns (51-30 B.C.)

Birth of Jesus

Chariot introduced by Hyksos invaders and adopted by Egyptians for warfare during New Kingdom

Old Kingdom building and art styles copied

Tutankhamen moves royal court back from Amarna, site of the new capital, to Thebes and Memphis

Temples dedicated to Amun-Ra built at Karnak and Luxor

Greatest period of expansion into Syria and Palestine

Massive military campaigns by the Egyptians

Groups of people from Greece and the Mediterranean islands raid Egypt

Egypt halts expansion

Ramses III, the last warrior pharaoh, defeats Mediterranean Sea peoples in battle

Persians occupy Egypt (525-404 B.C.) and return for a brief reign (343-332 B.C.)

Thebes ransacked by invading Assyrians

Alexander the Great of Macedonia invades Egypt (332 B.C.)

Egypt becomes a province of Rome (30 B.C.)

INTERMEDIATE PERIOD

NEW KINGDOM (1550 B.C.-1069 B.C.)

INTERMEDIATE PERIOD

LATE PERIOD (712 B.C.-332 B.C.)

The Fertile Nile River

The first Egyptians were **Stone Age** hunters, followed by settlers from the south and east who were attracted by the river valley's fertile soil. The ancient Egyptian civilization began over 5,000 years ago and lasted for more than 2,000 years before being wiped out by foreign invasions. Initially Egypt was divided into Upper and Lower Egypt (the valley and the **delta**). These were united in 3118 B.C. and ruled by a pharaoh called "Lord of the Two Lands."

▽ *The compass shows the direction of the flow of the Nile: south to north.*

▽ *Lower Egypt (Ta-mehu)*

Giza

Memphis

Nile Delta

THE MARSHY, TRIANGULAR DELTA of Lower Egypt, where the river divides into separate branches, was known as *Ta-mehu*—land of the papyrus plant. Upper Egypt, the long, narrow valley just 7 miles wide, was called *Ta-shema*— land of the reed. Ancient Egyptian civilization developed in these two fertile areas.

MEMPHIS was one of the most inhabited areas, not only of Egypt, but of the ancient world. It was the capital of Egypt during the Old Kingdom and its harbor and workshops played a key part in the country's foreign trade. Just south of Memphis is Giza, the site of the largest pyramid of all—the Great Pyramid.

THE SOURCE OF THE NILE is in the lakes and mountain springs of Ethiopia and Central Africa. From there it flows north to the Mediterranean Sea. Summer rains caused the floor of the Nile Valley to flood, creating a lush green corridor. In modern Egypt, the Aswan Dam, built in the 1960s, keeps the level of the Nile constant.

▷ *This aerial view shows the Nile Valley today. It is no longer a green strip as in ancient Egypt, because the Aswan Dam holds back the annual flood waters.*

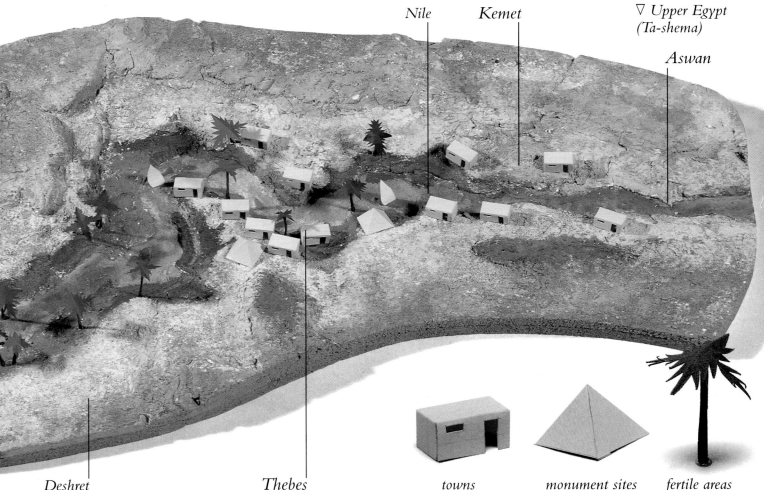

Nile

Kemet

▽ *Upper Egypt (Ta-shema)*

Aswan

Deshret

Thebes

towns

monument sites

fertile areas

THE RED LAND or *Deshret* was the desert that surrounded the river valley. There was nothing to sustain life and nobody lived there. For the ancient Egyptians, however, it provided several things: a barrier against invasion, safe trade routes to the rest of Africa, sandstone for building monuments, and gold for making jewelry.

THE BLACK LAND, known as *Kemet,* was the narrow strip of **silt** that runs along the river valley. It took its name from the rich, fertile soil in which crops flourished. The Egyptians called themselves *remet-en-Kemet*—people of the black land—and their language, *medet-remet-en-Kemet,* meant speech of the people of the black land.

Clothing

The clothes worn by the ancient Egyptians were light and cool. They were made from fine, undyed linen cloth and needed very little stitching as they were simply draped around the body. Color and decoration came in the form of elaborate jewelry, wigs, and makeup. No one wore underwear, and because it was so hot for most of the year, children often wore nothing at all.

OLD KINGDOM WOMEN wore a simple tube dress made from a rectangle of linen sewn down one side, with straps attached to the top edge. This simple dress style did not change, although during the Middle Kingdom colorful, patterned collars started being worn by both the rich and poor. New Kingdom fashion was more elegant, with a pleated, fringed robe worn over the tube dress.

MEN WORE SHORT KILTS to the knee during the Old Kingdom. The linen cloth was pleated and fastened at the waist, either with a knot or buckle. In the Middle Kingdom, the style of kilts changed to become straight and longer for all. Full–length cloaks kept winter chills at bay.

△ *This pleated dress is possibly the oldest existing garment in the world. It dates from the period of the first pharaoh, which was around 3000 B.C.*

By the New Kingdom, fringing and pleating became popular, adorning the sashes and aprons that men now wore.

MAKE A TUNIC

You will need: needle and thread, felt-tip pen, scissors, safety pin, fabric (5 x 3 ft.)

1 Wrap the fabric around the person you are making the tunic for, from under the arms to the knees.

2 Allow an overlap of at least half the width again. Mark the fabric and cut it. Use the leftover material to make two straps.

3 Use a safety pin to hold the tube together, by pinning it carefully at the top of the back (so that you can take it off and put it on).

MAKE A PAIR OF SANDALS

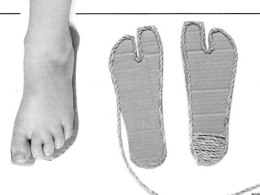
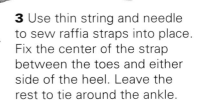

You will need: cardboard (1 x 1 ft.), pen, scissors, thin string, darning needle, glue, braided raffia

1 Place feet on the cardboard; draw around them carefully and cut out.

2 Glue the raffia around the edge of the sole and cut lengths to fit across the center, filling in the sole shape as shown.

3 Use thin string and needle to sew raffia straps into place. Fix the center of the strap between the toes and either side of the heel. Leave the rest to tie around the ankle.

PLEATING was the main form of decoration. The pleats were probably made by pressing the fabric onto a grooved board. Then they were attached with a form of starch.

▷ *This is the kind of tunic dress that would have been worn by a servant in a noble household.*

4 Sew the straps onto both shoulders and even up the hem using a pair of scissors.

5 By adding some elaborate decoration to the basic tunic you can transform it into a costume fit for royalty. Popular decorations of the time included feathers, rosettes, and sequins. A fringed border was also used to embellish the robes of noblewomen.

▷ *The two prisoners and nine bows depicted on these sandals represent the traditional enemies of ancient Egypt. This was so that they could be trampled underfoot with every step.*

LINEN WAS A COMMON material at the time because **flax**—the plant that produces linen threads—grew easily in the rich Nile silt. Also, cotton did not grow in Egypt, and Egyptian sheep were not the wool-bearing variety.

WHITE WAS THE COLOR OF PURITY, and white linen cloth was mostly used for clothing during the Old and Middle Kingdoms. At this time, the Egyptians sometimes used brown and blue dyes to color the linen, but were unable to use other, brighter colors, such as red and green, as they needed a special fixative to color the cloth. By the New Kingdom the method for fixing dyes had been discovered. After this clothes became much brighter and designs more elaborate.

ANCIENT EGYPTIANS LIVED in the northeast corner of Africa. They were not tall, had dark eyes, straight, black hair, and coppery skin.

MAKEUP and perfumed oils were used by men and women and kept in beautiful caskets. Oils softened their skin and stopped it from burning and cracking in the sun and sandy winds.

EYELIDS were colored with green pigment, made from a crushed soft stone called malachite. Eyes were outlined with black **kohl**, made of lead ore mixed with water, to make them look larger, and to protect them from the sun's glare.

CHEEKS AND LIPS were stained red with **ochre**. **Henna**, made from the powdered leaves of a plant, was used to color hair, as it still is today.

MIRRORS WERE ESSENTIAL for all this making up and hairdressing. Egyptian mirrors were round and made from highly polished metal disks, usually bronze. Their shape and brightness made the ancient Egyptians think of the life-giving sun, and so mirrors were important as religious objects, too. By the New Kingdom the back of the mirror was often decorated with sacred motifs.

▷ *This bronze mirror dates from the New Kingdom. The handle is in the shape of a papyrus plant.*

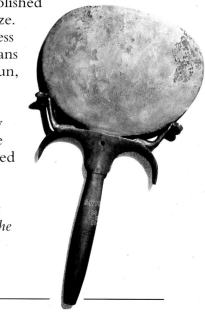

MAKE A WIG

You will need: 3 sheets of black craft paper (24 x 16 in.), scissors, glue, ruler, thin and thick doweling, and modeling clay, or wig stand

1 Make wig stand using thick doweling as shown. Cut paper strips for wig base to the width of a ruler. Fit, cut, and glue base band. Make crosspieces as shown. Glue.

2 Cut long, thin strips of paper. Wrap each strip around the thin doweling and run your hand along it. Remove the doweling and you will have a tightly curled ringlet.

CHILDREN'S heads were shaved, except for one long, braided lock which hung at the side. It was known as the "lock of youth."

◁ *On important occasions, the pharaoh wore a false beard of braided and knotted hair, hooked around the ears.*

FACIAL AND BODY HAIR was thought by many to be unclean. Women used tweezers to pluck their hair and shape their eyebrows. Noblemen at court sometimes wore short beards, although most men were clean shaven. Priests kept their heads and bodies completely hair-free.

You will need: black eyeliner, green eye shadow, red lipstick

1 Make sure that your face is clean and tie your hair back. Apply eye shadow from the eyelid to the brow.

2 Draw a heavy line around the eyes with the eyeliner, taking care to avoid any smudging.

3 Darken the eyebrows with eyeliner to form a straight line.

4 Apply lipstick carefully, following the outline of your mouth.

5 To take off the makeup, wipe with cotton wool dipped in an oily makeup remover.

◁ *The higher a person's status, the more makeup and clothes worn. Servants were scantily dressed.*

3 Put the base on the wig stand and glue ringlets to base, starting at the base band. Use shorter ringlets for the front, and trim the fringe with scissors.

READY-DRESSED WIGS
were worn by many Egyptians who shaved their heads or kept their hair short. Elaborately curled and beaded wigs were worn on special occasions. The base was made from a net of woven hair with individual strands looped into the netting.

JEWELRY WAS WORN by rich and poor, men and women, and even some sacred animals. Elaborate costume jewelry was worn to adorn otherwise plain clothing and as a sign of social position.

GOLD AND SEMIPRECIOUS STONES were used to make expensive jewelry. Cheaper versions were made of glass and **faience**, a glazed composition made by heating powdered quartz, or sand, in molds. Jewelry often served a dual purpose: as decoration for the body and as **amulets**, or charms, to protect the wearer from harm. From earrings to anklets, the ancient Egyptians decorated almost every part of the body.

STONES such as carnelian, lapis lazuli, and turquoise were thought to have charmed powers.

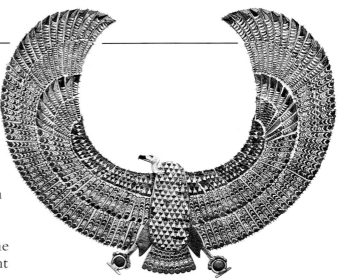

△ *This collar was found on the mummy of the pharaoh Tutankhamen. Made of colored glass, it shows Nekhbet, the vulture goddess of Upper Egypt.*

∼ MAKE A PECTORAL

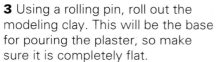
You will need: paper (8 x 7 in.), pencil, compass, thin cardboard strips ³/₄ in. wide, glue, tape, rolling pin, modeling clay, plaster of paris, paints

1 Using a compass for the circles, copy the shape above onto a piece of paper. Next, stick the strip that runs across the top of the wings and the body with modeling clay.

2 Starting with the body, cut, curve, and glue the cardboard strips so that they follow the lines of the drawing. Secure with tape if necessary.

3 Using a rolling pin, roll out the modeling clay. This will be the base for pouring the plaster, so make sure it is completely flat.

4 Place the cardboard outline on the modeling clay, pushing down gently so that no plaster escapes under the cardboard walls. Prepare the plaster.

5 Pour the plaster into the mold and let dry overnight. Remove the modeling clay, turn the pectoral over, and paint as shown right.

MAGIC MOTIFS included figures of the gods and, most significantly, the **scarab**—a representation of the dung beetle. To the ancient Egyptians, this was a powerful symbol of the sun god and life being reborn from dust. Children sometimes wore a fish pendant in their braids to protect them from drowning. Pregnant women wore figures of the hippopotamus goddess Taweret, meaning "the great one," to help them in childbirth.

GOLD-WORKING TECHNIQUES were quite varied. Most gold jewelry was made by hammering out thin sheets that were then cut to shape. These were decorated by punching on designs with a sharp chisel and making indentations to hold stones or jewels. The sheets were also cut into thin strips to make gold wire. Expensive, solid pieces of jewelry were made by pouring molten, or liquid, gold into molds.

▷ *This falcon pectoral with outstretched wings shows the god Re-Harakhty, the sun god in one of his many forms.*

talons clutch the "shen" symbol, meaning eternity

PECTORALS were worn on the chest for protection as well as decoration and often took the shape of falcons or scarabs. They were made using a technique now known as **cloisonné**, where semiprecious stones or colored glass are held in place by fine metal strips.

▷ *These gold bracelets show the god Horus as a child sitting on a lotus flower, between two cobras.*

From Pharaoh to Laborer

Egyptian **society** was well ordered and administered by law-enforcers, courts, and judges. All classes paid their taxes in goods or services, which were then used to pay government officials and the army. Scribes were the only members of society who could possibly rise through the ranks to become noblemen.

THE PHARAOH, meaning "great house," was absolute ruler. He could have many wives, but only one queen could be the Great Royal Wife. His symbols of office were the double crown of Upper and Lower Egypt, the **crook** and the **flail**, an implement used for threshing grain.

COURT OFFICIALS AND NOBLEMEN held high office in ancient Egypt and helped the pharaoh to rule the country. The pharaoh would often reward loyal nobles with gifts of land, so that they would have their own income from taxes.

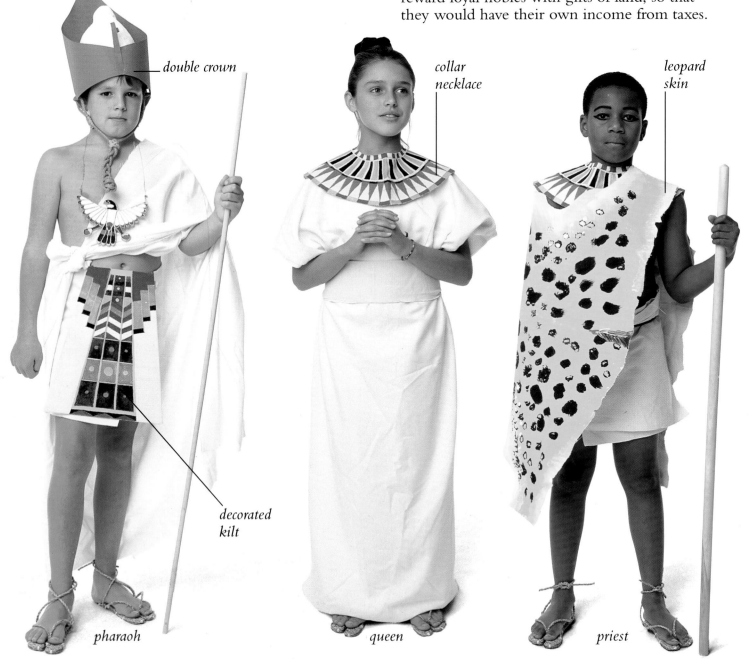

double crown

collar necklace

leopard skin

decorated kilt

pharaoh

queen

priest

PRIESTS AND PRIESTESSES looked after the temples and held religious ceremonies. The high priest ran his temple with the help of musicians, dancers, and assistant priests. People paid taxes directly to temples.

SCRIBES were the civil servants of ancient Egypt. They administered the law, collected taxes, and oversaw government projects. Parents were eager to send their children to scribal school (see page 103) so they would learn to read and write. They could then enter government or royal service where they might become rich and powerful.

ARTISTS AND CRAFTSMEN worked in organized workshops using simple techniques and tools and were employed by the pharoah, the government, or the temples. Blind people often worked as musicians during the Old Kingdom and dwarfs were traditionally employed as jewelers.

SOLDIERS AND UNSKILLED LABORERS came from the same social class. The laborers worked on farms during the growing season and paid their taxes in labor by joining the army or working on government projects during the flooding season when farming was impossible.

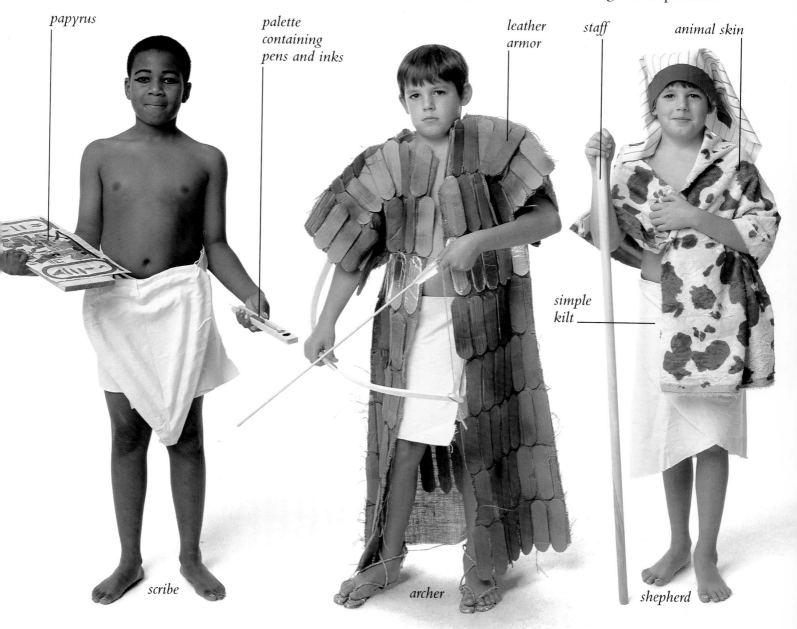

papyrus

palette containing pens and inks

leather armor

staff

animal skin

simple kilt

scribe

archer

shepherd

Homes and Villas

The majority of Egyptians lived in towns and villages strung out along the Nile Valley. To escape the effects of the annual flooding, towns were built on the edge of the desert and on patches of high ground within the cultivated valley. Until the New Kingdom, houses, palaces, government offices, and even temples were built from dried mud bricks, quite a fragile building material. As buildings crumbled, the occupants would knock them down and rebuild on top of the remains, so that gradually the high ground became even higher and therefore safer from the floods.

△ This model "soul house" is based on a typical village house. It was placed in a burial tomb to provide a home for the deceased in the afterlife.

〰 **GRANARIES, BAKERIES, AND BREWERIES** were important features of any town. Models of these buildings were made and buried with people when they died, as it was thought that they would need sustenance in the afterlife.

sun shield

silos for storing grain

silo

external stairs leading to roof

courtyard

outside granary

TOWN HOUSES were built with a shelter on the roof to catch cool north breezes. Families would sometimes live there during hot weather. Inside, houses were often cramped and quite dark as windows were small and high up to keep out the sunlight. Kitchens were usually situated on the top floor so that the heat and cooking smells could drift out through an opening onto the roof terrace.

— temple

△ *The earliest homes and temples found in Egypt were made of reeds. The houses were shaped like beehives.*

SUPPORTING BEAMS and pillars were made of wood, covered in plaster and then painted. Columns were made of several tree trunks bound together with a rope made of **papyrus**, a tall reed. Houses were covered with a white limestone plaster to deflect the heat of the sun.

"TO START A HOUSE" was the Egyptian term for marriage, which was not marked with any kind of ceremony. Families would get together to arrange their children's marriages, and once a written agreement had been drawn up, the couple set up house together (see page 86).

∿∿ MAKE A VILLA

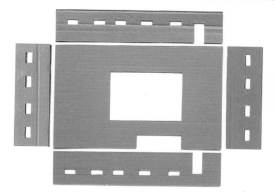

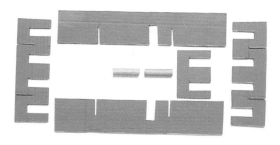

You will need: cardboard, craft knife, masking tape, doweling, plywood base, plaster of paris, sand, spatula, small pieces of wood

1 Ask an adult to help cut the shapes from cardboard as shown: lower floor walls and roof—12 x 8 x 2½ in., and top floor—8 x 6 x 2½ in.

2 Cut out interior walls for the top floor as shown above. Cut two pieces of doweling to the height of each ceiling. This is the column.

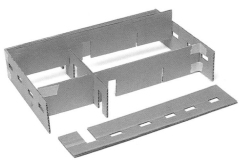

3 Assemble the lower floor and internal walls as shown. Fix the corners with masking tape. Glue column in position as shown on page 82.

4 Add the lower floor roof, then assemble and attach the walls of the upper story with masking tape. Glue column in place and add the roof.

5 Prepare the plaster of paris and apply a thin layer with a spatula. When dry, trim plaster from doors and windows with a craft knife.

A NOBLEMAN'S VILLA was home to family, servants, and livestock, as well as being a place of business. Like most Egyptian buildings, it would have been a low, white-plastered construction with a flat roof. Usually, this would have been approached through beautiful landscaped gardens with terraces, ponds, shady trees, and flowers. The vegetable gardens, stables, and granaries were situated around a courtyard at the back of the house with the servants' quarters and the kitchen.

▷ *The finished villa (see previous page) with part of the roof and walls cut away to reveal the interior. You could paint your villa, make simple palm trees, or use sand to decorate it.*

PRIVATE ROOMS were at the back of the house and were much more simple. This is where the bedrooms were situated and where children played without getting in anyone's way.

cool, enclosed central hall

thick, wooden columns

sun shelter

pool

dining area

shaded corridor

main gate

PUBLIC ROOMS
were at the front and center of the house. This is where guests would be received and business was conducted. These were the grandest rooms, with high ceilings and decorated columns often inlaid with semiprecious stones. Walls were plastered and painted and hung with painted cloths. Floors were decorated with glazed tiles.

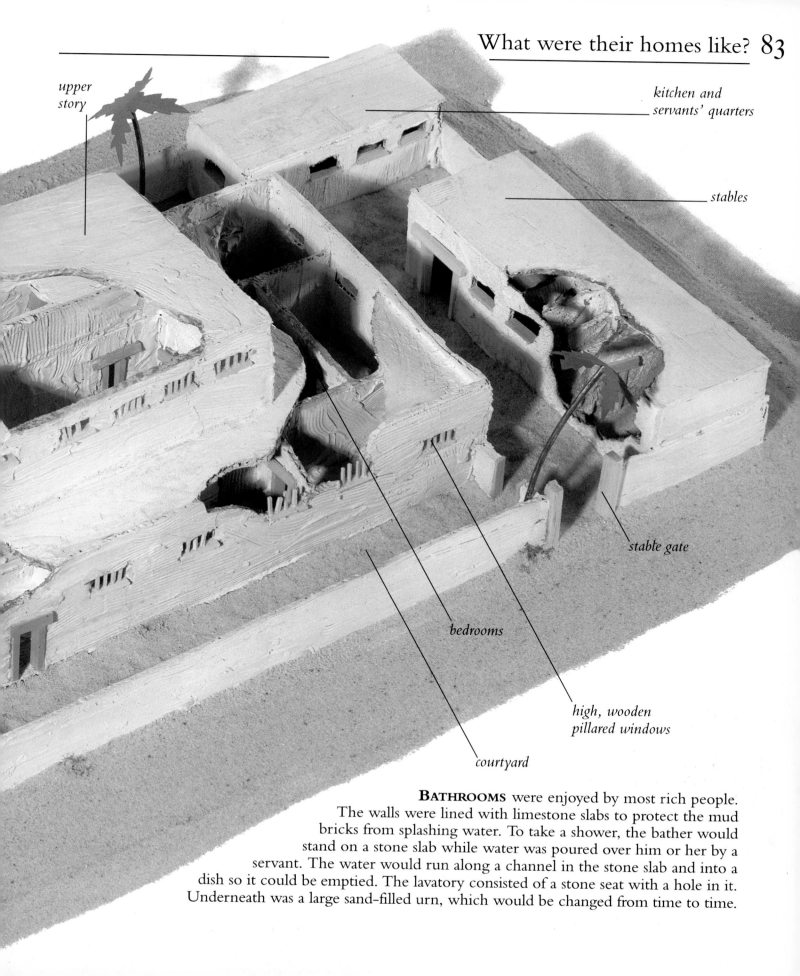

upper story

kitchen and servants' quarters

stables

stable gate

bedrooms

high, wooden pillared windows

courtyard

BATHROOMS were enjoyed by most rich people. The walls were lined with limestone slabs to protect the mud bricks from splashing water. To take a shower, the bather would stand on a stone slab while water was poured over him or her by a servant. The water would run along a channel in the stone slab and into a dish so it could be emptied. The lavatory consisted of a stone seat with a hole in it. Underneath was a large sand-filled urn, which would be changed from time to time.

FURNITURE, such as stools, tables, beds, and chests, was simple and made in workshops by carpenters. Poorer people either made their own basic furniture or squatted on the floor on mats or cushions.

CHAIRS had carved wooden frames and low seats made from braided cord. The legs were often carved to resemble a lion's paw or a bull's hoof.

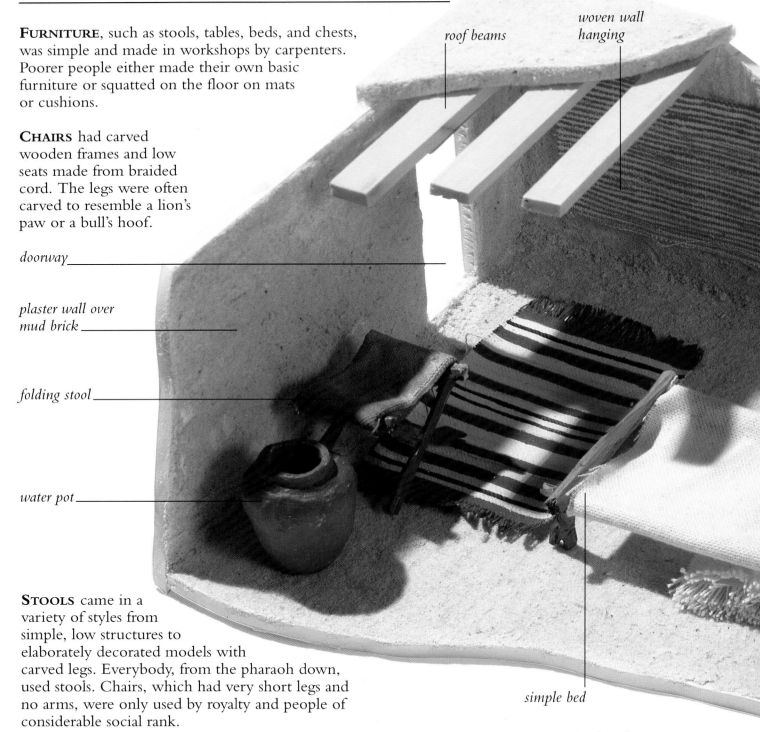

roof beams

woven wall hanging

doorway

plaster wall over mud brick

folding stool

water pot

simple bed

STOOLS came in a variety of styles from simple, low structures to elaborately decorated models with carved legs. Everybody, from the pharaoh down, used stools. Chairs, which had very short legs and no arms, were only used by royalty and people of considerable social rank.

LAMPS were stone or pottery bowls filled with palm-nut oil and a wick made of flax. They were lit in the evenings, only for the short time between sundown and bedtime, as people went to bed as soon as it got dark and got up at sunrise to make the most of the daylight.

MATS AND CURTAINS were made of woven reeds and decorated with colored fabric.

〰 **SHRINES** to household gods were often a feature of Egyptian living rooms. Among them were Bes, the dwarf god of marriage and family prosperity, and Imhotep, the god of medicine.

CHESTS were used to store everything as there were no cupboards. Some were made of wood—sycamore, fig, or imported ebony—and some of woven reeds. They ranged from the plain and simple to finely carved pieces, inlaid with ivory and faience.

terracotta pot

high window

pot stand

mud floor

chest

△ *Most headrests were wooden. They were carved into a crescent shape to fit the back of the head comfortably.*

BEDS had wooden frameworks and bases of woven rushes. Bedclothes were made of linen, and instead of pillows people used curved wooden or stone headrests, padded by cushions. These allowed air to circulate below the neck and were cool in the sticky Egyptian climate.

▷ *This ebony chair, inlaid with semiprecious stones, was the throne that the pharaoh Tutankhamen used for religious ceremonies.*

Everyday Life

Ancient Egyptians had a strong sense of family and generally married someone in their own social group or extended family. Historians once thought that brothers and sisters sometimes married, but, apart from the royal family, it seems that this was not true. The words "brother" and "sister" in ancient Egyptian were simply terms of affection. Marriage was fairly straightforward and divorce was legal, but costly.

DAILY LIFE centered around the marketplace, with stalls filling squares and lining streets. This is where the wealthy would send their servants to shop. The ancient Egyptians did not use money, relying instead on a **barter** and exchange system of trade. They used everything for this— from storage jars and furniture to grain, flax, or copper ore. Prices rarely went up, which meant that the value of things tended to remain the same. As a result, people knew what to expect in exchange for their goods.

△ *This Old Kingdom tomb model of a woman and her husband, Hetepheres and Kaitep, dates from 2500 B.C.*

INTERMARRIAGES often took place within the extended family, such as between cousins. Children played an important role in society and were thought to be a great blessing. Parents prayed to the gods for many children who were expected to look after their parents during old age.

CHILDHOOD was short as children were sent to learn a trade, or the privileged few to be educated at scribal school when they were just eight or nine years old. Girls married when they were as young as 12 years old and boys at 14. The average life expectancy was 40 years, although mummies of officials and rulers show that some lived much longer.

cattle

market stall

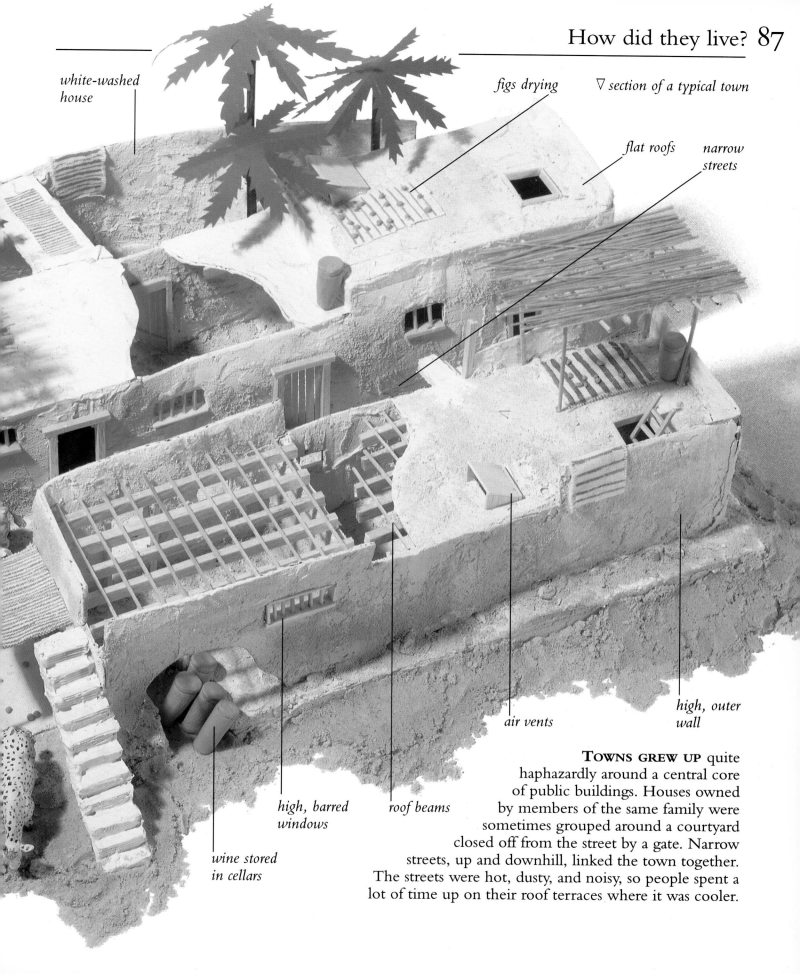

white-washed house

figs drying

▽ section of a typical town

flat roofs

narrow streets

high, outer wall

air vents

high, barred windows

roof beams

wine stored in cellars

TOWNS GREW UP quite haphazardly around a central core of public buildings. Houses owned by members of the same family were sometimes grouped around a courtyard closed off from the street by a gate. Narrow streets, up and downhill, linked the town together. The streets were hot, dusty, and noisy, so people spent a lot of time up on their roof terraces where it was cooler.

Work on the Land

Ancient Egypt was a wealthy country because most years the rich and fertile soil yielded magnificent crops. This was due to the annual flooding of the Nile River between July and October. During this time, little farmwork was done and poorer families paid their taxes in labor by working on government projects.

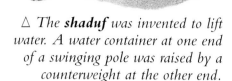

△ *The **shaduf** was invented to lift water. A water container at one end of a swinging pole was raised by a counterweight at the other end.*

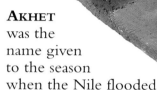

AKHET was the name given to the season when the Nile flooded the river plain, soaking the dry soil and leaving behind a fertile layer of black silt. If too little water covered the land, crops would suffer, while too much severely damaged houses.

WORK STARTED when the flood-waters began to recede. **Irrigation** channels had to be repaired and boundaries re-established. Farmers marked out their fields to avoid ownership arguments and to make it easier to calculate what they owed in taxes each year.

Nile

The annual flooding of the Nile irrigated and fertilized the soil of nearby fields.

Irrigation channels allowed the floodwaters to reach those fields farther away from the river.

PERET was the growing season and ran from November to February. Water had to be kept flowing in the irrigation channels to water the crops. Small boys chased off birds, but plagues of insects and flash floods were a constant threat to the crops.

SHEMU was the period between March and June, during which crops were harvested. Children worked, too, picking up the ears of wheat or barley missed by the harvesters. The work was overseen by tax assessors or scribes who calculated how much the farmers owed in taxes and rent.

THE LAND WAS PLOWED, once it had been cleared, by a simple wooden plow pulled by cows. The most important seeds sown were wheat and barley for making bread and beer, flax for making linen cloth and linseed oil, and emmer, an ancient variety of wheat.

HARVESTED CROPS were taken away to be stored in granaries once all dues had been paid to the government. Those who did not pay were often beaten without mercy. Finally, offerings were made to Renenutet, goddess of the harvest, as thanks for a plentiful crop.

The parched soil of the plains was covered with a fine layer of silt.

Deeper channels had to be dug in order to irrigate higher ground.

Towns and villages were located on high, dry ground to avoid flooding.

Food and Drink

The Egyptians loved good food and drink. Almost all their food was homegrown, and the staple food was bread. Most people drank beer, brewed from barley, and the rich drank wine. Even poor people enjoyed a healthy diet of vegetables, fruit, and fish from the Nile, while the wealthy supplemented their diet with meat—mainly from calves and oxen—and poultry such as duck, pigeon, goose, and stork. Meat was expensive because there were few grazing pastures as land was needed for growing crops.

△ *This coffin painting of a man offering a feast to the gods gives us an idea of what the Egyptians used to eat.*

EGYPTIANS DINED at low tables and ate with their fingers. Ordinary people ate off earthenware dishes, but the rich were attended by servants who served them on dishes of silver, bronze, gold, or faience.

During banquets the servants would tie a cone of scented grease on the head of each guest. These would melt and run down the guests' hair and wigs, leaving them sweetly perfumed.

MAKE FIG CAKES

You will need: food processor, 1⅓ cup fresh figs, water, ⅓ cup walnuts, ⅓ cup almonds, honey, ground cardamom

1 With an adult's help, use a food processor to grind the almonds and walnuts separately. Set them aside.

2 Chop the figs roughly and put them in the food processor, adding just a little water.

BEER WAS MADE by first half-baking loaves of barley bread, then crumbling the loaves into a mixture of barley and water. The jars were sealed and left to ferment, and the resulting thick, lumpy beer was strained through a sieve before being served.

THE GRAPEVINE was one of the main garden crops, and was used mainly for wine. Grapes were trampled to extract the juice in troughs big enough to hold six men. It was poured into clay jars and sealed and labeled with the date and the name of the vineyard, much as it is today.

▷ *Once grain had been harvested, it was threshed (trampled by oxen) and winnowed, to separate the grains from the chaff, or casing. Then it was stored in silos until it was ground down for cooking.*

storing grain in silos

threshing grain

COOKING was done outside or on the rooftops, because it was too hot and dangerous to cook over an open fire indoors. Fires were started by rubbing a bow string vigorously against a stick.

MEAT from cows and sheep was broiled over the open fire or stewed. Some pigs were kept, although priests associated them with the evil god Set, and they refused to eat them. Fish and ducks caught from the Nile were sometimes salted and dried to preserve them. Bees were kept in clay pots to produce honey, which was used as a sweetener in baking.

3 Add the walnuts and cardamom and blend again, adding a little water if the mixture is too sticky.

4 Spoon the mixture out of the food processor onto a clean surface. Shape the mixture into balls.

5 Roll the balls in honey and sprinkle with ground almonds.

BREAD was the mainstay of most people's diet, but it was a bit of a mixed blessing. The texture of Egyptian bread was fairly tough as it was often full of sand and grit that became mixed up in the grinding of the grain. Studies on mummies show that it was so coarse that it wore down the teeth of those who ate it!

Fun and Games

Tomb paintings and the **artifacts**, or implements made by people, that were buried with the ancient Egyptians show that they enjoyed themselves in many ways. Music was very popular, and performers were in great demand at celebrations.

MUSICIANS were mostly male during the Old Kingdom, but mainly female by the New Kingdom. Blind men were sometimes employed as harpists. Being blind was not a disadvantage because music was memorized by sound rather than written down. Children of rich families were also taught to play instruments for their own pleasure.

∿∿ MAKE A HARP

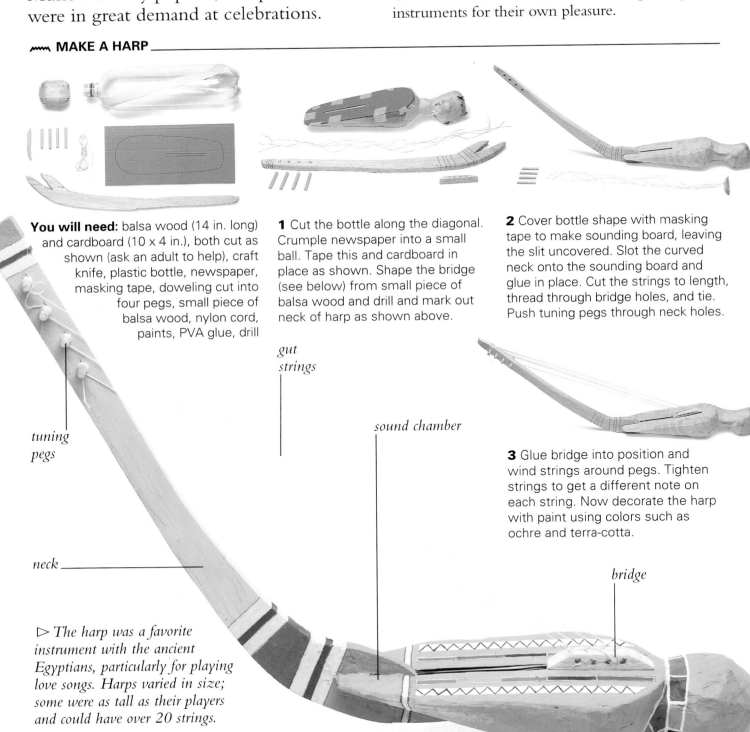

You will need: balsa wood (14 in. long) and cardboard (10 x 4 in.), both cut as shown (ask an adult to help), craft knife, plastic bottle, newspaper, masking tape, doweling cut into four pegs, small piece of balsa wood, nylon cord, paints, PVA glue, drill

1 Cut the bottle along the diagonal. Crumple newspaper into a small ball. Tape this and cardboard in place as shown. Shape the bridge (see below) from small piece of balsa wood and drill and mark out neck of harp as shown above.

2 Cover bottle shape with masking tape to make sounding board, leaving the slit uncovered. Slot the curved neck onto the sounding board and glue in place. Cut the strings to length, thread through bridge holes, and tie. Push tuning pegs through neck holes.

3 Glue bridge into position and wind strings around pegs. Tighten strings to get a different note on each string. Now decorate the harp with paint using colors such as ochre and terra-cotta.

gut strings

sound chamber

tuning pegs

neck

bridge

▷ *The harp was a favorite instrument with the ancient Egyptians, particularly for playing love songs. Harps varied in size; some were as tall as their players and could have over 20 strings.*

⌁ MAKE A SISTRUM

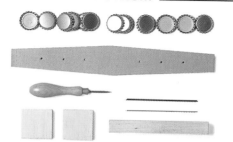

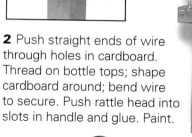

You will need: balsa wood (8 x 1 in.), PVA glue, saw, awl, pliers, thin wire, wire cutter, cardboard (16 x 3 in.) cut and holes made as shown, bottle tops, paint

1 Glue both squares of wood onto handle as shown. Use awl to pierce a hole in each bottle top. Cut the wire into three, using pliers to bend up one side. Make saw cuts into the top of the handle as shown above right.

2 Push straight ends of wire through holes in cardboard. Thread on bottle tops; shape cardboard around; bend wire to secure. Push rattle head into slots in handle and glue. Paint.

MUSICAL INSTRUMENTS fell into three groups: strings, wind, and percussion. They became more complex during the New Kingdom as new musical ideas arrived from the East. The harp, lyre, and lute were the main string instruments; early forms of the flute, oboe, and clarinet made up the wind section; rattles, castanets, and tambourines were popular percussion instruments.

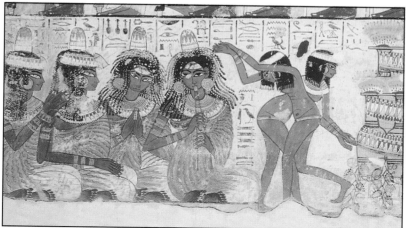

△ *Dancing girls and musicians are in full swing at a banquet in this wall painting. The hieroglyphs show the song being performed.*

EGYPTIAN BANQUETS were rowdy and fun, and religious festivals were equally lively. Enormous amounts of food and wine were consumed, and for guests who overindulged, a servant was always on hand with scented water or a sick bowl!

PROFESSIONAL DANCERS, acrobats, magicians, and storytellers were attached to the royal court and to noblemen's homes. The dancers were mainly women who started their training when young. Other performers worked in troupes for hire.

△ *Noblewomen and priestesses carried a sacred rattle, or sistrum, at ceremonies.*

HUNTING was a favorite pastime of men. The pharaoh and his nobles hunted lions, wild bulls, and leopards. Accompanied by professional hunters, they took off into the desert in horse-drawn chariots in pursuit of prey. Alternatively, they would lie in wait around a water hole, ready to attack beasts with bows and arrows.

IN THE MARSHY RIVER DELTA, waterbirds were killed with throwing sticks, and hippopotami with lassoes and harpoons. Hippos were a menace to farmers as they flattened crops. Only the brave hunted crocodiles.

▷ *Hippo-hunting on the river*

THE RIVER was also a place to relax. Egyptians would take their reed boats down to the water, enjoy a picnic, go fishing, or catch waterbirds.

CHILDREN played leapfrog and tug-of-war and practiced wrestling and gymnastics. **Senet** was a favorite board game played by everyone.

MAKE A SENET GAME

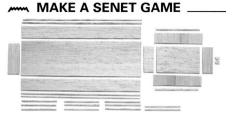

You will need: balsa wood, craft knife, PVA glue, paint, felt-tip pens, self-hardening clay, ruler, sandpaper

1 With an adult's help, cut wood as shown (12 x 4 in. base). Larger pieces (left) for board; smaller pieces (right) for drawer.

2 Make five pieces for each player (Senet is a game for two players) and a couple of spares, from the clay. When the clay is dry, paint five of the pieces black and five white.

3 Glue together the drawer and handle from balsa wood as shown. Then glue the drawer runners to the bottom edge of the side pieces. Mark the top board into 30 squares.

TO PLAY SENET

The object of the game is for one player to get his/her pieces around and off the board before his/her opponent. Players throw the four dice sticks to find out how far to move when it is their turn:

One flat side up = 1   Four flat sides up = 4
Two flat sides up = 2   Four round sides up = 6
Three flat sides up = 3

RULES

● Throwing a 1, 4, or 6 wins a player another throw.
● Pieces move up and down the board lengthwise: row one, left to right; row two, right to left; row three, left to right.
● Landing on a square occupied by an opponent means the opponent's piece must move back to the square his attacker has come from.
● Two pieces of the same color cannot occupy one square, but next to each other they cannot be attacked.
● Three pieces in a row cannot be passed by an opponent.
● The square marked means a player must go back to the square marked ⌾, and if that is occupied, go back to the start.
● The squares marked ↓↓↓, ≋, and 👥👥 are safe from attack.
● A player cannot move a piece off the board until all his pieces are off the first row.

START OF PLAY

1 Place a white piece on every other square of the first row and five black pieces on the squares in between.

2 The first player to throw a 1 moves the last black piece on the first row one square down. Then he throws again, free now to move any of the black pieces.

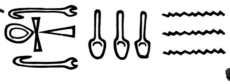

start   *finish*

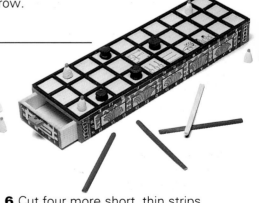

3 When the white player makes his first move, he must use the last white piece in the first row.

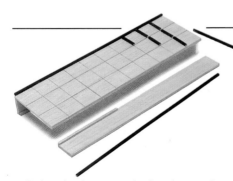

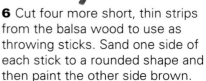

4 Paint the long vertical strips and shorter dividing sticks black. Cut the dividing sticks into short strips and glue firmly in between the vertical ones as shown above.

5 Copy the images above onto the top of the board. It is important that each sits on the correct square as shown right. Decorate the board's sides with felt-tip pens and paint.

6 Cut four more short, thin strips from the balsa wood to use as throwing sticks. Sand one side of each stick to a rounded shape and then paint the other side brown.

Artwork

Many beautiful objects have survived from ancient Egypt, indicating that the Egyptians were skilled and creative. They made papyrus sheets to write on, and the rich adorned their houses with ornaments and fabrics. Many workers were employed solely as craftsmen to meet their needs.

WEAVING was one of the earliest Egyptian crafts. Scraps of woven linen have been discovered that date back 6,000 years. Linen fibers come from the flax plant. The stems were soaked in water until only the fibers were left. These were combed into fine strands and spun to make a continuous thread.

TO MAKE PAPYRUS SHEETS, papyrus reeds, which grew abundantly along the Nile, were harvested. First the green outer skin of the stem was peeled away. The inner core was then cut into strips and soaked in water. The wet strips were placed in a frame, side by side and just overlapping, and another layer of strips going the other way was laid on top. The paper sheet was pressed, dried, rolled, and polished.

MAKE A LOOM

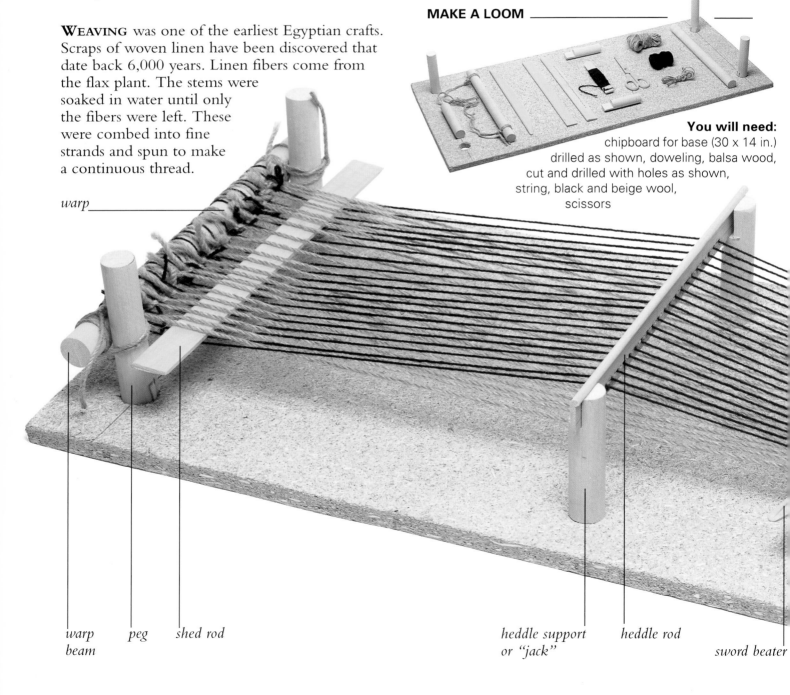

You will need:
chipboard for base (30 x 14 in.) drilled as shown, doweling, balsa wood, cut and drilled with holes as shown, string, black and beige wool, scissors

warp

warp beam   *peg*   *shed rod*

heddle support or "jack"   *heddle rod*   *sword beater*

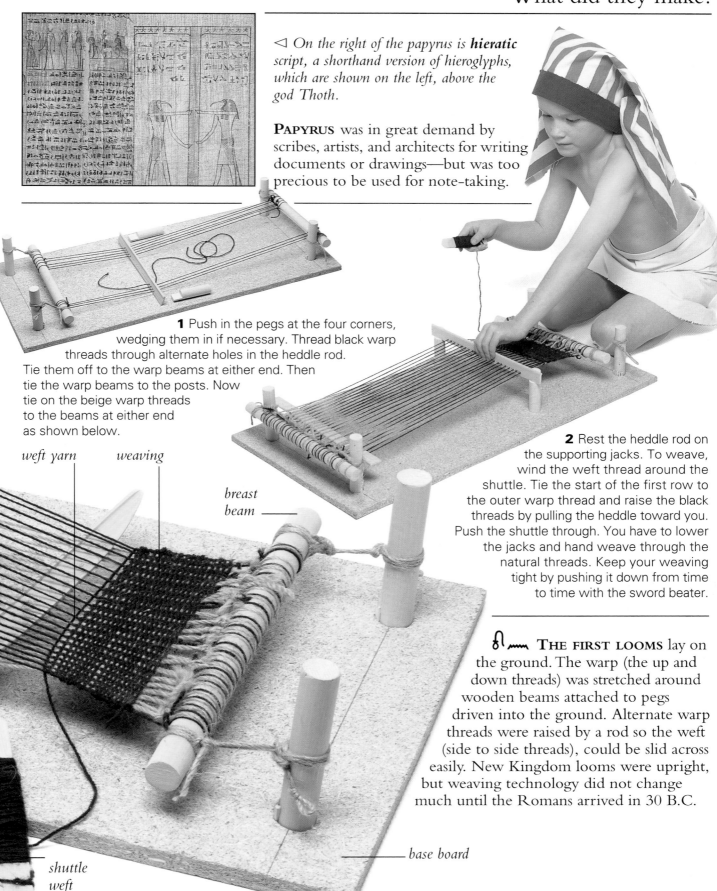

◁ *On the right of the papyrus is* **hieratic** *script, a shorthand version of hieroglyphs, which are shown on the left, above the god Thoth.*

PAPYRUS was in great demand by scribes, artists, and architects for writing documents or drawings—but was too precious to be used for note-taking.

1 Push in the pegs at the four corners, wedging them in if necessary. Thread black warp threads through alternate holes in the heddle rod. Tie them off to the warp beams at either end. Then tie the warp beams to the posts. Now tie on the beige warp threads to the beams at either end as shown below.

weft yarn

weaving

breast beam

2 Rest the heddle rod on the supporting jacks. To weave, wind the weft thread around the shuttle. Tie the start of the first row to the outer warp thread and raise the black threads by pulling the heddle toward you. Push the shuttle through. You have to lower the jacks and hand weave through the natural threads. Keep your weaving tight by pushing it down from time to time with the sword beater.

𓂧𓏤 **THE FIRST LOOMS** lay on the ground. The warp (the up and down threads) was stretched around wooden beams attached to pegs driven into the ground. Alternate warp threads were raised by a rod so the weft (side to side threads), could be slid across easily. New Kingdom looms were upright, but weaving technology did not change much until the Romans arrived in 30 B.C.

base board

shuttle weft

◁ *This Middle Kingdom jug shows a kneeling woman nursing a baby. Scholars believe that it could even be a representation of the goddess Isis feeding her son Horus. A mother's milk was thought to be a potent remedy for illness and was often stored in jars and pots.*

HOUSEHOLD POTS were made from river clay. The clay was first prepared by adding fine sand to make it easier to work. The potters then shaped the vessels using the coil method and smoothed them inside and out to a remarkably even thickness. The outsides of the pots were often rubbed with a flat stone before firing to give them a shiny red look. Others were painted with black designs or rippled by dragging a comb across the surface.

WOOD-BURNING KILNS were used to fire the pots. They were beehive-shaped and made from mud bricks. They needed constant attention to keep the temperature high and even.

MAKE A CLAY POT

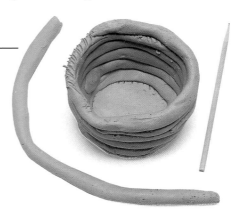

You will need: self-hardening clay, sharp pencil, paints

1 Knead the clay until it is easy to work. Make a flat, round base for your pot. Keep the remaining clay in a ball so it does not dry out.

2 Take some clay from the ball and roll out two long coils of the same thickness. Score the rim of the base with a pencil so the clay will stick properly.

3 Use the coils to build up the sides of the pot as shown. Make a third coil before using the second, and so on, to ensure they are all the same length. Score every layer as you go.

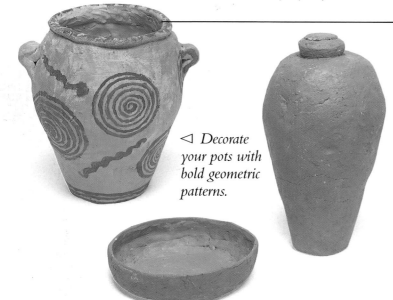

◁ *Decorate your pots with bold geometric patterns.*

A TAPERING BASE was given to many vessels. This meant they could be rested in a stand or fitted into a depression in the ground. Early on, they were decorated with geometric patterns on a red surface, or spiral and mottled designs to mimic vessels that had been carved from stone.

DECORATIVE VASES and stylized sculptures of human and animal figures were made in the New Kingdom period. Instead of the red and black decoration of earlier times, pots were also painted with a bold shade of blue, a pigment extracted from copper or cobalt.

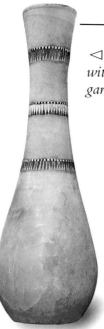

◁ *A New Kingdom alabaster vase with a long neck inlaid with floral garlands made of glass paste.*

△ *This calcite "wishing cup" was one of the first finds by the excavators venturing into Tutankhamen's tomb.*

METAL VASES, BOWLS, and open containers were made of gold, bronze, and copper by hammering sheets of metal around an anvil, a heavy wood or stone block. Statues, tools, and weapons were cast by pouring the molten metal into a pottery or stone mold. All metals were considered rare and precious because, even if there was an adequate supply, mining was an expensive, difficult, and lengthy process.

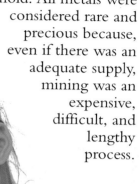

4 When you get to the widest point, stop and smooth both the inside and outside of your pot. Score the top before you restart with the coils.

5 When you have completed your pot, smooth the outside and inside for a perfect finish. Add a rim and, if you like, a pair of handles. Then allow to dry according to the directions on the package.

6 Paint your pot dark red to look like terra-cotta from the Nile Valley. When that is dry, paint on some black geometric designs.

STONE VESSELS were made from the large outcrops of attractive mottled stone found in the desert and hills bordering the valley of the Nile River. First, blocks of stone were cut out using a saw, and these were then shaped on the outside with chisels, **bow drills**, and **rasps**. Finally, the insides were drilled and chiseled out. Vases with narrow necks were made in two separate pieces and then cemented together.

△ *This is a replica of a wall painting taken from the tomb of a powerful overlord from the Middle Kingdom. The painter may have first used a system of grids.*

THE BEST PRESERVED paintings were painted onto the plaster walls of the sealed tombs of the wealthy. Evidence shows that houses were painted with colored murals and patterns, also.

MAKE A TOMB PAINTING

You will need: plaster of paris, water, bowl, nail, polystyrene tray (6 x 4 in.), pencil, ruler, paper and tracing paper, paints, steel wool

1 Put the plaster into a bowl and add water gradually, stirring all the time, so that there are no dry patches of powder left. Mix the plaster with your fingers and get rid of any air bubbles.

2 When you have a smooth paste, pour the mixture into the polystyrene tray. Leave to set until it has formed into a plaque as shown above right.

3 Copy or draw your own Egyptian scene on tracing paper. If you prefer, you can use the ancient Egyptian method of using a grid to help you get the figure(s) in proportion.

4 When the plaque is dry, put your tracing paper over it and draw over every line, pressing hard. Scratch away the lines on the plaque with a nail to leave a clear outline.

5 Paint the plaque using earthy, natural colors. Then, using the steel wool, gently rub away small bits of the picture so that it passes for being about 3,000 years old, as shown right.

◁ *A wall painting from the tomb of the pharaoh Horemheb that was discovered in the Valley of the Kings. The goddess Isis faces the pharaoh, and the god Harsiese is on the right.*

DRAWING, and the rules that went with it, evolved alongside writing. Artists drew and painted not what they saw, but what they knew was there. So if, for example, they were painting a chest that they knew contained a necklace in one of the drawers, they might show a side view of the chest with the necklace placed on top. And when they drew a scene, it did not simply record what they saw from their own viewpoint, but included everything and everyone that they knew to be present.

DEFINITE RULES applied to art because it had a definite purpose: to come to life in the next world. The people and objects in the afterlife had to be perfect, so tomb and temple paintings never portrayed death, disease, or old age.

PEOPLE AND OBJECTS were drawn flat, from whatever angle made them instantly recognizable. People were nearly always drawn with their faces, arms, and legs in profile (because they are easier to identify), but the eye and shoulders faced the front. Men were often shown as having dark skin, as they worked in the sun, whereas women were fair-skinned as they spent more time indoors.

PROPORTIONS were laid down so that people could be recognized by the gods in the afterlife and to provide guidelines for apprentice artists. Most apprentices used a squared grid as a guide. One Middle Kingdom scale measured the standing human figure as 18 squares from the ground to the hairline, so the shoulders started in square 16, the waist in square 12 and the knees between 6 and 7.

PAINT COLORS were made from powdered minerals and other natural materials. These are just some examples:

Black	charcoal
Red	ochre
White	powdered limestone
Blue	copper/cobalt
Green	malachite
Yellow	iron oxide

▷ *Malachite, an oxide of copper, was ground to make a soft green eyeshadow.*

◁ *Copper was mined in Nubia, Sinai, and the Eastern Desert. It was used to make tools as well as pigment.*

Reading and Writing

One reason we know so much about the ancient Egyptians is because they had a written language and recorded everything. All legal and business agreements were documented, so the few who could read and write were in great demand. They were called **scribes**. Instead of an alphabet, they used 27 **hieroglyphs**, or signs, to represent sounds. There were an additional 700, which could be used in various combinations to give particular meanings or else to represent groups of two or three consonants.

ANCIENT EGYPTIAN belongs to a family of languages that spread across northern Africa and western Asia. Some languages in that family, such as Arabic, are still spoken today. But ancient Egyptian is a dead language, except where it survives in a form within the Coptic Church.

THE ROSETTA STONE was the key to deciphering hieroglyphs. This black stone is inscribed with text in three different languages: Greek, **demotic** script, and hieroglyphs. It was discovered in 1799, near Rosetta in the Nile Delta and later decoded by the French scholar Jean-François Champollion in 1822.

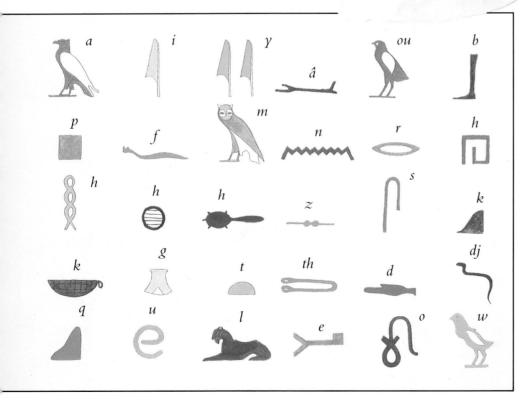

a   i   y   â   ou   b
p   f   m   n   r   h
h   h   h   z   s   k
k   g   t   th   d   dj
q   u   l   e   o   w

△ *The use of hieroglyphs made writing complex and difficult to learn.*

HIEROGLYPHS were carved into stone on monuments, painted on walls of burial tombs, and used for making up a **cartouche**, or personal seal, which could be used as a signature.

△ *The top section of the Rosetta Stone is in hieroglyphs, the middle in demotic, and the bottom in Greek.*

hieroglyphs   demotic   Greek

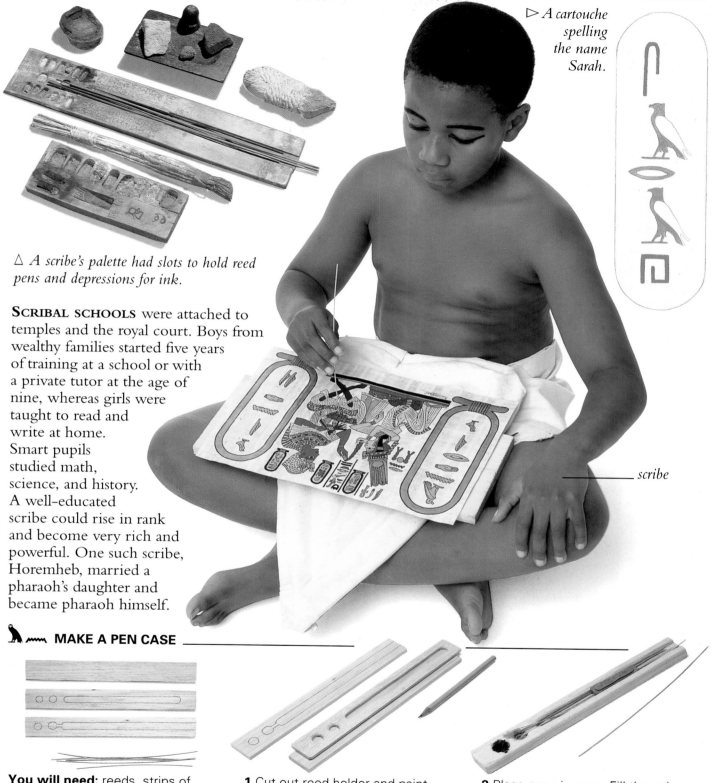

△ *A scribe's palette had slots to hold reed pens and depressions for ink.*

▷ *A cartouche spelling the name Sarah.*

scribe

SCRIBAL SCHOOLS were attached to temples and the royal court. Boys from wealthy families started five years of training at a school or with a private tutor at the age of nine, whereas girls were taught to read and write at home. Smart pupils studied math, science, and history. A well-educated scribe could rise in rank and become very rich and powerful. One such scribe, Horemheb, married a pharaoh's daughter and became pharaoh himself.

MAKE A PEN CASE

You will need: reeds, strips of balsa wood (10 x 2 in.), marked as shown, PVA glue, powder paints, craft knife

1 Cut out reed holder and paint wells as shown and sandwich together the layers of wood. Glue into place. Leave to dry.

2 Place pens in case. Fill the paint wells with powder paint to look like ground-up minerals. Now your scribe's palette is complete.

Egyptian Inventions

The Egyptians were clever, curious people who invented many things we recognize today. In addition to their complicated form of picture writing (see page 102), they had advanced ideas about medicine, measuring time, mathematics, and astronomy.

THE ANCIENT EGYPTIANS were the first people to organize the year into 365 days and the days into 24 hours. The Egyptian year was divided like this:

10 days = 1 week   3 weeks = 1 month
4 months = 1 season   3 seasons + 5 holy days = 1 year

THE WATER CLOCK, the most common Egyptian clock, was a vessel marked with lines on the inside. Time was measured against these levels as water dripped through a hole in the base. Sun poles, ideal in the sunny climate, were used by people of learning, such as priests, to tell the time.

MAKE A WATER CLOCK

You will need: pot made from self-hardening clay, painted and varnished inside to make it waterproof, awl, wax crayon, water jug filled with water, cup or glass

1 Make a small hole with an awl in side of pot near to base as shown left. Place glass or cup under pot to catch water dripping out of the hole. Pour water into pot, filling it up.

EGYPTIAN DOCTORS were surprisingly advanced for their time. Papyrus manuals reveal that they had a detailed knowledge of bodily systems such as digestion, circulation, and the nervous system. This was gained largely through centuries of **embalming** the dead. They also studied the symptoms of sick people in order to understand illness and disease and used plants and herbs, such as garlic and juniper berries, as cures.

MAGICIANS were valued for their healing powers, too. Spells were chanted as cures and to ward off injury, sickness, and danger.

▷ *The mummified head of Nebera, chief of the royal stables of Thutmose III. Embalming taught doctors a lot about **anatomy**.*

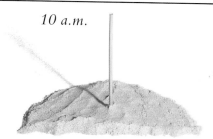

7 a.m.

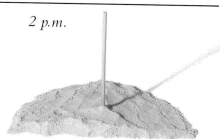

10 a.m.

2 p.m.

You will need: wooden post, watch

1 Find a spot outside that is sunny all day.

2 Push the post into the ground and mark where the shadow falls at 7 a.m. Check the shadow's position every hour, marking it each time.

3 After a full day of sun, with a mark on the ground for every hour, your sun pole will be all set to tell you the time when the sun next appears.

2 Time the water as it drips out, using a crayon to mark the water level on inside of pot every five minutes. Once empty, refill pot and time again, checking marks for accuracy.

MEASUREMENTS were related to the human body. The main one was the cubit, equal to the distance from the elbow to the tip of the middle finger. It was further divided into palms and digits (the width of a finger).

MATHEMATICAL CALCULATIONS involving sophisticated **geometry** were used for building pyramids. The Egyptians had no signs for numbers between two and nine.

1= | 10 = ∩   100 = ℮   1,000 = 𝑋

so 13 was written like this: ∩ | | |
146 like this: ℮ ∩ ∩ | | |
                ∩ ∩ | | |

▷ *The Egyptian measuring system worked like this:*

distance from elbow to outstretched fingertip = 1 cubit

cubit = seven palms

palm = four finger widths

elbow to fingertip = 1 cubit

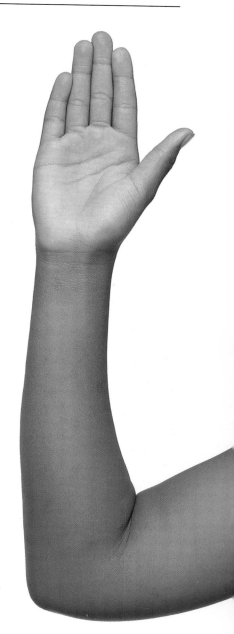

Boats and Chariots

The Nile was the highway of Egypt. Boats could drift downstream with the current to the north of the country and sail upstream with the help of the northerly wind to the south. The Egyptian hieroglyph for traveling north is a boat with no sail or mast, and for traveling south it is a ship in full sail.

𓃀 **EARLY BOATS** were made from papyrus reeds, bound with string made from reed fibers. By 3200 B.C. timber was being imported from Lebanon, and boatyards on the Nile were building wooden ships.

◁ *A gilded wooden sculpture showing the pharaoh Tutankhamen as a harpooner on a papyrus raft.*

deckhouse

forestay

bow

𓃀 MAKE A REED BOAT

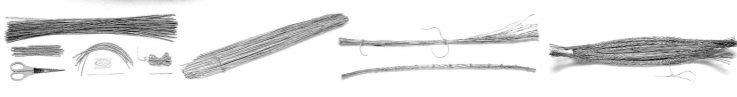

You will need: bundle of thin reeds or dried grasses 18 in. long, scissors, thin string, darning needle, balsa wood, cut as shown into handle and blade for steering oar, six lengths of basket cane for deckhouse (6 in. long), glue, scissors

1 Tie a small bundle of reeds with string at regular intervals. Prepare seven or eight bundles in the same way and sew them together. Trim the ends so the boat base looks like the example above left.

2 Make two longer bundles for the sides, as shown above left. Sew them on securely using the string and darning needle. Fill in the center with more bundles if necessary and sew them to the boat base as above.

FERRIES were used by most Egyptians wanting to cross the Nile, which had no bridges. A constant traffic of ferryboats rowed across from side to side, carrying people and goods.

GRAND BOATS owned by nobles and government officials were used for business as well as pleasure.

stern

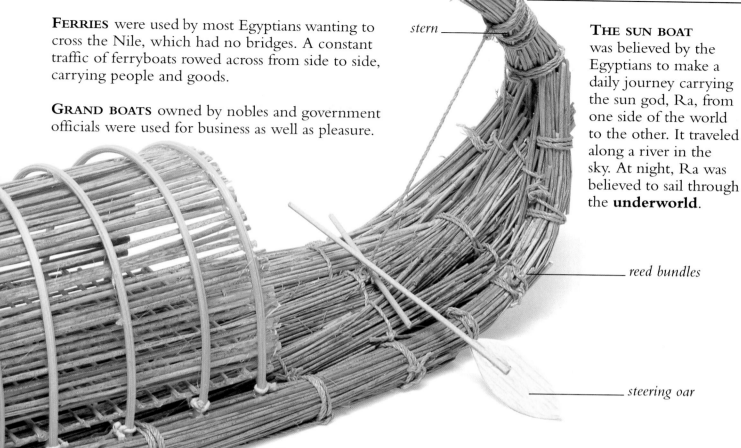

THE SUN BOAT was believed by the Egyptians to make a daily journey carrying the sun god, Ra, from one side of the world to the other. It traveled along a river in the sky. At night, Ra was believed to sail through **the underworld**.

reed bundles

steering oar

CARGO BOATS were a common sight. All heavy cargo, such as slabs of stone or **obelisks**, was moved on huge river barges, towed by a fleet of small boats.

CATTLE BOATS were special wide boats with flat decks. They were made to transport an Egyptian farmer's most treasured possession— his cattle. These animals were the true measure of his wealth and worth protecting at all costs.

FUNERAL BARGES were used to carry bodies across the river to the embalmers' workshops. The crossing was conducted with great ceremony and dignity.

ROYAL BOATS ensured that the pharaoh traveled in great style and comfort. Huge, canopied boats protected royal families from the glare of the sun and the inquisitive stare of their subjects.

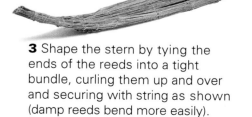

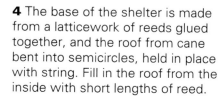

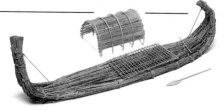

3 Shape the stern by tying the ends of the reeds into a tight bundle, curling them up and over and securing with string as shown (damp reeds bend more easily). Shape the bow in the same way.

4 The base of the shelter is made from a latticework of reeds glued together, and the roof from cane bent into semicircles, held in place with string. Fill in the roof from the inside with short lengths of reed.

5 Glue the base of the shelter onto the boat and fix the roof on top. Glue together the oar handle and paddle. The stick at the stern is a support for the steering oar, so it can be held still. Now the boat is ready to float!

SEAGOING BOATS had to be bigger and stronger than river boats, although they followed the same basic design. They were built of wood, mainly cedar wood, which came from the hillsides of a seaport in Lebanon called Byblos. Seagoing boats were known as "Byblos-boats."

ORDINARY EGYPTIANS traveled very little. Some ventured as far as the next village and, if they could afford it, made a once-in-a-lifetime pilgrimage to Abydos, a religious center in the south. Generally, people were very suspicious of foreign places, and thought it far better to stay at home. Their greatest fear was to die in a foreign country where they would not have a proper burial, and so arrive unprepared for the afterlife.

△ *A model sailing boat found in Tutankhamen's tomb, complete with oars and linen sails.*

FOREIGN TRADE was the prize that tempted Egyptians to travel. To the south lay Nubia (now Sudan), rich in gold, copper, and semiprecious stones. Strange animals such as monkeys, giraffes, and panthers were brought back, too.

TO THE NORTH lay the Mediterranean Sea. However, the Egyptians stuck to the more familiar northeast coastline and traded with what are now Israel, Lebanon, and Syria. Syrians traveled to Egypt, too. Quite different in appearance, their colorful clothes and beards seemed strange to ancient Egyptians.

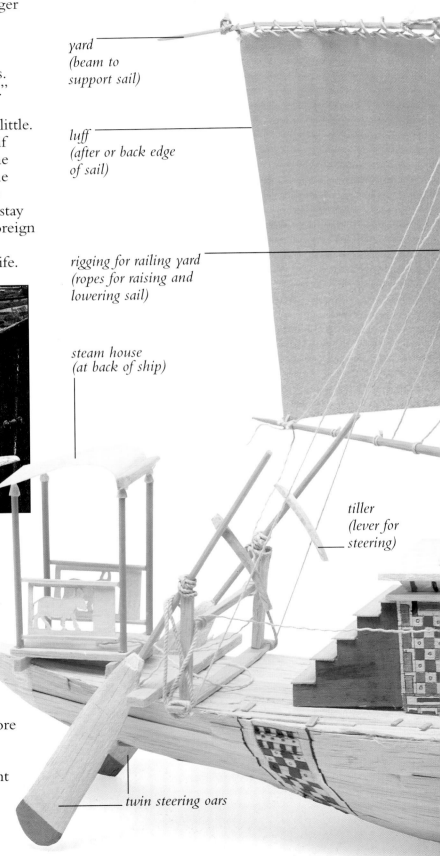

*yard
(beam to
support sail)*

*luff
(after or back edge
of sail)*

*rigging for railing yard
(ropes for raising and
lowering sail)*

*steam house
(at back of ship)*

*tiller
(lever for
steering)*

twin steering oars

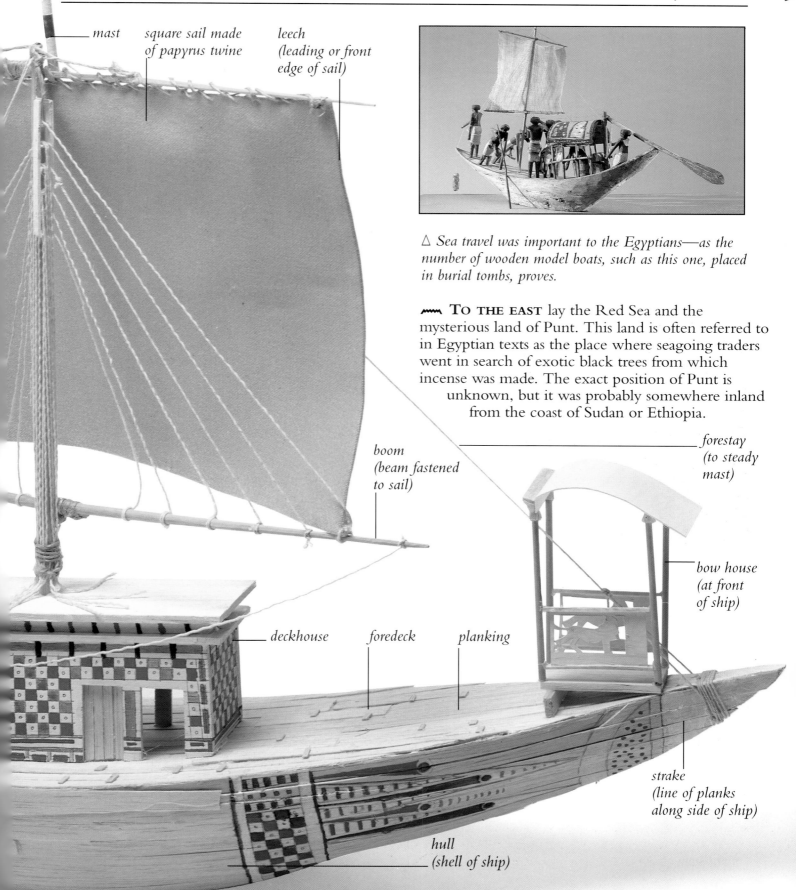

mast

square sail made of papyrus twine

leech (leading or front edge of sail)

△ Sea travel was important to the Egyptians—as the number of wooden model boats, such as this one, placed in burial tombs, proves.

〰 **To the east** lay the Red Sea and the mysterious land of Punt. This land is often referred to in Egyptian texts as the place where seagoing traders went in search of exotic black trees from which incense was made. The exact position of Punt is unknown, but it was probably somewhere inland from the coast of Sudan or Ethiopia.

boom (beam fastened to sail)

forestay (to steady mast)

bow house (at front of ship)

deckhouse

foredeck

planking

strake (line of planks along side of ship)

hull (shell of ship)

THERE WERE NO PROPER ROADS in ancient Egypt. There was no point as the annual floods would have washed them away. Unless they were lucky enough to own a donkey, ordinary people had to walk everywhere. Very rich people were carried around by servants on platforms with thronelike seats.

THE EASTERN DESERT, which lay between the east bank of the Nile and the Red Sea, provided overland routes to present-day Syria and Lebanon. Trade with these countries was important since they had a wealth of metals and semiprecious stones. The Eastern Desert also yielded raw materials, such as copper and tin.

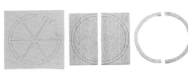 **MAKE A CHARIOT**

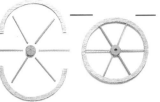 

To make the wheels you will need: paper, pencil, compass, balsa wood, thin doweling for spokes and pegs, thicker doweling for axle, wood circles for hubs, PVA glue, craft knife

1 Draw template for wheels as shown. Use the compass to mark two sections for each wheel onto wood (6 in. diameter). Ask an adult to help cut them out.

2 Assemble wheels, fitting spokes into holes drilled in hub and gluing them onto inside rim of wheel. Fix axle with peg as shown. Paint.

HEAVY OBJECTS, such as stones and statues, were tied onto sleds and pulled by men with ropes. Water or oil was poured under the front of the sled to make it slide along more easily.

horse yoke

TO THE WEST lay a desert area populated by **nomadic** tribes and known, during the years of the Old and Middle Kingdoms, as *Tjemehu.* Today it is Libya. Below Tjemehu was the endless stretch of the Western Desert, which protected Egypt from raiding neighbors. It also provided the ancient Egyptians with limestone which they quarried from the areas close to home.

yoke pole

LONG OVERLAND journeys were made to carry out these trading operations with neighbors to the east, and for mining and quarrying operations to the west. Donkeys were laden with goods and taken on long treks across the desert. Camels, ideal animals for desert travel, were not introduced until the beginning of the Roman period in 30 B.C. when raiding tribesmen descended upon the fertile Nile Valley on these strange, swift-footed beasts.

◁ *This relief in the rock, from the temple of Ramses II, shows the pharaoh riding into battle on a chariot while conquering Nubia, situated to the south.*

THE CHARIOT was introduced to Egypt by the Hyksos from southern Palestine. They invaded the delta area of Egypt at the end of the Middle Kingdom period. The rich were the only people able to afford chariots. They used them for hunting and traveling around on business.

CHARIOT WHEELS were a technological marvel, given the few tools available. They were made from curved segments of wood, bound together with a leather hoop. Initially, all chariots ran on four-spoked wheels, but during the New Kingdom, an extra two spokes were added.

To make the cage you will need: balsa wood, cut and sanded as above, uprights and axle fittings as above right, string, basket cane, PVA glue

3 Glue pieces of wood together as shown. Fix cane handrail onto top of uprights with string. Glue and tie cane front struts to form Y-shape.

To complete the chariot you will need: canvas (8 in. sq.) cut as shown, glue, weaving cane, thin string, darning needle, paint, felt-tip pens

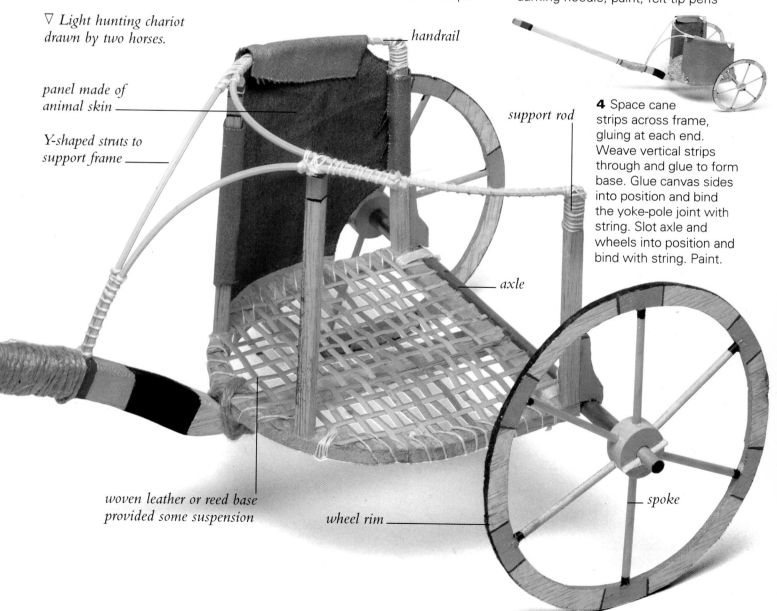

▽ *Light hunting chariot drawn by two horses.*

handrail

panel made of animal skin

Y-shaped struts to support frame

support rod

axle

4 Space cane strips across frame, gluing at each end. Weave vertical strips through and glue to form base. Glue canvas sides into position and bind the yoke-pole joint with string. Slot axle and wheels into position and bind with string. Paint.

woven leather or reed base provided some suspension

wheel rim

spoke

Guarding the Frontiers

△ *Daggers often boasted sheaths overlaid with gold.*

Ancient Egypt was the first rich and powerful civilization in history. Naturally it attracted the envy of neighbors who wanted some of Egypt's wealth for themselves. The pharaohs of Egypt would rather have conquered by influence than by war. But they were certainly prepared to push out the boundaries of Egypt, building fortresses for protection and dealing harshly with intruders if necessary.

MAKE A SHIELD

You will need: thick cardboard (30 x 18 in.), scissors, paint, canvas, pencil, string, PVA glue

1 Cut out cardboard in the shape of a shield as shown above. Then, cut out a piece of canvas, the same shape, only larger.

2 Glue canvas to cardboard. Draw a wide border around the edge. Paint the area inside the border white with brown patches to look like cowhide.

◁ *Arrowheads were commonly made of copper and designed to kill the victim instantly.*

THE ROYAL ARMY, during the Old and Middle Kingdoms, consisted of a small group of professional soldiers and the pharaoh's bodyguards. If a campaign was being mounted, laborers would be called up from the fields. At this time, the army was made up of foot soldiers armed with either bows and arrows or axes and spears and protected by large shields of wood or leather.

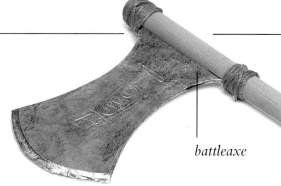

battleaxe

BY THE NEW KINGDOM, warfare had become much more organized. The army was larger and better run, with horses and chariots providing extra speed. Soldiers were well trained and were allowed to take slaves and goods from conquered armies after a successful campaign.

A golden fly was the pharaoh's award for bravery on the battlefield.

SEVERAL DIVISIONS existed within the royal army. Each division consisted of 4,000 foot soldiers and an elite corps of 1,000 charioteers. It was then subdivided into 20 companies of 250 men—200 foot soldiers (in four units of 50 men) and 50 charioteers.

CHARIOTEERS fought two to a chariot and were regarded as superior to other soldiers. They had their own barracks and were only temporarily assigned to a company.

AXES AND SPEARS had wooden handles and bronze blades. Soldiers wore protective tunics with metal scales or wrapped bands of leather around their chests.

CAMPS were set up when the army was on the move. A moat was dug around the outside and the soldiers' shields were used to make a wall.

OFFICERS' TENTS were comfortably furnished and they had cooks and scribes to organize supplies and keep a daily record of the battle.

MAKE A BATTLEAXE

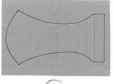

You will need: craft knife, glue, doweling, pencil, string, silver foil, saw, cardboard

1 Mark out and cut the blade shapes from cardboard. Cut two shapes per blade and trim one side a little shorter than the other.

2 Ask an adult to help you saw down the doweling to the depth of the blade as shown. Score a design on the blade with a pencil.

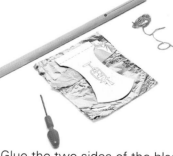

3 Glue the two sides of the blade together with the longer side underneath. Cover the blade with foil, rubbing over the design. Slot blade into the doweling and secure with string as shown left.

Gods and the Afterlife

The ancient Egyptians believed strongly in many gods who ruled everything from the sun and moon, to love, wisdom, and war. Some were national gods, worshiped in grand temples all over the country, but most were local gods with temples in their own home town. Their strongest belief was that the Egyptians would enjoy a wonderful, trouble-free life after death, in other words a perfect version of life on earth. To be prepared, the dead were buried with all their possessions and food for the journey to the afterlife.

THE SUN GOD, RA, is involved in most Egyptian legends about the creation of the world. In one version, the world is nothing but a black ocean. Then a mound of dry land emerges out of the mud and a sacred blue lotus flower grows. It opens up and out steps Ra, who goes on to create all things.

▷ *An Old Kingdom group statue of the pharaoh Mycerinus between the goddess Hathor, regarded as the ideal of beauty, and Hu, the personification of a province of Upper Egypt.*

ANIMAL GODS were worshiped from the Old Kingdom onward. The Egyptians often associated the character of an animal with that of a god. By the New Kingdom, most gods continued to be depicted with the head or body of an animal.

◁ *A solid gold statuette of Amun-Ra, a New Kingdom god who was a powerful combination of the sun god Ra and Amun the creator.*

Montu, god of war

Amun, creator god

Khons, god of the moon

Thoth, god of knowledge

Horus, royal protector

Hathor, goddess of love

Anubis, god of the **necropolis**

Osiris, god of the underworld

HUNDREDS OF GODS and goddesses were worshiped by the Egyptians, and many of them were related. Shu, son of Ra, was god of the air. Shu's daughter, Nut, was the sky goddess. Her body stretched across the horizon, held up by her father. She married Geb, her brother and god of the earth. Their heirs were Isis and Osiris (god of the underworld), and together they ruled Egypt.

Set, brother of Osiris and Isis, and god of evil, was jealous. He murdered Osiris and cut up his body. Anubis, god of embalming and the dead, gathered the pieces and the goddess Isis restored him to life.

TEMPLES were the earthly homes of the gods and goddesses. Only priests and priestesses could enter, while ordinary people prayed at the gates.

〰 **MAKE ANUBIS**

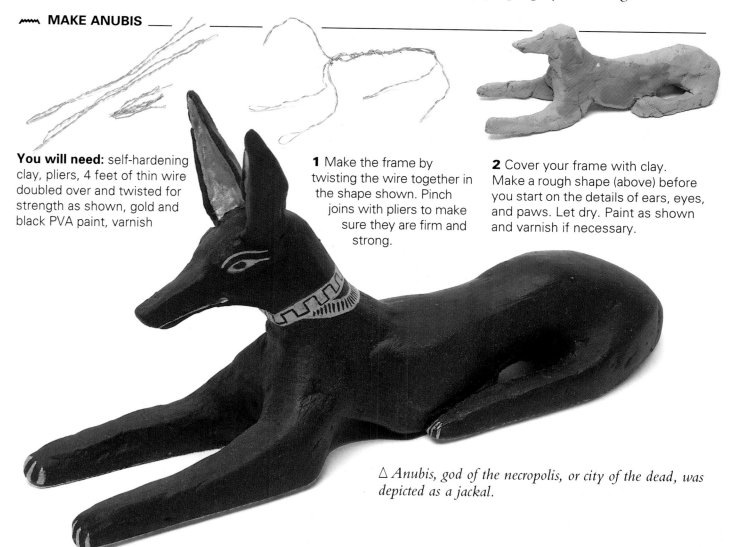

You will need: self-hardening clay, pliers, 4 feet of thin wire doubled over and twisted for strength as shown, gold and black PVA paint, varnish

1 Make the frame by twisting the wire together in the shape shown. Pinch joins with pliers to make sure they are firm and strong.

2 Cover your frame with clay. Make a rough shape (above) before you start on the details of ears, eyes, and paws. Let dry. Paint as shown and varnish if necessary.

△ *Anubis, god of the necropolis, or city of the dead, was depicted as a jackal.*

△ *The magnificent death mask of the young pharaoh Tutankhamen represents him as Osiris, god of the underworld. It is made of inlaid sheet gold and measures 21 inches high and weighs over 27 pounds.*

THE UNDERWORLD, called Duat, was believed to be a land full of dangers. The **Book of the Dead** was buried in tombs with the dead. This guidebook to the underworld, and a knowledge of all the right spells, guaranteed safe passage through the underworld to the Hall of Two Truths.

THE AFTERLIFE, an ideal version of Egypt, was where everyone wanted to go when they died. Upon death, an Egyptian arriving in the Hall of Two Truths would be led to a set of scales by Anubis, god of the dead and of embalming. Here, after being interrogated, his or her heart was weighed against the feather of truth. If honest, the person was granted safe passage to the afterlife by Osiris. The hearts of the dishonest were devoured by a goddess known as Devourer of the Dead. Paradise was no place for spirits without a heart.

GRAVES of ordinary people have been found, and it seems they were buried in reed or wooden chests along with their possessions and food, to ensure they reached the afterlife.

THE BODIES OF THE RICH were buried with a supply of worldly goods for eternity and models of servants to work in the fields of the gods to pay off heavenly taxes. Models of bakeries, workshops, scribes, and priests were also placed in tombs, so the dead would have all the help and guidance they needed. They also believed that the dead needed a body in the afterlife, which is why corpses were preserved.

ᴡᴡᴡ MAKE A DEATH MASK

You will need: plywood base (16 x 12 in.); modeling clay modeled into a face, neck, and beard as shown above; petroleum jelly; papier-mâché made from strips of torn newspaper and wallpaper paste; masking tape

1 Cover the clay head with a layer of petroleum jelly, so the papier-mâché does not stick to it.

2 Cut out cardboard shapes for headdress as shown.

3 Start covering the clay head with the papier-mâché. Keep the layer of papier-mâché over the face as smooth as possible so the details of the features are not lost.

A BODY FOR BURIAL took 70 days to prepare. First the brain and internal organs (all except the heart) were removed and placed in **canopic jars**.

THE LAST CEREMONY to be performed before burial was the opening of the mouth. The priest touched the mouth of the mummy with ritual instruments so the deceased would be able to eat, speak, and breathe in the afterlife.

◁ *The mummy of an adult woman which dates from around 1000 B.C.*

NATRON CRYSTALS (a type of salt) were packed around the body, which was left to dry for 40 days. Then followed a period in which the body cavity was stuffed with linen and sawdust, and false eyes were put in the sockets. The body was massaged with lotions and coated with resins. Finally, 15 days were spent wrapping the body with bandages and charms to ensure that the form was properly preserved.

A DEATH MASK completed the mummy. Royal masks were made of gold, while others were made of linen or papyrus and painted to look like gold.

THE COFFIN, of either wood or stone, had inscriptions and prayers carved into it and usually a pair of eyes painted on the outside so the dead could see out. A little door was painted on the inside through which the spirit could leave.

4 Slot the cardboard headdress piece flat on the board, behind the ears. Place the top of the headdress over the forehead of the model and attach to back of headdress with masking tape.

5 Cover rest of mask with papier-mâché. Leave to dry. Ease the clay head out from the back. The beard and ears may be difficult to remove, so be careful. Now paint.

Pyramids and Burial

Pharaohs believed that they became gods in the afterlife, so their tombs had to be very grand. Pyramid tombs were built during the Old Kingdom. The shape represents the mound of earth that rose out of the dark ocean at the beginning of time, from which the creator god Ra emerged (see page 114). The biggest pyramid is The Great Pyramid of Giza. It is still one of the largest man-made structures in the world.

△ The Great Pyramid of Giza, the tomb of the pharaoh Cheops, was originally 480 feet high and took over 20 years to build.

△ Some experts believe that a long, shallow, mud and rubble ramp was used to haul huge building blocks up to the pyramid on sleds.

△ As the pyramid got higher, the ramp would get longer, to keep an even gradient.

covered causeway, nearly 1,000 yards long

valley temple

Nile

MARKING OUT the ground was the first step. It involved complex mathematics. To set out the corner blocks, the height of the pyramid and the angle of the sloping sides had to be calculated carefully. This ensured that the top would be dead center.

TO CUT STONES the Egyptians used copper and bronze tools (iron was very scarce). Another method was to make small holes in a block of stone, along the line to be cut. Wooden wedges were forced into the holes, and water was poured over the dry wood to make it swell up and crack the stone along the line.

TO SMOOTH THE SURFACE of the pyramid, great triangular facing blocks of the best quality polished limestone were cut and added to each course, from the top down. These facing stones gleamed white in the sun. The stone cutters were so skillful at cutting and fitting the blocks (they did not use cement) that even today a piece of paper cannot be slipped between two blocks.

◁ Pyramid complex of Sahure at Abusir

subsidiary pyramid (for queen)

enclosure wall

mortuary temple

ARCHAEOLOGISTS have various theories on how the Egyptians heaved two-and-a-half-ton stone blocks up a pyramid.

THE ONE-RAMP THEORY suggests that a mud ramp was built and the stones dragged up it. But for the angle of the ramp to be shallow enough, it would have had to be three times as long as the pyramid, and no rubble has been found to indicate that such a structure ever existed.

THE FIRST LAYER, or course, of stones was laid out all over the base. Side blocks were then laid out, meeting each of the corner stones. The next course was laid on the first, and so on up to 200 courses, until a single capping stone was placed on top. (In the case of the Great Pyramid of Giza, this was coated in gold.) Meanwhile, tomb chambers, anterooms, and access tunnels inside the pyramid were beaten out of the blocks with hammers made of a hard stone called dolerite.

THE ANGLED-RAMP THEORY states that the internal core of the pyramid was built in steps, and series of ramps were built from step to step. The steps were then filled out later with smaller stones, and the facing stones set into them.

THE LEVER THEORY proposes that teams of skilled workers levered the stones up the courses.

△ *The Great Sphinx at Giza is 4,500 years old. Over 240 feet long and 65 feet high, it guards the way to the pyramid of the pharaoh Khafre.*

INSIDE THE PYRAMID a series of passages snaked up and down and led to caverns and chambers, some lined with granite. Escape shafts meant the burial party could get out of the pyramid after sealing up the burial chamber and treasure stores.

△ *The coffins of royalty or noblemen were placed in a sarcophagus. By the New Kingdom, they would have the figure of a protective goddess carved into each corner.*

THE BURIAL CHAMBER was usually dug deep beneath the pyramid. Here, the coffin of the dead pharaoh was put into a stone box called a **sarcophagus**. Around the room were piled chests full of possessions, food and furniture, and models of anything an important person might need in the afterlife. On the walls, hieroglyphic spells gave the pharaoh safe passage in the afterlife.

ANTECHAMBERS were filled with treasures, so the pharaoh could enjoy a rich and comfortable afterlife. Boats were also buried with the pharaoh in case his spirit needed to travel.

AFTER THE BURIAL, the priests left the chamber, sweeping away their footprints as they backed toward the door. Then the door was sealed so that no one could enter.

THE MORTUARY TEMPLE was usually an unsealed chamber aboveground. Here, priests dedicated to caring for the dead pharaoh's spirit could leave food and offerings to the gods.

▷ *Coffins carried spells written in hieroglyphs, to protect the dead on their journey to the afterlife.*

TOMB ROBBERS have been raiding tombs for their gold, jewels, and precious oils ever since they were first built. The Great Pyramid at Giza, for instance, is thought to have been robbed of almost everything when royal power collapsed at the end of the Old Kingdom.

New Kingdom pharaohs felt that pyramids were too easy to break into, so they had their burial chambers built into solid rock. Corridors and chambers were dug deep beneath the ground and the pyramid entrance was well concealed.

◁ *Inside the Great Pyramid at Giza. The burial chamber was very deep to protect it from thieves.*

white capstone at apex, 480 feet high

limestone

pharaoh's chamber

second burial chamber

grand gallery

limestone blocks

deep corridor

bed rock

first burial chamber

〰 **THE VALLEY OF THE KINGS**, on the west bank of the Nile, was the site of the pharaonic tombs. However, over the centuries all have been robbed except one—the famous tomb of the pharaoh Tutankhamen.

An Amazing Discovery

△ *The entrance to Tutankhamen's tomb in the Valley of the Kings.*

THE DISCOVERY OF TUTANKHAMEN'S tomb in the Valley of the Kings was one of the most exciting archaeological finds of the century. The tomb had lain hidden from robbers since 1327 B.C.

annex—stored wine jars, oils, and food

We know a lot about the ancient Egyptians largely because they buried so many artifacts with them for use in the afterlife. As a result, their tombs reveal an enormous amount of information from which archaeologists have been able to piece together a detailed picture of their daily life. Also, Egypt's hot and dry climate is ideal for preserving these ancient sites and artifacts.

antechamber

descending corridor

sealed first doorway

FIRST EVIDENCE of the tomb was discovered in early November 1922, when an expedition, led by British archaeologists Lord Carnarvon and Howard Carter, uncovered a flight of stone steps cut into the rock face, leading downward.

stepped entrance to tomb

A SEALED ENTRANCE was found at the bottom of the steps; the door was plastered over and its seals were still intact. The corridor beyond the door was filled with stone rubble. Another door, the same as the entrance door, was also sealed.

THE ANTECHAMBER was a stunning vision of glimmering gold. When, on November 26, 1922, Carter opened this doorway and held up his candle, he could hardly believe his eyes. The room was piled high with chests, caskets, statues, beds, chairs, chariots, and weapons. Clearing the chamber and cataloging all the objects took until February 1923.

THE PHARAOH'S BODY was brilliantly hidden. Bolted doors in the side of the shrine revealed another shrine and another. There were four in all, then a sarcophagus. Fitting inside this, like Russian dolls, were three coffins. The last, made entirely of gold, was opened in October 1925. It contained the 3,000-year-old mummy of Tutankhamen, wearing a mask of solid gold inlaid with jewels and garlanded with flowers.

burial chamber

first outer shrine hood

△ *Carter chips off the hardened black ointments that had been poured over the gold coffin.*

second shrine with wooden frame and gilded surface

third and fourth shrines made of gilded wood

treasury — canopic jars containing Tutankhamen's insides, removed before embalming, were found here

THE BURIAL CHAMBER was finally entered through a blocked doorway flanked by statues of the pharaoh, in February 1923. The room was filled by a giant gold and blue shrine. The top reached to the ceiling and there was only about half a yard between the shrine and the walls.

sarcophagus

inner coffins of solid gold containing mummy of Tutankhamen

THE
ROMAN
EMPIRE

The Ancient Romans

All human beings need food and shelter to survive. They also need a system of beliefs that gives shape and meaning to their lives. Throughout history, people have developed different ways of meeting these basic needs. By studying the people of **ancient Rome**, we can learn how they used the resources around them to create a sophisticated way of life, many traces of which survive to this day.

IN THIS BOOK, we look at the **civilization** of the ancient Romans, a people of Italian origin. Two thousand years ago, they conquered most of Europe, North Africa, and the Middle East, creating one of the biggest empires in the world.

△ *Underwater archaeologists have explored many Roman shipwrecks in the Mediterranean Sea.*

WE KNOW ABOUT THE ROMANS thanks to the many books and letters that have survived from their time. The remains of Roman cities, villas, forts, and shipwrecks help **archaeologists** to build up a picture of daily life in ancient Rome.

THE EARLIEST ROMAN HISTORY is not known, so the Romans used the ancient legend of Romulus and Remus to explain how their city was founded. Legend has it that they were the twin sons of Mars, the god of war. They were abandoned at birth and rescued by a she-wolf. Romulus later became the first ruler of Rome, and the city was named after him.

▽ *Today, statues of Romulus and Remus and the she-wolf can be seen all over Rome and other Italian cities.*

ROME was founded as a tiny farming settlement on the banks of the Tiber River. The date of its founding is traditionally given as 753 B.C. At the time, Italy was a land of many different peoples, speaking different languages. There were the **Etruscans** and Umbrians north of Rome, and Greek settlers in the south. The first Romans belonged to the **Latin**-speaking peoples of central Italy.

◁ *The* **fasces** *was a bundle of rods tied around an ax. It was an Etruscan symbol of power that was later used by the Romans.*

THE ETRUSCANS were a powerful people. In the 500's B.C., Rome came under their influence and was ruled by a series of Etruscan kings. The Etruscans were good builders, and they gave Rome its first large temples.

THE GREEKS were another important influence on the Romans. They founded cities around the coast of southern Italy. The Romans copied Greek buildings and sculpture, and were influenced by Greek legends and ideas.

ROMAN CIVILIZATION lasted for many centuries. To help make sense of it, we have divided it into different periods. Each period has been given a **symbol**, to show when information relates to that time. If there are no symbols, the information covers all periods.

The Republic refers to that period in Roman history when Rome was ruled by elected officials, and the Roman territory started to increase. By 27 B.C., the Republic had ended and was replaced by the rule of **emperors**. Under their rule, the Empire continued to expand. Later, the Empire was divided into two parts: the Eastern and Western Empire.

KEY FOR SYMBOLS

(eagle)   **Roman Republic**
509–27 B.C.

(wreath)   **early imperial period**
27 B.C.–A.D. 284

(Chi-Rho)   **late imperial period**
A.D. 284–476

THE MAKE IT WORK! way of looking at history is to ask questions about the past and to discover some of the answers by making copies of the things people made. However, you do not need to make everything in the book in order to understand the Roman way of life.

▽ *This map shows how, in Rome's earliest period, the ancient Romans were influenced by different peoples.*

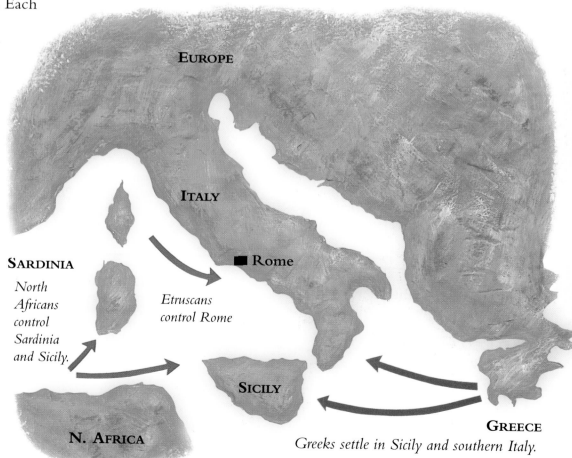

EUROPE

ITALY

SARDINIA

North Africans control Sardinia and Sicily.

Etruscans control Rome

■ Rome

SICILY

N. AFRICA

GREECE

Greeks settle in Sicily and southern Italy.

A Conquering Force

In the year A.D. 117, the Roman Empire reached its greatest size. It stretched 2,500 miles (4,000 kilometers) from east to west, 2,300 miles (3,700 kilometers) from north to south, and had a population of over 50 million.

🦅 🏵 THE WESTERN half of the Empire was conquered as a result of rivalry between the Romans and the people of Carthage. The Carthaginians were a powerful seafaring people in North Africa who also controlled Sardinia, parts of Sicily, and southern Spain. During a series of wars, Rome defeated Carthage and claimed its territory. The Romans later moved into northern Europe, conquering northern Spain, France, parts of Germany, and Britain.

🦅 🏵 THE EAST mostly came under Roman control during the last two centuries B.C. The Romans first went east to fight a people from northern Greece who were allied with Carthage. After defeating them, many more wars of conquest followed. By 30 B.C. most of the lands around the Mediterranean were part of the Roman Empire. Roman rule put an end to fighting between rival states and brought peace.

▷ *This is a map of the Empire during the A.D. 100's. Some important provinces are marked in capital letters. Provincial capitals, important cities, and army bases are given with their Roman names. You could compare the names to those on a modern map of Europe.*

BRITANNIA

Londinium

Isca

Colonia Agrippina

GERMANIA

Mogontiacum

Calleva

GAUL

Legio

IBERIA

Massilia

Lugdunum

Toletum

Roma

Ostia

Emerita Augustus

ITALIA

Hispalis

Mediterranean Sea

Carthago

Thugga

MAURETANIA

AFRICA

KEY TO SYMBOLS

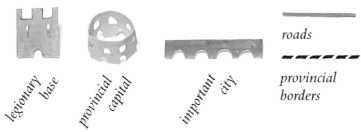

legionary base   *provincial capital*   *important city*   *roads*   *provincial borders*

TWO LANGUAGES held the Empire together. In the west, educated people learned to speak Latin; in the east, they spoke Greek. The Romans looked down on all other languages. Foreigners who could not speak Latin or Greek were called **barbarians**, because their speech sounded to Romans like a string of meaningless "bar-bar" sounds.

ROMAN CITIZENSHIP was given to the most important people in the conquered lands. This meant that they were allowed to become Romans. Citizens had many rights denied to noncitizens. A male citizen could vote in local government, or stand for election. Becoming a citizen was like taking on a new identity: a citizen even had to take a Roman name and learn how to wear Roman clothes.

THE NUMBER OF ROMAN CITIZENS grew steadily over time. In 28 B.C., there were four million: 80 years later, the figure had risen to six million. Finally in A.D. 212, the Emperor Caracalla allowed all free men and women, including former slaves, to become citizens.

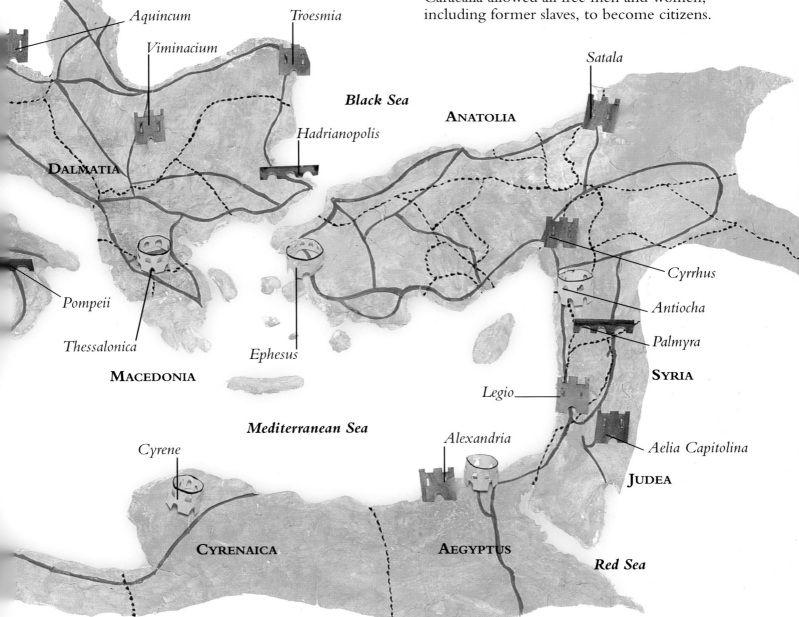

Aquincum

Troesmia

Viminacium

Satala

Black Sea

ANATOLIA

Hadrianopolis

DALMATIA

Cyrrhus

Pompeii

Antiocha

Palmyra

Thessalonica

SYRIA

Ephesus

Legio

MACEDONIA

Mediterranean Sea

Alexandria

Cyrene

Aelia Capitolina

JUDEA

CYRENAICA

AEGYPTUS

Red Sea

From Emperor to Slave

The people of Rome belonged to separate groups and classes, each with different rights. During the early imperial period, the most important distinction was between Roman citizens and noncitizens, or **provincials**. Citizens had more rights than provincials and even dressed differently.

SLAVES were men, women, and children who were owned as property and who were bought and sold in the market-place. Some were captured in wars, others were the children of slave parents. Household slaves could be secretaries, tutors, entertainers, cooks, or servants. These slaves were far better off than those who worked on farms or down in the mines.

double pipes

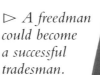

△ A household slave who is also a musician.

▷ A provincial farmer from northern Europe.

▷ A freedman could become a successful tradesman.

ROMAN SLAVES who had been given their freedom were called **freedmen** and **freedwomen**. Many slaves saved money and bought their freedom; others were freed by their owners as a reward for loyal service.

PROVINCIALS, or non-citizens, had different degrees of wealth and status. Unlike slaves, they could serve in the army in special support, or "auxiliary" units. After many years of service, **auxiliaries** and their families were usually given Roman citizenship. This was one way in which the number of citizens steadily increased.

trousers were worn in the cold north

◁ A centurion was a middle-ranking Roman citizen.

WOMEN had fewer rights than men. They could not vote or follow careers in politics or law. Most wealthy Roman women looked after children and the home, and gave orders to slaves. However, women could own property, and some ran their own businesses. Other women played important roles as priestesses in the temples (see page 157).

THE EMPEROR had enormous power. He was the chief priest of the Roman religion and the overall commander of Rome's armies. He appointed governors to rule the different provinces of the Empire. Statues of him stood in every city, and his face appeared on every coin.

▷ A noblewoman and priestess.

laurel wreath

purple **toga**

altar for making offerings to the gods

ROMAN CITIZENS were divided into different "orders" or ranks, depending on their wealth and family background. At the top were the wealthy nobles who belonged to the order of **senators**. They were the generals, chief priests, and governors of the most important provinces. Below them were **equestrians**, wealthy people who became civil servants, high-ranking officers, or governors of smaller provinces. Lower still were ordinary citizens. They ranged from **centurions** and **legionaries**, to wealthy traders and poor farmers.

△ The emperor was the most important person in Roman society.

Togas and Tunics

Roman men, women, and children wore a simple tunic made of wool or linen, with a belt around the waist. Some had sleeves, like a T-shirt; others had armholes. This was the one item of clothing that everyone, rich and poor, wore. Women's tunics were longer than men's, reaching to below the knees.

MALE ROMAN CITIZENS were supposed to wear a **toga** in public. The toga was a huge, semicircular, woolen sheet that was wrapped around the body and arranged in folds. It took time and skill to put it on properly. Slaves and noncitizens wore the simple tunic, or *tunica*.

DIFFERENT-COLORED TOGAS were also a sign of status. Men working for election wore a pure white toga. This has given us the word *candidate,* from the Latin word *candidus* (white). **Magistrates** and the young sons of wealthy families wore a *toga praetexta*, which was white with a purple border. The emperor wore a *toga picta*, which was purple with gold embroidery.

△ *This group of senators are all wearing togas. The Roman on the far right also holds the* fasces *symbol.*

WOMEN had a greater variety of clothing to choose from. Over the *tunica* they wore many different kinds of robes and dresses. Richer women wore clothes of brightly colored Chinese silk and Indian cotton, decorated with jewelry.

FOOTWEAR included various kinds of leather sandals. Slaves and citizens in warmer provinces wore simple sandals, like modern flip-flops. Soldiers wore stronger sandals with hobnails on the soles.

MAKE A TUNICA

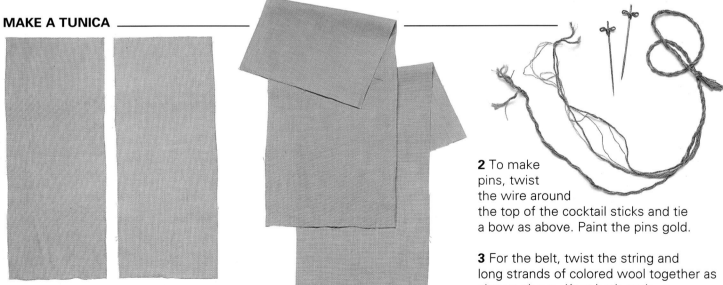

You will need: needle, thread, scissors, an old cotton sheet cut in half lengthwise, string, colored wool, long cocktail sticks, thin wire, gold paint

1 Fold over a third of the material on each piece. You could hem the edges to prevent fraying. You will need to hold the material as shown above, up to your shoulders, in the final stage.

2 To make pins, twist the wire around the top of the cocktail sticks and tie a bow as above. Paint the pins gold.

3 For the belt, twist the string and long strands of colored wool together as shown above. Knot both ends.

4 Ask a friend to help you put on the *tunica*. Push the pins through the folded fabric at the shoulders. Tie the belt at the waist and over the flaps of material.

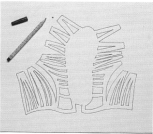

You will need: brown felt or a square piece of leather, laces, pen, paper, scissors

1 If possible, enlarge the design shown above on a photocopier to fit your foot. Or copy the design onto paper.

2 Cut out the design and draw around it on the fabric.

3 Turn the paper over and copy the design again, for your other foot. Then cut out both shapes.

4 Stand on the center of each piece of fabric. Use laces, or strips of spare fabric, to lace up the loops in the sandal, as shown above.

PURPLE DYE was specially valued by the Romans. It came from a sea snail called the murex, found in parts of the Mediterranean.

WEAR A TOGA

△ *This is a simple way to put on a toga. In reality togas were more difficult to put on.*

You will need: semicircular piece of fabric with a straight edge of 13 ft. (4 m)

1 Hold the straight edge of the fabric behind you. Drape half over your left arm. Tuck this section into your belt.

2 Pass the right half of the *toga* under your right arm and around the front. Tuck a little fold in your belt.

3 Now pass the rest of the fabric over your left shoulder.

Dressing to Impress

Wealthy Romans went to great lengths to keep up with changing fashions. They started each day in front of a mirror, attended by slaves who dressed their hair, applied their makeup and perfume, and plucked out unwanted hair with tweezers.

◊ **WOMEN'S HAIRSTYLES** became more and more elaborate over time. They wore wigs and hairpieces curled with heated tongs and piled up high in rows of curls. Hairpins, made of bone or metal, held the curls in place. Some women wore wigs so that they could change the color of their hair. Blond wigs were made with hair clipped from German slave girls, and black wigs were made with hair imported from India.

▷ *A wealthy or noble Roman woman spent a lot of time making her hair look beautiful.*

🦅 ◊ **MEN WORE LAUREL WREATHS** on their heads as a mark of rank. Victorious generals wore them on their return from successful campaigns, and Roman emperors wore them as crowns.

🦅 ◊ **MAKE A LAUREL WREATH**

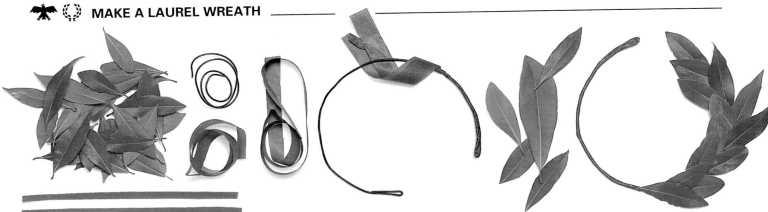

You will need: fresh bay (laurel) leaves or leaves made from green cardboard, strips of green tissue paper, scissors, glue, plastic-coated wire, red ribbon

1 Shape the wire into a headband. Wind and glue strips of tissue paper around the band. Starting at one end, glue the leaves to the tissue paper as shown above right.

2 When you have reached halfway around the headband, start at the other end and glue on the rest of the leaves. Finally, snip the ends of the ribbon in a V-shape, and glue as shown at right.

◊ **WEARING MAKEUP** was important to noblewomen. They used paint made from chalk and white lead to whiten the face and forearms, and powdered ashes to blacken the eyebrows. Red ocher (from earth), or red wine leftovers were used as rouge for cheeks and lips. Women also used face packs made from damp bread, which they hoped would prevent wrinkles.

◁ *Many women wore beautiful metal bracelets shaped like coiling snakes.*

MAKE A ROMAN BROOCH

You will need: cardboard, glue, safety pin, fine string, tape, paints, paintbrush

1 Draw two flower shapes on the cardboard—one a little larger than the other. Draw four petal shapes, lots of little stamens and a small circle. Cut out the shapes carefully.

2 Glue pieces of string around the petals and the circle. Glue lengths of string to the tips of the stamens.

3 Paint all the cardboard shapes and pieces of string gold.

4 When dry, paint the insides of the petals different colors.

5 Glue the smaller flower on top of the larger one. Bend the edges inward slightly. Glue the stamens onto the center of the flower. Then glue on the petals and the circle as shown.

6 To wear your brooch, tape a safety pin onto the back, as shown above.

▽ *Brooches like these were used to fasten cloaks.*

▽ *The laurel-wreath crown was a symbol of military success and power.*

⚜ ✳ **MEN'S HAIRSTYLES** were influenced by the emperor, whose portrait was engraved on coins (see page 173). Until the A.D. 100's, men shaved their chins, or had them plucked with tweezers by a barber. This style changed when Emperor Hadrian, who had an ugly scar on his chin, let his beard grow to hide it. Men all over the Empire followed his example.

Some men took just as much trouble over their appearance as women. This is how the historian Suetonius described Emperor Otho:
"He was as fussy about his appearance as a woman. His entire body had been plucked of hair and a well-made wig covered his practically bald head… He used a poultice of moist bread to slow down the growth of his beard."

Life in the City

Many Romans lived in the large cities of the Empire. These cities were often built near rivers or close to the sea, because it was much easier to move heavy goods by water than by road. Cities were the main trading centers. There was a constant movement of wagons, pack animals, and merchant ships arriving and departing.

ROMAN CITIES were often built on a grid system. Blocks of buildings called **insulae** were divided by straight streets. Each *insula* was packed with houses, stores, and workshops. To save space, these buildings often joined onto each other, like a row of terraced houses.

▽ *This is a model of a typical Roman town. Most towns and cities had the same key buildings.*

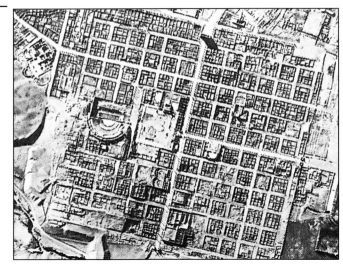

△ *This is an aerial photograph of the Roman town of Timgad in Algeria. The grid system can be seen clearly.*

FRESH WATER was brought into the city by an **aqueduct**. A lot of water was needed for drinking and for the public baths, where Romans went to relax. Many cities also had sewers, and public toilets flushed by water.

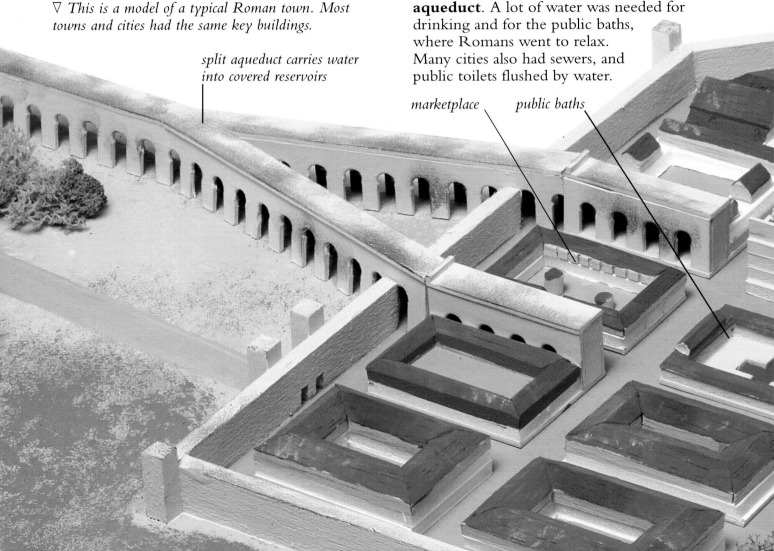

split aqueduct carries water into covered reservoirs

marketplace   public baths

AT THE HEART OF EVERY ROMAN CITY was the **forum**. This was a large open area, used as a market and a public meeting place. Along one side there was a long hall called a *basilica*. This was the law court and the place where merchants and wealthy Romans met to do business.

A smaller building nearby, the *curia*, was where the local council met. The council was responsible for putting on public entertainment, keeping law and order, raising taxes, and looking after the roads, public buildings, and the water supply.

TEMPLES for worshiping the most important gods and the Roman emperor were also built in the forum. Temples to local gods were scattered across the town. Wealthy Romans helped to pay for building temples, and in return had their names carved on them.

PUBLIC ENTERTAINMENT was an important part of city life. There were theaters for plays, and **amphitheaters** where fights between **gladiators** were held (see pages 160–161). Some of the bigger cities even had a racecourse for chariot racing.

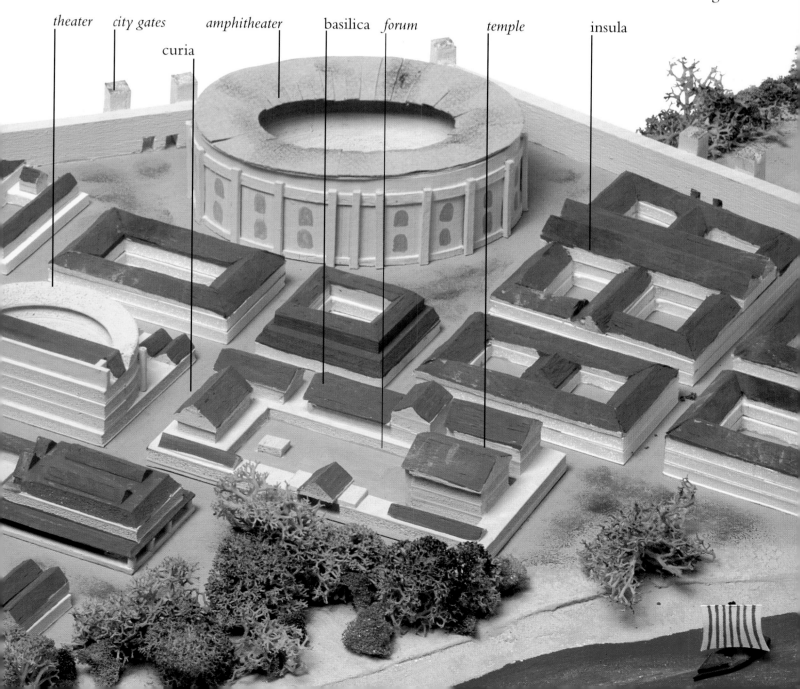

theater   city gates   amphitheater   basilica *forum*   temple   insula

curia

POMPEII is a town in Italy that was buried under ash when the volcano Vesuvius erupted violently in A.D. 79. Over the past 200 years, the houses and stores of Pompeii have been slowly uncovered. As a result, we have a picture of a whole Roman town as it was on an August day nearly 2,000 years ago.

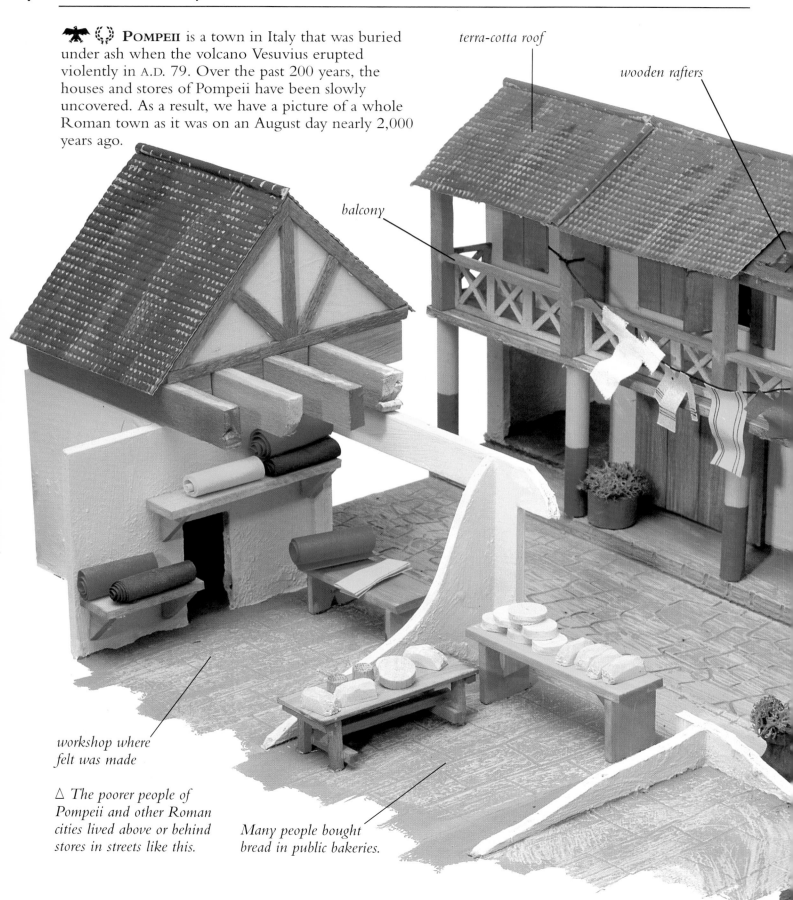

terra-cotta roof

wooden rafters

balcony

workshop where
felt was made

△ *The poorer people of Pompeii and other Roman cities lived above or behind stores in streets like this.*

Many people bought bread in public bakeries.

🦅 🏵 THE STREETS of Pompeii were lined with a variety of stores and bars. These were often run by freedmen who had their own slaves working for them. Each store had a large open front that was closed up with wooden shutters at night. There was a counter at the front where goods were displayed to customers in the street. Taverns had stone counters with jars set into them for snacks and hot drinks.

△ *In this excavated street in Pompeii, you can see the deep ruts in the road made by oxcarts.*

🦅 🏵 THE SIDEWALKS IN POMPEII, like those of many Roman cities, were raised above the level of the road. This prevented oxcarts from knocking over pedestrians. The road sloped slightly so that rainwater and sewage ran into the gutters. Stepping stones were laid across the road to allow people to cross without getting their sandals dirty, and also to slow down the carts.

MOST PEOPLE IN THE EMPIRE were poor, although those who were in charge were very rich. In the larger cities, poor people lived in rented rooms in blocks of apartments. In smaller towns, rich and poor alike lived in the *insulae*, or blocks of housing. A rich family might own a large part of the *insula*, whereas a poor family rented perhaps only one or two rooms.

Inside the homes, furniture was very simple. The poet Martial described a typical room: "There was a little three-legged bed and a two-legged table, with a lamp and a bucket... The neck of an **amphora** held back a little cooker covered in green rust." Most homes did not have bathrooms. Instead, people used chamber pots, which they emptied out of their windows onto the street below.

public drinking fountain

a one-room apartment

tavern

raised sidewalk

gutter

stepping stones

WEALTHY ROMANS lived in very different conditions from the poor. From the outside, the houses of wealthy Romans looked very plain. Because of the risk of burglary, most houses had only a few windows. Rooms were arranged around courtyards and gardens, and openings in the roof let in the maximum amount of light.

△ *In the evenings, homes were lit with pottery lamps. The lamps burned oil made from olives, nuts, or fish.*

THE FIRST ROOM people entered in a Roman house was called the **atrium.** It was a cross between an entrance hall and a courtyard. It had a high ceiling with a skylight in the middle. Below this, in the center of the *atrium*, was an ornamental pool to collect rainwater.

THE DINING ROOM was called a **triclinium,** meaning "three couches." The houses of the rich sometimes had two *triclinia*; a sheltered one for winter, and one with a view of the garden for summer.

THE RECEPTION ROOM was the **tablinum.** This was a cross between a living room and an office where guests were received. Important papers and valuables were kept there, safely locked in a strongbox.

A ROMAN HOUSE was often a crowded place. There were household slaves running errands, children playing with toys, and older women spinning wool (see pages 152-153). There was also a stream of daily visitors or **clients** who came to ask advice and favors from their "patron," who was the head of the house. These were generally people who were less well off. For a wealthy Roman, the day began with a visit from his clients. The more important a Roman was, the greater the number of clients who visited him.

▷ *A wealthy Roman might have lived in a town house like this*

bedroom (*above* tablinum)

peristyle garden (see page 145)

BEDROOMS were often alongside the *atrium*. Apart from the bed, there was little furniture—perhaps a chair and a table, and a pottery chamber pot kept underneath the bed.

CLIENTS were expected to arrive in a clean toga and to call their patron "my lord." They would wait in the *atrium* until they were summoned by a slave to the *tablinum*, where the patron would receive them.

These wealthy patrons were themselves the clients of still richer men. After they had greeted their clients, they might have to visit their own patron. The only man who did not have a patron was the emperor.

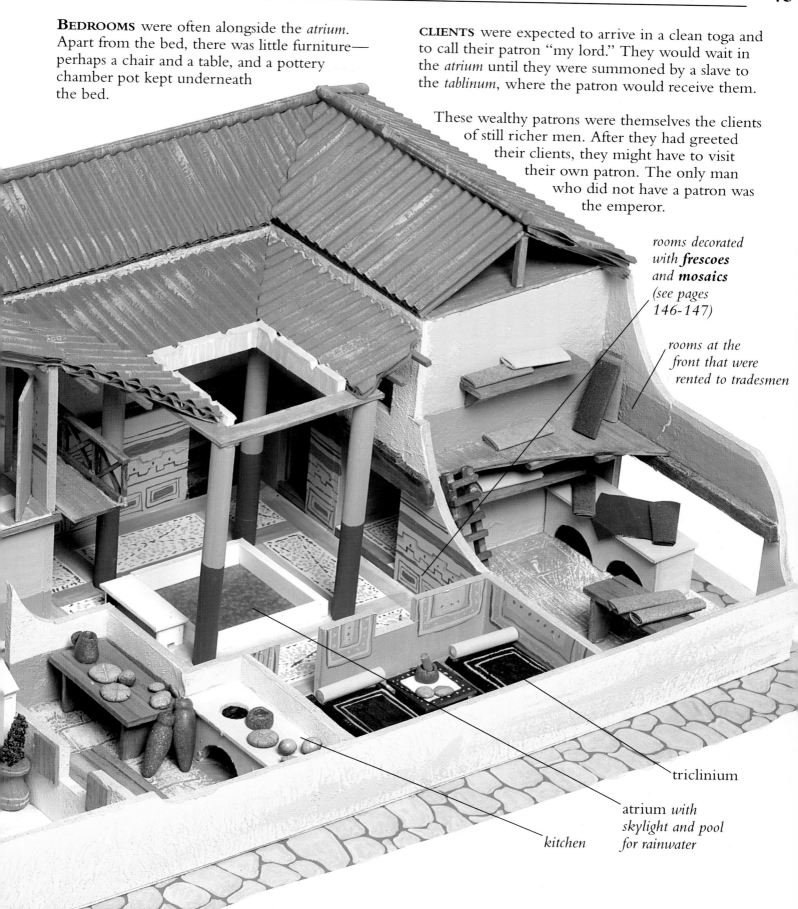

rooms decorated
with **frescoes**
and **mosaics**
(see pages
146-147)

rooms at the
front that were
rented to tradesmen

triclinium

atrium *with
skylight and pool
for rainwater*

kitchen

Gardens, Mosaics and Frescoes

Wealthy Romans loved their gardens. They were neatly laid out with rows of clipped hedges and paths, and filled with fountains, pools and statues. A garden was a place to relax on a sunny day, to read or write or just do nothing.

▷ The gardens of a Roman town house or country villa may have been circular, like this one, or rectangular.

MANY GARDENS have been discovered at Pompeii. Although the plants there disappeared long ago, their roots have left spaces in the soil. Archaeologists make plaster casts of these spaces to find out what kinds of trees and bushes were planted there.

hedges trimmed to look like birds

lemon tree

small bust of a forest spirit

fountain

FOUNTAINS and ornamental pools were carved from marble. Pliny the Younger, a writer, described the fountains of his garden: "A fountain plays in a marble basin, watering the plane trees round it and the ground beneath them with its light spray… Another has a bowl surrounded by tiny jets which make a lovely murmuring sound."

 **STATUES** of gods and fighting animals were popular garden ornaments. The "House of Stags" in Herculaneum in southern Italy is named after two sculptures of stags being attacked by dogs. There were also statues of forest spirits such as *satyrs*, who were young men with the legs, ears, and horns of goats.

△ Oscilla *were decorated with carvings of gods and satyrs.*

THE PERISTYLE was a type of garden surrounded by roofed columns that provided shade. White marble or terra-cotta disks called *oscilla* were hung between the columns for decoration. They flashed like tiny mirrors as they caught the sun.

SLAVES who were skilled gardeners looked after the garden. They clipped bushes into the shape of animals, birds and gods. The wealthiest Romans also liked to have fish tanks in their gardens, filled with fish, eels and other seafood. They provided a fresh supply for the dinner table! Exotic birds were also popular. Peacocks were imported from India and were thought to be the sacred bird of the goddess Juno.

GARDEN WALLS were sometimes painted with pictures of trees, birds and flowers to make the gardens look bigger. If a house had no real garden, Romans painted garden scenes on a wall, to give the impression of one. Some of these still survive today. They show us what kind of plants the Romans liked to grow.

△ *This mosaic from Pompeii shows a scene from the banks of the Nile River in Egypt. The Romans hunted many of these animals and brought them back to Rome for the games (see pages 160-161).*

THE TOWN HOUSES AND COUNTRY VILLAS of wealthy Romans were full of color. The walls of important rooms, such as the *triclinium* and *tablinum*, were covered with bright paintings called frescoes. The floors were decorated with mosaics—pictures made from thousands of tiny colored tiles and pieces of glass.

MOSAICS were fashionable throughout the Empire. The Romans used the technique, developed by the Greeks, of making black and white patterned floors with pebbles. Later, colored floors became popular. By cutting stones, glass, tiles and shells into little pieces known as *tesserae*, the Romans could make mosaics as detailed as paintings. There were scenes from everyday life, flowers, and different figures such as the gods, gladiators, and actors. One house in Pompeii had a mosaic of a snarling dog in the doorway, with the words *cave canem*—"beware of the dog"—written into the mosaic.

MAKE A MOSAIC

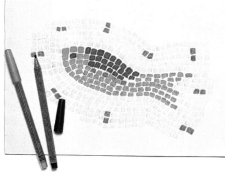

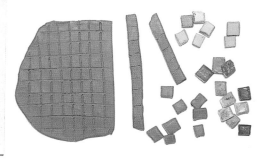

You will need: paper, felt-tip pens, scissors, modeling clay, paints, paintbrush, stiff cardboard, rolling pin, tile adhesive, sponge or stiff brush, varnish (optional)

1 Draw a fish or another animal. Then cut a piece of stiff cardboard, large enough to cover the whole design.

2 Draw your design on a piece of paper and choose the colors you would like to use.

3 Roll out the clay with the rolling pin until it is about ⅛ in. (3 mm) thick.

4 Use a pair of scissors to mark the clay into small squares, as shown above right.

5 Cut the squares to make small tiles, or *tesserae*. Let them dry.

6 Paint them in your chosen colors.

7 To create a more textured effect, you could dip a sponge in the paint and dab it gently onto the tiles. Or you could flick paint onto them, using a stiff brush.

FRESCOES were painted on a freshly plastered wall that was still damp. The color soaked into the plaster and became fixed as it dried. The finished wall was given a protective coat of melted wax mixed with a little oil. Finally, the surface was polished to give it a glossy appearance.

THE FIRST PAINTERS had only a few colors to work with: black from soot, white from chalk, and red and yellow ocher from earth. As the Empire grew, more colors became available. The Egyptians showed the Romans how to make a rich shade of blue from copper. Vermilion, a bright scarlet, came from a mineral called cinnabar that was mined in Spain. Even more exotic and expensive colors were brought by sea from India. You could tell how wealthy Romans were simply by looking at the colors on the walls of their houses.

STYLES OF PAINTING came and went. Until about 80 B.C., walls were painted to look as if they were made of colored marble. Then, architectural scenes with columns and statues became popular. The aim was to make a room look bigger than it really was.

△ *This fresco was discovered on the wall of a town house in Pompeii. The young woman is holding a writing tablet in one hand and a* **stylus** *in the other (see page 155).*

△ *Mosaics of sea creatures were sometimes used to decorate* triclinium *floors.*

8 Cover the stiff cardboard with a layer of tile adhesive. Press the tiles into the adhesive, following your paper design. Begin with the center tiles and work outward until the design is complete.

9 Let the mosaic dry. You could varnish it later.

Food and Feasting

The staple food of most Romans was a type of stew made of wheat, barley, beans, or lentils. However, rich Romans had a more varied diet. They ate food grown on their own farms, and more expensive dishes imported from all over the Empire.

COOKING was a luxury for most people who lived in cities. Because of the risk of fire in their wooden apartments, the poor bought their meals from stalls in the street instead of cooking. Wealthy Romans had their own kitchens and slaves who cooked for them.

food cooked on a raised hearth

amphorae

MAKE A HONEY OMELET

You will need: 5 eggs, ground pepper, ⅓ oz. (10 g) butter, 5 tablesp. (75 ml) milk, 1 teasp. (5 ml) honey, 1 oz. (25 g) almonds, dash of anchovy essence or soy sauce

1 Whisk the eggs in a bowl. Then add the honey, pepper, and milk.

2 Ask an adult to put the almonds on a baking tray and bake them in a hot oven at 325° F (165° C) for 20 min.

3 When cool, ask an adult to chop the nuts with a sharp knife. Now add them to the egg mixture.

4 Stir the anchovy essence or soy sauce into the egg mixture.

5 Melt the butter in a frying pan and pour in the egg mixture. Cook until the omelet is firm, turning once.

BRICK OVENS were used for baking and roasting. A fire was lit inside, heating the bricks. When the fire died, the ashes were raked out and bread or meat was put in the oven. The entrance was covered and food cooked by the heat of the bricks.

◁ *A wealthy Roman had a kitchen like this one.*

flour

bowl for grinding spices

POTTERY JARS, or *amphorae*, leaned against the kitchen walls. They held the most commonly used ingredients—olive oil, vinegar, wine, and fish sauce.

THE MOST POPULAR FOOD FLAVORING was a spicy fish sauce called *garum*. It was made from the blood and internal parts of mackerel, an oily type of fish. The fish parts were salted, mixed with vinegar and herbs, and left in the sun until they turned into liquid. *Garum* had a powerful flavor. Only a tiny amount was needed to flavor a dish.

THE ROMANS COOKED in ways rather different from how we cook today. They used honey to sweeten food, because they did not have sugar. They also loved pepper, which came from India. They even sprinkled it on desserts and mixed it with wine.

MAKE GRAPE PUNCH

3 Ask an adult to help you heat the mixture. Stir it continuously over a low heat for half an hour.

4 Let cool before serving.

You will need: 4 tablesp. of honey, crushed bay leaf, 2 dates, 1 qt. (1 l) white grape juice, pinch of cinnamon, ground pepper, saffron, and lemon for flavor and decoration

1 Chop the dates fine. Discard the pits.

2 Place all the ingredients in a saucepan.

▷ *The Romans served this spiced punch cold before a meal, or warm during a meal.*

ENTERTAINING generally took place in the evening, when wealthy Romans invited guests to dinner. They ate in the *triclinium*, or dining room, stretched out on three couches.

◁ *The Romans made beautiful glassware, which they used when they entertained.*

EACH COUCH could seat three people, so the perfect number of guests at a dinner party was nine. The couches were arranged to make three sides of a square, with the fourth side left open for the slaves who brought the dishes.

DORMICE were a popular dish. They were kept inside pottery jars and fattened until they were ready to cook. Then they were served sprinkled with honey and poppy seeds!

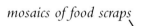
mosaics of food scraps

THE PLACE OF HONOR was on the right-hand side of the host, who was in the center of the middle couch. The guests propped themselves up on their elbows and ate with their fingers. Between courses they washed their hands in finger bowls and dried them with napkins. Guests often brought their own napkins, so that they could take away any of the delicious food they had been unable to finish.

ROMANS SHOWED OFF THEIR WEALTH by serving food brought from all the corners of the Empire. Certain provinces were famous for particular delicacies. Libya, for example, was the place to find truffles, while Syria was known for its delicious pears.

burning lamps for light

▽ *A Roman dinner party in the* triclinium.

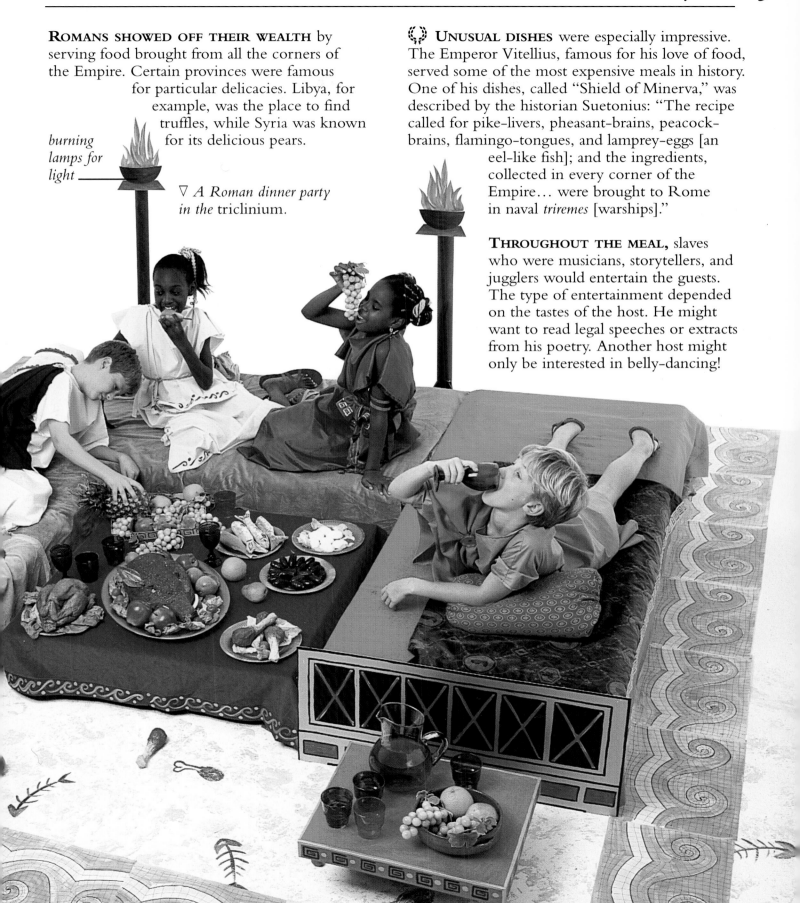

UNUSUAL DISHES were especially impressive. The Emperor Vitellius, famous for his love of food, served some of the most expensive meals in history. One of his dishes, called "Shield of Minerva," was described by the historian Suetonius: "The recipe called for pike-livers, pheasant-brains, peacock-brains, flamingo-tongues, and lamprey-eggs [an eel-like fish]; and the ingredients, collected in every corner of the Empire… were brought to Rome in naval *triremes* [warships]."

THROUGHOUT THE MEAL, slaves who were musicians, storytellers, and jugglers would entertain the guests. The type of entertainment depended on the tastes of the host. He might want to read legal speeches or extracts from his poetry. Another host might only be interested in belly-dancing!

Family Life

The word *family* is Roman and comes from the Latin word *familia*. In Roman times, a family meant the household, which included slaves, freedmen, and freedwomen.

POORER ROMANS were rarely educated. Unlike the wealthy, they did not write books and could not afford carved tombstones for their graves. Most of what we know about the daily lives of Romans comes from these sources. Because the rich were generally interested only in their own lives, not much is known about poorer Romans.

▷ *Young children played with terra-cotta rattles shaped like animals. This jewel-studded pig probably belonged to a child with wealthy parents.*

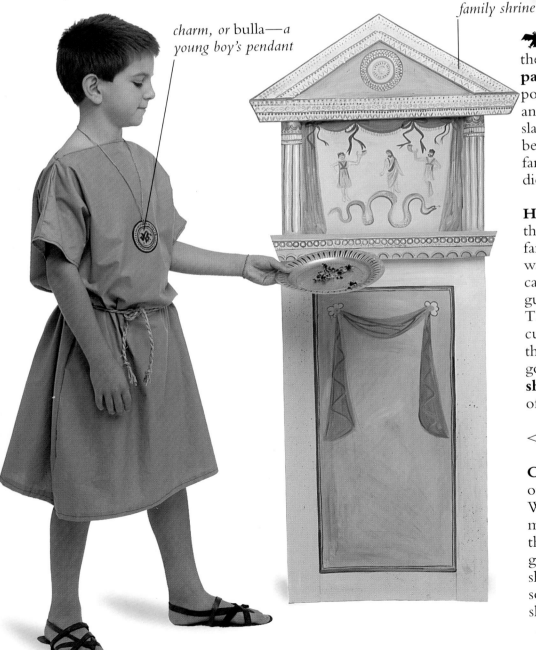

charm, or bulla—*a young boy's pendant*

family shrine

THE FAMILY HEAD was the father. He was known as the **pater familias.** He had total power over all family members and had the right to sell them into slavery, or even to kill them. Sons became the *pater familias* of their families only when their fathers died.

HOUSEHOLD GODS were thought to watch over every family. The head of the house was protected by a guardian spirit called his *Genius*, while his wife's guardian spirit was called her *Juno*. The *Penates* looked after the food cupboards, and the *Lares* protected the home. Small statues of these gods were kept in a household **shrine** and the family made offerings to them.

◁ *A boy offers a tuft of hair to the gods.*

CHILDREN made their own offerings to the household gods. When girls became engaged to be married, they left their toy dolls at the shrine as a sign that they were grown up. When boys were first shaved by the barber, they offered some of the hair to the gods to show that they had become men.

MAKE A ROMAN TOY DOLL

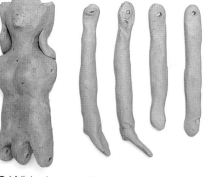

You will need: modeling clay, needle, string, paints, paintbrush

1 Model the clay into the parts of a doll: two arms, two legs, a body and head, as shown above right. At the base of the body, make two indents for the legs.

2 With the needle, make holes in the top of the arms and legs, through the base of the body, and right through the chest. The holes must be large enough for the string to be threaded through.

3 Let the clay parts dry.

4 Paint your doll as shown. Add a pattern around the neck, waist, and hair for decoration. Let it dry.

5 Thread string through the holes in the chest and arms. Knot the ends. Do the same with the legs.

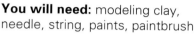

▷ *Roman children played with spinning tops, carved wooden animals, hoops, and dolls like this one.*

MARRIAGE had a dramatic effect on the lives of Roman women. In early times, when a young girl married, she had to leave her own *familia* and join her husband's. This meant that she had to live by the rules of a new *pater familias*. But by the end of the Republic, the Romans had invented a new system of marriage in which a wife legally remained part of her own *familia*. This gave her more freedom. She kept control of her own property and if her husband divorced her, he had to return her possessions to her.

DIVORCE was common, especially among wealthy Romans. A husband could divorce his wife if the marriage was childless, or if he wanted to marry someone else. But wives did not have the right to divorce their husbands.

WIVES were responsible for running the household, giving orders to slaves and looking after the children. They also spent a lot of time spinning thread from wool to make clothes. In marriage ceremonies, a bride often carried a spindle for hand-spinning as a symbol of her duties as a wife.

Education and Trades

Life for the sons and daughters of wealthy Romans was very different from the lives of poor children. Children of the wealthy were educated at home or at school, while poorer children went out to learn a trade.

POOR CHILDREN did not go to school. From an early age, they were expected to help their parents at work. A young boy aged eight or nine would either follow in his father's footsteps or work as an apprentice in the trade of a family friend. To begin with, child workers were usually given the most unpleasant tasks, but by watching and helping, boys learned the skills of blacksmiths, bakers, launderers and goldsmiths. Girls stayed with their mothers and helped in the store, the workshop, or the kitchen.

▷ *This is a Roman inkpot and pen from the first century A.D.*

RICH CHILDREN began their education at home, where they were taught by a well-educated slave called a *pedagogue*. At the age of 11, some boys and girls went to a school run by a *grammaticus*, or grammar teacher, to study literature. They learned to speak Greek and memorized Greek and Latin poetry, taking turns to recite it. Roman noblemen and women loved quoting poetry in their conversations and letters.

PUBLIC SPEAKING was considered to be essential for all young men wishing to become politicians or lawyers. A tutor called a *rhetor* taught pupils how to present an opinion in a logical way and how to speak persuasively. Pupils practiced these skills by imagining they were taking part in law cases, either defending or accusing.

◁ *In Pompeii, young boys were employed in laundries to clean cloth in large vats by treading it with their feet.*

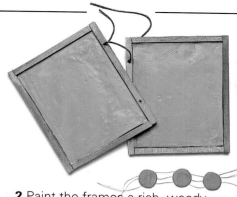

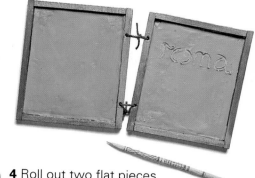

You will need: balsa wood, red and green modeling clay, craft knife, ruler, glue, string, paint, awl, stick

1 For both frames cut a flat piece of wood 7 x 5½ in. (18 x 14 cm), four thick strips of wood: two measuring 7 x ⅓ in. (18 x 1 cm), and two measuring 5½ x ⅓ in. (14 x 1 cm). Glue together as shown above right.

2 Paint the frames a rich, woody color. With the bradawl, make two holes in one side of each frame. Thread string through the holes and tie the frames together.

3 Make seals to decorate. Cut three 8-in. (20-cm) lengths of string. Press the string into three red clay disks. Glue to the back of the tablet.

4 Roll out two flat pieces of green clay and glue inside each frame as shown.

5 To make a *stylus*, ask an adult to help you sharpen the end of a stick. Use it to write on the tablet. Smooth over the clay to use again.

ROMAN NUMERALS

1	I	7	VII	40	XL
2	II	8	VIII	50	L
3	III	9	IX	60	LX
4	IV	10	X	90	XC
5	V	20	XX	100	C
6	VI	30	XXX	500	D
				1,000	M

▷ *A noblewoman reads a letter written on a wax writing tablet.*

ROMANS used letters to represent numbers, and they are still used today on many clocks and watches. Each letter has a different value and can be combined with other letters to make bigger numbers. I is used for 1, X for 10, C for 100, and M for 1,000. For example, 1,326 is shown as MCCCXXVI. This made it quite tricky to do calculations with large numbers, especially multiplication and long division.

PUPILS wrote on thin sheets of wood using pens made of reeds or brass. They also wrote on beeswax tablets using a pen called a *stylus* to scratch letters onto the tablet. One end of the *stylus* was flat, so that the wax could be smoothed over and reused.

IN SOME ROMAN TOWNS walls were covered with advertisements, so it is likely that many of the poor could read. Despite the lack of formal teaching, many poorer Romans learned to read and write a little—enough to sign their name and write a few simple documents.

Gods of the Empire

The Romans believed in many gods and goddesses who were thought to watch over different aspects of their lives. From very early times the Romans adopted Greek myths, linking the legends of the Greek gods with their own. They told the same stories about Jupiter that the Greeks told of their god, Zeus.

THE MOST IMPORTANT GODS were Jupiter, ruler of gods and men, and king of heaven; his wife Juno, queen of heaven and goddess of women and marriage; and Jupiter's daughter Minerva, goddess of wisdom and art. Together, they shared the Temple of Jupiter Capitolinus in Rome. Temples were places to worship the gods. They were also places to leave valuables for safekeeping, like banks today. It was thought that thieves would not dare to rob the house of a god.

▽ *Musicians herald the arrival of the procession.*

long, curved horn called a cornu

double pipes

▽ *The* victimarius *(sacrificing priest) carries an ax.*

a sheep is led to the altar as an offering to the gods

RELIGIOUS CEREMONIES were conducted by a priest or priestess in front of the temple building. Processions of people brought gifts as offerings to a particular god. In return they hoped to win the god's favor. Bulls, sheep, and pigs were decorated with flowers and led to the temple. The priest or priestess sacrificed the animal on an altar in front of the temple, and then burned some of the meat. The rising smoke was supposed to carry the offering up to the god.

PREDICTING THE FUTURE was an important part of religion. The Romans believed that the gods sent messages to warn of coming disasters, or as a sign of good luck. There were different ways of reading these messages. **Augurs** were priests who told the future by studying birds. **Haruspices** were men who examined the inner organs of a sacrificed animal to find out if the god had accepted the offering.

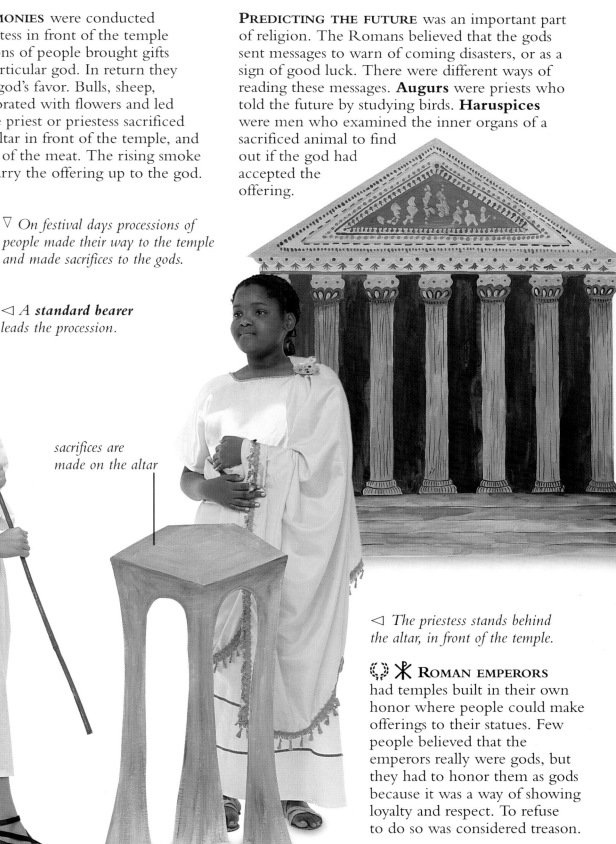

▽ *On festival days processions of people made their way to the temple and made sacrifices to the gods.*

◁ *A **standard bearer** leads the procession.*

sacrifices are made on the altar

◁ *The priestess stands behind the altar, in front of the temple.*

☆ ✳ ROMAN EMPERORS had temples built in their own honor where people could make offerings to their statues. Few people believed that the emperors really were gods, but they had to honor them as gods because it was a way of showing loyalty and respect. To refuse to do so was considered treason.

△ *This statue depicts Mithras slaying a mythical bull. The bull's blood was believed to be the source of all life.*

() **AS THE EMPIRE EXPANDED,** the Romans came into contact with people who worshiped different gods. Some of these foreign gods were just like their own. Other gods, like **Mithras** and Isis, seemed very different, partly because they offered the promise of life after death.

() **THE CULTS OF MITHRAS AND ISIS** were spread throughout the Empire by merchants, traders, soldiers, and slaves. These gods were worshiped at secret ceremonies, unlike Roman gods who were worshiped in public. Mithras was the god of light from Persia (ancient Iran). He was worshiped by men who met by torchlight in underground rooms.

Isis was an Egyptian mother goddess and the special protector of seafarers. Followers of Isis were persecuted until the Emperor Caligula allowed people to worship Isis and built a temple to her.

MAKE A VOTIVE OFFERING

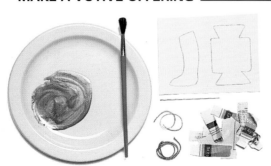

You will need: thin cardboard, strips of newspaper, flour, water, salt, wire, large needle, ribbon, bronze paint, paintbrush

1 Draw a leg or hand and a candy shape on cardboard as shown, then cut them out.

2 Make a paste from flour and water. Add a pinch of salt. Cover the cardboard with a few layers of newspaper strips dipped in the paste. Let dry.

3 Paint the cardboard shapes bronze.

4 You could write your name in Roman capital letters with a needle as shown at right.

5 Coil pieces of wire into rings. Make a hole at the top and bottom of the candy shape and thread the rings through.

6 Make a hole in the leg or arm shape and attach it to the bottom ring. Tie the ribbon to the top ring.

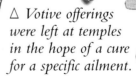

△ *Votive offerings were left at temples in the hope of a cure for a specific ailment.*

() **VOTIVES,** or dedicated offerings, were used in temples throughout the Empire. Romans believed that the gods had the power to cause and cure illness, so people who were sick went to the temple to pray. As offerings to the gods, they left a small model that showed the part of the body that needed healing, with a few words inscribed on it.

() **SOME RELIGIOUS PRACTICES** are shrouded in mystery. Face pots, some containing ashes of the dead, have been found at Roman sites in Britain and Germany. They were discovered in graves, under buildings, and in streams. No one knows what the faces mean: they may represent a dead person, a god, or a mask.

() ✳ **MAKE A FACE POT**

You will need: modeling clay, poster paints, paintbrush

1 Roll the clay into several long sausage shapes. Coil a length of clay into a round base shape as shown above.

2 Carefully add another coil of clay and build up your pot in this way. Use your thumbs to smooth the outside of the pot and merge the coils.

3 Make little clay petal shapes for the rim of the pot. Then make a mouth, eyes, eyebrows, nose and ears.

4 Add the petal shapes and facial features. Smooth the pot at the joined places. Let it dry. Paint it brown.

() **CHRISTIANITY** spread from Palestine in the Eastern Empire during the first century A.D. Like Mithras and Isis, Christ was seen as a god who promised eternal life. Unlike those gods however, his religion was open to everyone, including slaves and the poor. At first, Rome's rulers tried to stamp out this new religion because Christians refused to pay respect to the Roman gods, or worship the emperor.

✳ **ATTITUDES TO CHRISTIANITY CHANGED** when the Emperor Constantine came to power. He became a Christian, and in A.D. 313 he gave Christians the freedom of worship and encouraged Romans to convert.

△ *Face pots, or funerary urns, were used in burial rituals.*

At the Games

The Romans had very bloodthirsty tastes in entertainment. They loved watching people and animals killing each other in the amphitheater. There were many amphitheaters in the Empire, but the greatest was the Colosseum in Rome.

🏵 **THE COLOSSEUM** in Rome opened in A.D. 80 and held up to 50,000 people. The games usually began with bloody battles between wild animals. Then the gladiatorial contests followed. To celebrate the opening of the arena, 5,000 animals were slaughtered in the arena on the first day.

▽ *The Colosseum in Rome.*

△ *Romans hunting animals in North Africa for the games*

DURING THE FIRST HALF OF THE GAMES, wild animals, such as rhinoceroses, lions, elephants, and bulls were pitted against gladiators, and each other, or let loose on criminals.

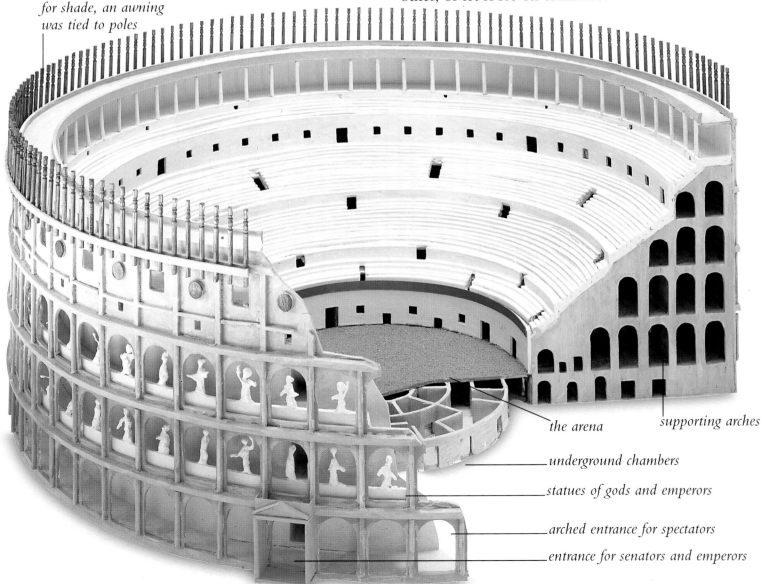

for shade, an awning was tied to poles

the arena

supporting arches

underground chambers

statues of gods and emperors

arched entrance for spectators

entrance for senators and emperors

GLADIATORS were usually slaves or criminals, although some freedmen also earned their living this way. A gladiator's life was short and hard; the majority survived only a few fights.

SUCCESSFUL GLADIATORS were treated rather like the film stars of today. They were well-trained champions who were taught combat techniques at special schools. There were different types of gladiators: the *retiarius* was armed as a fisherman, with a net and a trident—he was often pitted against a *murmillo*, the fishman. Each type of gladiator had its own group of devoted fans.

A CONTEST LASTED until one gladiator was killed or badly wounded. The wounded man threw away his weapons and begged for mercy. The crowd would shout a verdict. If the gladiator had fought well, the emperor would give a "thumbs-up" sign and spare his life. If he had not fought well, the emperor gave the "thumbs-down" sign. Then the victorious gladiator would kill the loser. An attendant dressed as a demon clubbed the loser on the head and dragged his body out through the "gate of death."

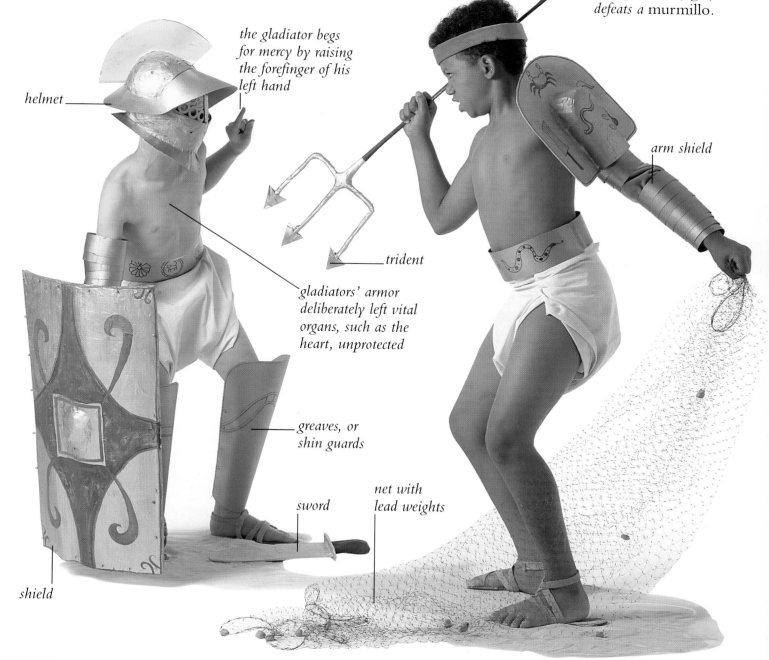

▽ *A retiarius gladiator (right) defeats a* murmillo.

the gladiator begs for mercy by raising the forefinger of his left hand

helmet

gladiators' armor deliberately left vital organs, such as the heart, unprotected

trident

arm shield

greaves, or shin guards

sword

net with lead weights

shield

CHARIOT RACING was the most popular entertainment in the larger cities of the Empire. The Romans may have taken the sport from the Greeks, who had been racing horses for over a thousand years.

RACES TOOK PLACE on a long track called a **circus**. The biggest of all, Rome's Circus Maximus, could hold 250,000 spectators. The circus was a place to meet friends, to gamble on the horses, and to enjoy a dangerous and spectacular show.

▷ *Chariots were made of lightweight pieces of wood, lashed together with thongs. This bronze statue once depicted a two-horse chariot.*

▽ *Watching chariot racing at the Circus Maximus in Rome was a favorite pastime for many Romans.*

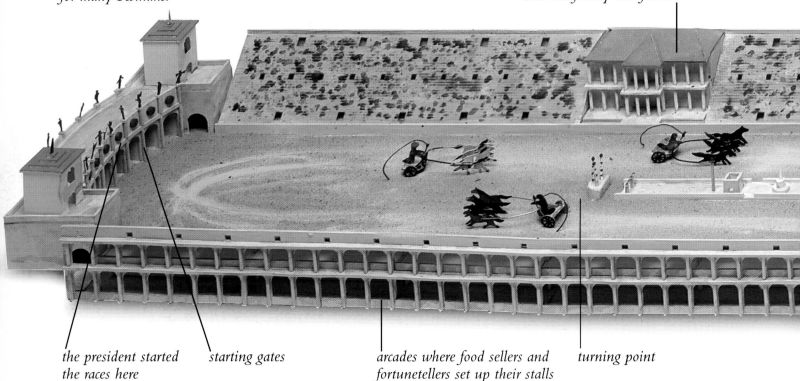

the emperor sat in the imperial box with his family and friends

the president started the races here

starting gates

arcades where food sellers and fortunetellers set up their stalls

turning point

THERE WERE FOUR TEAMS—the Whites, Reds, Blues, and the Greens. Each team had its own horses, riders and stables, staffed with trainers, veterinarians, and slaves. Like football fans of today, racegoers supported one particular team. They gambled money on their team and wore its colors. The Blues and the Greens had the most supporters. Their rival fans hated each other so much that the races sometimes ended in riots.

THE RACE TRACK was the only public place where men and women could sit together. According to the poet Ovid, the circus was a good place to find a girlfriend: "Sit as close as you like; no one will stop you at all. In fact, you have to sit close—that's one of the rules at the race track… Ask her, 'Whose colors are those?'—that's good for an opening. Put your bet down, fast, on whatever she plays… Girls, as everyone knows, adore these little attentions."

THE PRESIDENT OF THE RACES sat at one end of the circus, and it was his responsibility to get the race underway. At the blast of a trumpet, he stood up and held out a white napkin, which he dropped onto the track. At this signal, the starting gates flew open and the chariots came racing out.

The starting gates were situated at one end of the circus. Two or four chariots raced seven times around a long, narrow structure called a *spina* that had turning points at each end. The race finished opposite the judges' boxes about halfway along one side.

THE MOST DANGEROUS MOMENT was turning the chariots at the end of the track. If they were too close to the turning posts, they might crash into each other, or overturn. If they were too far away, the charioteers could lose their position.

CHARIOTEERS were mostly slaves. If they won races they could buy their freedom and grow very rich. The teams paid their stars huge salaries to stop them from joining a rival team. The fans admired their skill and courage so much that they kept busts and portraits of the charioteers in their homes. However, many charioteers died young, crushed under the hooves of the galloping horses.

spectators' seats   *charioteers*   *triumphal arch where the chariots entered the circus in a procession*

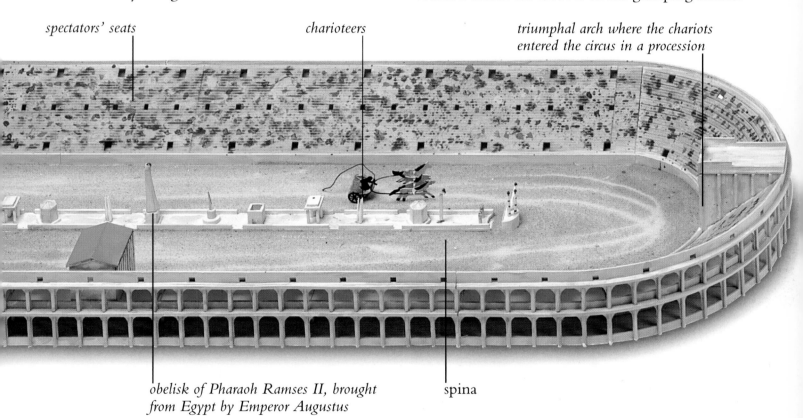

obelisk of Pharaoh Ramses II, brought from Egypt by Emperor Augustus   *spina*

THE CENTRAL "BACKBONE," or *spina*, of the circus, was decorated with statues of the gods and goddesses who were thought to watch over sport. There were also seven large wooden eggs and seven bronze dolphins on the *spina*. At the end of every lap, an egg was removed and a dolphin was reversed to show how many laps remained. Each end of the *spina* was marked by three tall posts.

THE BEST HORSES were also treated like stars. The Emperor Caligula had a favorite horse called *Incitatus* (Speedy) that raced for the Greens. He went to great lengths to keep his horse happy. On the day before a race, troops surrounded the stable, making sure that no one made any loud noises that might disturb *Incitatus*. Caligula even gave the horse a house complete with furniture and slaves!

Romans Relaxing

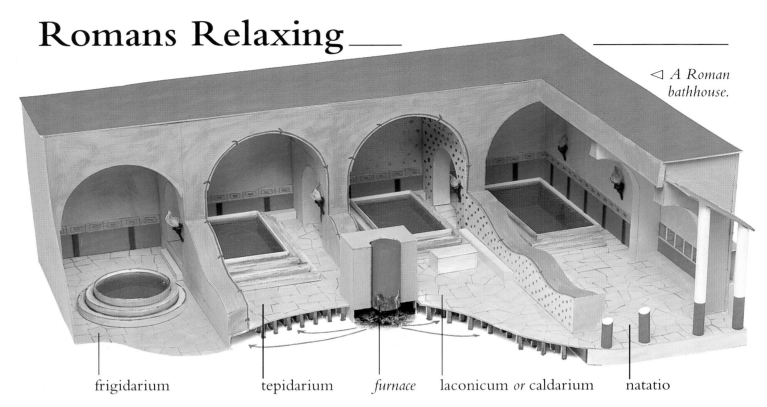

◁ *A Roman bathhouse.*

frigidarium   tepidarium   *furnace*   laconicum *or* caldarium   natatio

Every Roman town had at least one large public bathhouse. This was a place where people could go to wash the dust off, to exercise, or just to relax. Men and women visited the bathhouse separately, either at different times or in different areas. It cost very little to go to the baths, so only the poorest people could not afford to visit them. Many Romans went every day.

▷ *Oils were kept in the small pot, and the long, curved* **strigil** *was used for scraping off the oil and dirt.*

THE BATHHOUSE had a large exercise yard where people played ball games, lifted weights, and wrestled. After exercising, they went to a series of heated rooms to wash and relax.

THE ROOMS and bathwater were heated by a furnace stoked by slaves. Hot air from the fire passed through spaces under the floors and inside the walls. The hottest room was the one closest to the furnace.

Once inside, the bathers first went to an icy plunge pool called a *frigidarium*. From there they passed to a warmer room—the *tepidarium*. This was where oils were applied to the skin and then scraped off, so that the bather would be thoroughly clean.

INSTEAD OF SOAP, Romans used olive oil. They rubbed it all over their bodies and scraped it off with a curved metal tool called a *strigil*. Wealthy Romans had personal slave attendants to scrape them down. Poorer Romans had to rub their backs against the walls to scrape the parts they couldn't reach!

FINALLY, THE BATHERS went to a steam room, called a *caldarium*, or to the *laconicum*, or hot room. Then they were clean enough to swim in the swimming pool, or *natatio*. Around the pool there were entertainers, hairdressers and people selling food and drink. Businessmen even held meetings at the baths.

KNUCKLEBONES, or *astragali,* was a popular game at the baths. Players used the small anklebones of a sheep, which have six sides. It was an easy game to play: a player would throw the bones up into the air and try to catch them on the back of the hand. Knucklebones could also be played like dice, with each side of the bones having a different value. Wealthy Romans played with knucklebones made of marble, silver, or precious stones.

MAKE KNUCKLEBONES

You will need: modeling clay, poster paints, paintbrush

1 Mold the clay into 10 knucklebone shapes with 6 sides as shown above.

2 Paint the knucklebones and give five to each player.

The basic way to play knucklebones is described on the left. Each player should throw in turn. Try and catch as many bones on the back of your hand as possible. Keep count of the number you manage to catch.

▽ *Roman girls and women loved to relax at the baths by playing knucklebones.*

△ *This mosaic from Pompeii shows actors and musicians getting ready for a performance.*

MASKS were worn in most types of play. These larger-than-life masks showed the sex of the character, as well as his or her mood. Thanks to the masks, the audience could tell at once if an actor was meant to be an angry old man, a comical slave, or a beautiful woman. Masks for tragedy showed an expression of horror or despair.

PANTOMIME was a performance in which a single actor mimed several parts, using a series of masks with closed mouths. It was like a solo ballet dance and demanded a great deal of skill. With their faces covered, the actors relied on movement to show their feelings. Pantomime actors were the big stars of the Roman stage.

▽ *This is a mask that an actor might have worn in a tragic play.*

THEATER was invented by the Greeks. The Romans borrowed two main types of plays from them: the first was tragedy, a serious play showing the sufferings of a great hero or heroine, usually from a Greek myth. The second was comedy, a light-hearted play about everyday life. Many Roman plays were set in Greece and performed by Greek actors.

AUDIENCES were often very noisy. People either cheered the actors or shouted insults at them. The producer of *The Mother-in-Law*, a comedy by Terence, described his lively audience: "I was successful in holding the audience— at least to the end of the first act. But then a rumor spread that some gladiators were going to perform—and my audience flew off in a huge crowd, pushing, shouting, fighting to get a good spot at the gladiator performance."

You will need: two lengths of cardboard measuring 2⅓ x 35 in. (6 x 90 cm), paint, paintbrush, yarn, glue, double-sided adhesive tape, a circle of fabric 12½ in. (32 cm) in diameter

1 Glue the ends of one of the pieces of cardboard together to make a circle. Stretch the fabric over the circle and glue down tightly around the edges to make the drum.

2 Stick a strip of adhesive tape along the other length of cardboard. Wrap around the drum.

3 Paint your drum as shown above.

4 Make four tassels with your yarn and glue them around your drum.

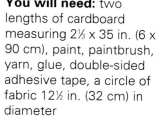

△ *This kind of drum was often used in Roman theater.*

SPECIAL EFFECTS were very popular with Roman audiences. Actors playing gods would swoop across the stage attached to wires. Even horses and carriages appeared in some plays.

MUSIC was very important in the theater. Musicians played the pipes, trumpets, cymbals, and drums, while the actors sang songs. Although we know what instruments were played, we have no way of knowing what Roman music sounded like.

◁ *This actor is wearing a comic mask. Actors used masks and hand gestures to show different characters.*

Amazing Architects

The Romans were among the best builders in history. They built things that served practical purposes, such as canals, bridges, sewers, harbors, and roads. But it was perhaps in constructing aqueducts that their engineering skills were most impressive.

▽ *Rome was served by eight aqueducts, each built using wooden scaffolding such as this.*

△ *This Roman aqueduct still stands in Segovia, in central Spain.*

covered water channel

AQUEDUCTS were developed by the Romans. They are channels for carrying water that were mostly dug into the earth, following the contours of hills. Where this was not possible, the Romans built arches made of concrete and stone. It took great skill to build an aqueduct. The water channel had to slope at exactly the right angle all the way along its length to give a steady flow of water.

AN ARCH is a curved structure that is able to support great weight. By using arches, the Romans found they could build high, strong walls using as little stone as possible.

CONCRETE was also a Roman invention. It was a mixture of volcanic sand and stone rubble, held together by mortar made from lime and water. It was strong, cheap, and much easier to use than stone blocks. Concrete and arches made it possible to build structures like the Colosseum.

PLINY THE ELDER described the work involved in giving Rome its water supply: "If we think of the abundant supply of water for public buildings, baths, settling tanks, pools, private houses, gardens, and country estates close to the city; and of the distance the water travels, the height of the arches, the tunneling through mountains, the leveling of routes across deep valleys; we can only conclude that this is a supreme wonder of the world."

▷ *This surveyor is using a* groma—*a wooden cross mounted on a pole, with weighted strings at the ends that hung vertically.*

wooden scaffolding supports arches as they are being built

THE SURVEYOR was the person who marked out the ground before building. To plot right angles, he used an instrument called a **groma.** The surveyor took sightings along each of the arms of the cross, using assistants who stood in the distance. He signaled to his assistants to move either left or right, so that they lined up. Then they laid out a long straight line of flags.

GOOD ROADS helped the Romans to expand their empire. Armies had to be able to move from place to place as quickly as possible with all their equipment. Before the Romans, roads were muddy tracks that were almost impossible to use in wet weather, especially for wheeled transport. The Romans made paved roads that could be used almost all year around. The surface was curved so that rainwater would drain off into ditches at the edges. Roman roads were usually as straight as possible, even if this sometimes meant tunneling through a cliff.

Feeding the Empire

Some of the best farmland in the Roman Empire was along the coast of North Africa. The soil there was good and the climate was excellent, with long, hot summers and regular rain in winter. It was the perfect place for growing wheat—in fact, North Africa produced two-thirds of the grain eaten in Rome.

△ *This mosaic from the A.D. 300's shows farm laborers gathering and treading grapes.*

ROMAN FARMS were often enormous and were owned by very wealthy people. In the first century A.D., half of North Africa was said to belong to just six men. Roman landlords spent most of their time in the cities, living extravagantly. They either rented the land out to tenants, or left their farms in the hands of a bailiff who was in charge of a gang of slaves.

FARM BUILDINGS included barns for storing grain and straw, stables for the animals, and various workshops—a blacksmith's forge for making and repairing tools, and a pottery for making storage jars. There were buildings for pressing grapes and olives, and a mill for grinding wheat. The type and quality of crops varied throughout the Empire. Olives could be grown only in the warm south. Grapes were grown in southern Britain, but they were not as good as those from Spain or Italy.

RELIGIOUS CEREMONIES played a big part in the farmers' year. The Romans believed that ceremonies were just as important as sowing or plowing at the right time. In May, for example, a pig, a ram, and a bull were led around the boundaries of the fields and then killed as a sacrifice to the god Mars. The farmer would say, "Father Mars, I pray that you keep disease and bad weather away from my fields and that you allow my harvest, my corn, and my vineyard to flourish."

▷ *A Roman farm on the north coast of Africa.*

team of oxen harnessed to a mechanical harvester

beehives

wheat

OLIVE TREES were grown all over North Africa, but the olives from Tripolitania (present-day Libya) were particularly famous. They were grown on dry hillsides, above fields of wheat. The olives could either be eaten or crushed in an oil press for their rich oil.

SLAVES did most of the farm work. A trusted slave called a *vilicus* was in charge of the field laborers. They had to work very hard: if not, they might be beaten or kept in chains. Farm work was used as a punishment for town slaves whose masters thought they were lazy.

▷ *Farmers' tools were simple but effective. These knives were used for pruning grapevines.*

stables

olive press

villa rustica, *or farmhouse*

slaves' quarters

olive grove

livestock

Trade and Transport

Wherever they went, the Roman armies built roads. Although they were for military use, Roman roads made it easier to transport goods on carts pulled by mules and oxen, no matter what the weather. Heavy goods were moved by water wherever possible—along rivers on barges pulled by oxen, or across the sea on merchant ships.

THE PEACE that was brought by Roman rule helped trade to flourish from one end of the Empire to the other. The demands of the wealthy also meant that luxury goods, such as silks and spices, were brought from distant lands.

△ *Coins were used throughout the Empire.*

WITHIN THE EMPIRE, the most important trade was in metals, luxury goods, and foods such as wine, olive oil, grain, and fish sauce.

Some goods were imported from beyond the Empire. Silk came from as far away as China along an overland route called the Silk Road. Spices for cooking were brought by sea from India, and incense, which the Romans burned on the altars of the gods, came overland from southern Arabia by camel caravans, or by ships sailing up the Red Sea.

KEY TO TRADE MAP

wild animals | wild animals | slaves | grain | wine | oil | gold | metals

▽ *This map shows where some of the goods traded around the Empire came from.*

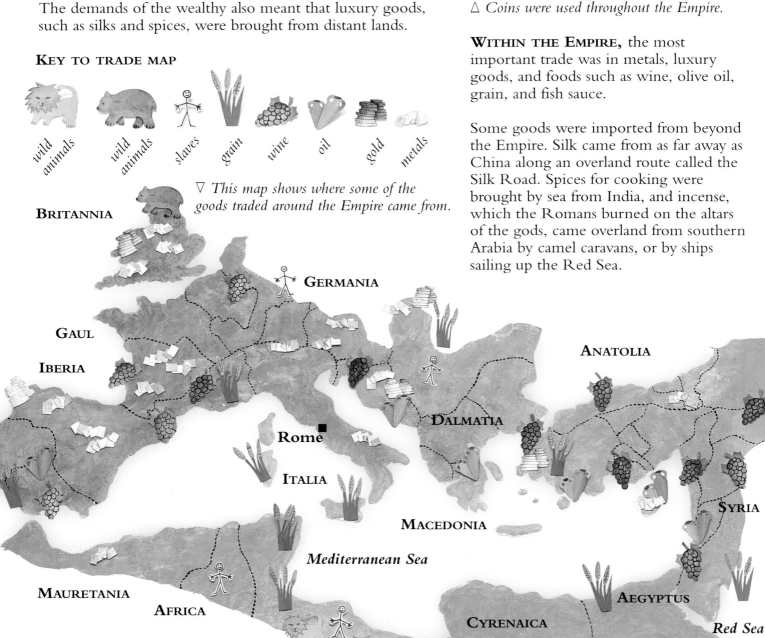

BRITANNIA
GERMANIA
GAUL
IBERIA
ANATOLIA
DALMATIA
Rome
ITALIA
SYRIA
MACEDONIA
Mediterranean Sea
MAURETANIA
AFRICA
AEGYPTUS
CYRENAICA
Red Sea

△ *Traders made healthy profits from transporting exotic animals around the Empire.*

☯ ✳ **PLINY THE ELDER** thought that foreign luxury goods were costing the Empire too much: "At the lowest reckoning, India, China, and Arabia carry off one hundred million *sestertii* a year from our Empire—such is the bill for our pleasures and our ladies."

WILD ANIMALS were brought from all parts of the Empire and from lands beyond for the games in Rome. Bears were shipped from Scotland and Ireland. Elephants came from Africa and India.

☯ ✳ **THE SAME COINS** were used throughout the Empire, making trading simple. The basic unit was a copper coin called an *as*. A larger copper coin, called the *dupondius*, was worth 2 donkeys; a bronze coin, the *sestertius*, was worth 4 donkeys; a silver *denarius* equalled 16 donkeys; and a gold *aureus* was worth 100 donkeys.

☯ ✳ **A ROMAN COIN** was like a tiny newspaper in some ways. One side was used by the emperor to announce important events, such as a military victory. He also used coins to try to win people's loyalty. The coin might show him speaking to his troops—giving people the impression that he was in firm command. Another coin might show the emperor as the chief priest, so that people would think that he had the support of the gods.

▷ *A merchant weighs some fruit using a set of scales.*

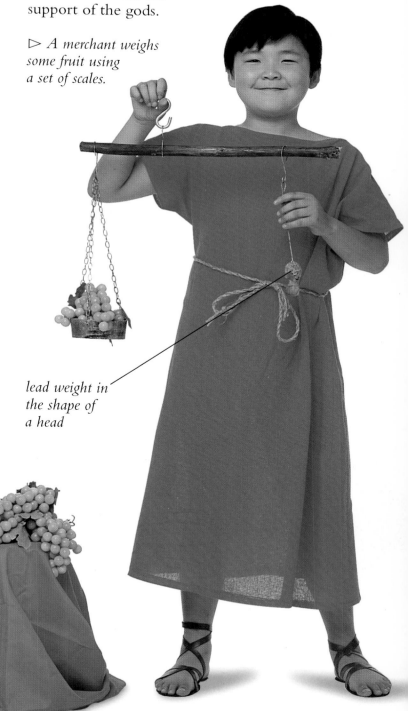

lead weight in the shape of a head

SHIPS were used to move people and goods around the Empire and beyond. As well as traveling for trade and religious reasons, some wealthy Romans went sightseeing, and some even had guidebooks.

▽ A Roman war galley.

sail was lowered before going into battle

underwater battering ram

up to five men manned each oar

WAR GALLEYS were slim, fast vessels. They were powered by oarsmen who sat on benches below deck, pulling in time to orders shouted by the helmsman. At the bow, or front, there was a battering ram made of wood covered in bronze. Galleys would try to ram enemy ships in the side. Then the crew of marines (naval soldiers) would jump on board the enemy ship for hand-to-hand fighting.

PIRATES were a menace in the first century B.C. Fleets of pirates based in the eastern Mediterranean raided coastal towns and seized any ships they could. They stole the cargoes and held the crews for ransom, or sold them as slaves. In 67 B.C., the Romans gathered a fleet of war galleys and hunted the pirates down to make the sea safe.

THE SAILING SEASON lasted from March to November. Few ships put out to sea in winter because of the risk of storms, and because of shorter daylight hours. However, the city of Rome needed wheat grown abroad to feed its people, so some huge grain ships had to make the dangerous winter journey from North Africa. When grain supplies ran low in the granaries, there was panic in Rome.

IN THE SECOND CENTURY A.D., the Greek writer Lucian described the *Isis*, one of the great grain ships that sailed out of Egypt: "What a big ship! About 180 feet [55 meters] long and something over a quarter of that wide… And then the height of the mast! And how the stern rises with its gentle curve, with its golden beak, balanced at the opposite end by the long rising length of the prow, with a figure of the goddess Isis on either side!"

▽ Merchant ships carried people, food supplies, and wild animals for the games.

yard

foresail, or steering sail

MERCHANT SHIPS were used to move goods around the Empire. These ships were large and round-bellied, to provide lots of storage space for all the sacks of grain and *amphorae*, or pottery jars, holding oil or wine. Because of their shape, these ships were stable but very slow. They had a big square sail on the mast with a smaller sail at the bow. Two large oars at the stern, or rear, were used for steering.

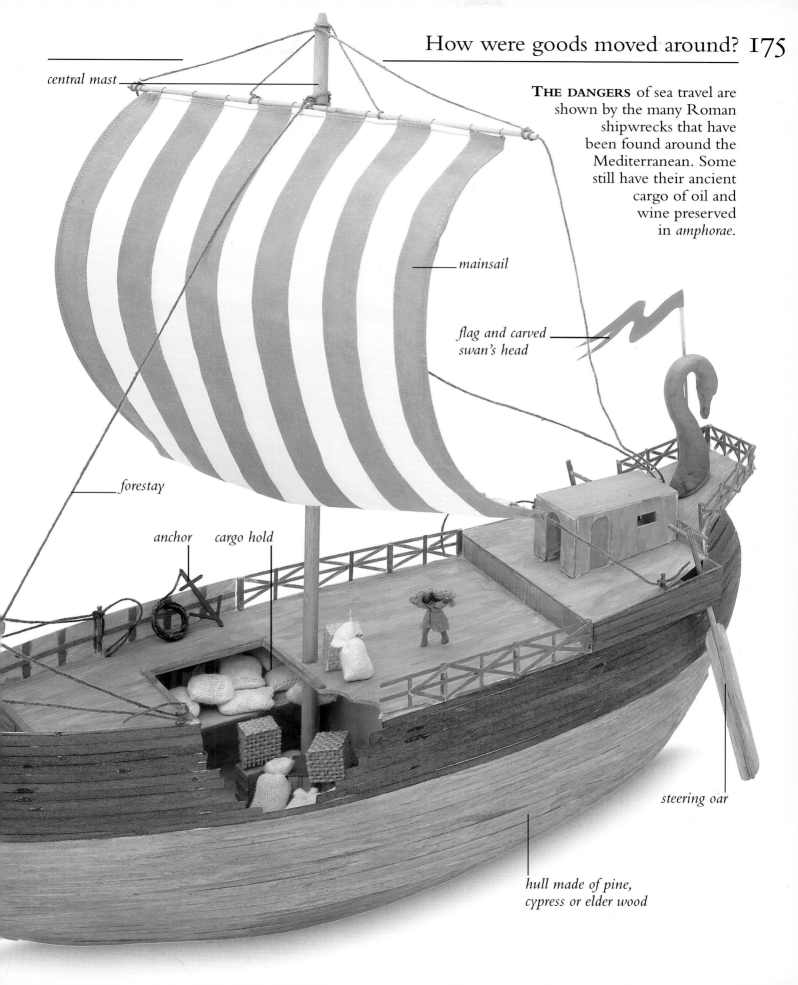

central mast

mainsail

THE DANGERS of sea travel are shown by the many Roman shipwrecks that have been found around the Mediterranean. Some still have their ancient cargo of oil and wine preserved in *amphorae*.

flag and carved swan's head

forestay

anchor   cargo hold

steering oar

hull made of pine, cypress or elder wood

The Roman Army

In the first century A.D., the Roman army was mostly made up of legionaries and auxiliaries. There were 28 legions, mainly stationed around the borders of the Empire. Each one had a number and a name that was either a nickname or the place where the troops were raised. For example, the sixth legion was called *Victrix*, or victorious; and the ninth legion was called *Hispana*, or Spanish.

lionskin headdress worn over a helmet

◁ *A legionary from the first century B.C.*

A LEGIONARY was a Roman foot soldier. On marches, they had to carry heavy loads of weapons, tools, and supplies. If they were not fighting or training, legionaries had to do building work. They cut down trees, quarried stone, and built roads, bridges, and forts.

▽ *A Syrian archer of the early A.D. 100's.*

Syrian archers wore long robes

△ *An aquilifer from the first century A.D.*

AUXILIARIES were soldiers who came from the provinces and who were not Roman citizens. They were poorly paid, earning only a third of the legionaries' rate. Auxiliaries fought using the familiar weapons of their own countries. Cavalry came from Gaul (France) and North Africa, slingers from islands off Spain, and archers from Syria. Auxiliaries supplied the extra fighting skills that the legions lacked.

THE AQUILIFER, or eagle bearer, carried the standard of the legion—a golden eagle on a pole. Smaller units also had standards, such as golden hands or busts of the emperor. These were used to rally the soldiers in battle. Aquilifers had to be very brave, for they led the men into the most dangerous places on the battlefield. The lionskins on their helmets were a symbol of their rank and courage.

long spear used for stabbing from horseback

▽ A cavalry officer from the A.D. 300's.

silver-plated helmet

▷ A centurion from around A.D. 50.

helmet with sideways crest

EACH LEGION had around 5,500 soldiers, including 120 horsemen who acted as messengers and scouts, keeping an eye on the enemy. The rest of the soldiers were divided into small units called centuries, each of about 80 men. Six centuries grouped together made a cohort.

silver and gold medals on chest

vine cane used to point at, or beat, the men

A CENTURION was an officer in charge of a century. To show his rank, he wore special armor made from silver-colored metal scales, and shiny greaves (shin guards). He also wore a helmet with a sideways crest as a sign of his status. He kept his men in order by beating them with a vine cane, either as a punishment, or to make them work harder.

CAVALRY played an even more important role during the later Empire, when large armies of soldiers on horseback fought alongside the legions. By the A.D. 300's, the cavalry carried long swords and round shields.

LEGIONARIES were full-time soldiers. They joined the army at about the age of 18, and had to serve for the next 20 to 25 years. It was a hard life, but it also offered security and regular pay to the poorest Roman citizens. Through good service, legionaries might be promoted to the rank of centurion. If they survived the battles they fought, they could retire and live a comfortable life.

New recruits had to swear an oath that they were free-born Roman citizens, not slaves. Sometimes, slaves tried to join the legions. If they were discovered, they were executed.

DRILLING AND MARCHING took up a large part of the legionary's day. In his book *Military Service*, the author Vegetius described the type of training program that legionaries were put through: "Every recruit, without exception, should in the summer months learn to swim, for it is not always possible to cross rivers on bridges… They should be accustomed also to leap and strike blows at the same time, to rise up with a bound and sink down again behind the shield… They must also practice throwing their javelins at the posts from a distance to increase their skill in aiming, and the strength of the arm."

MAKE A PAIR OF ARMORED SHOES

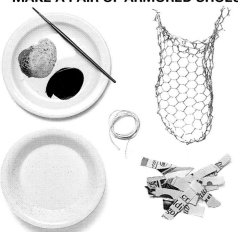

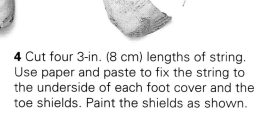

You will need: scissors, chicken wire, paper, string, flour, water, salt, paint

1 Ask an adult to help you mold the chicken wire to fit the top of your feet.

2 Make a runny paste of flour and water. Add a pinch of salt. Cover the shapes (inside and out) in layers of strips of paper dipped in the paste. Let them dry.

3 Cut off the tops of the toes as shown to make toe shields.

4 Cut four 3-in. (8 cm) lengths of string. Use paper and paste to fix the string to the underside of each foot cover and the toe shields. Paint the shields as shown.

5 Make two small holes in the sides of each shoe. Thread string through the holes and tie around your ankles.

PUNISHMENTS were harsh in the army. Soldiers who fell asleep on guard duty or ran away in battle were stoned to death. If a whole unit showed cowardice or refused to obey orders, it could be punished with decimation, which meant that one man in every ten was killed.

However, life was not all bad for a Roman soldier. At Vindolanda, a Roman fort in northern Britain, archaeologists found many letters written on thin sheets of wood. In one letter, dating from A.D. 120, a soldier complains that his unit has run out of beer!

▷ *This is a copy of foot armor that was found in the south of Italy, in an early Greek settlement.*

🦅 🏵 **BAGGAGE MULES** trotted alongside the marching soldiers. There was one mule for every eight men. It carried a leather tent and a millstone for grinding corn. Other mules were loaded with dismantled catapults, used for hurling stones at the enemy.

▽ *An early legionary shown with the equipment he was expected to carry on long marches.*

cloak

javelin or pilum

spear

wooden shield carried on legionary's back

supplies carried on a wooden cross on the legionary's back

cooking pots

🦅 🏵 **A JAVELIN,** or *pilum*, had a long metal tip that bent on impact. This meant that the enemy could not throw it back. Soldiers fought in tight formation, obeying trumpet signals. After throwing their javelins, they drew their short swords and thrust at the enemy from behind their shields.

water pouch

turf cutter

🦅 🏵 **WHEN ATTACKING** an enemy stronghold, soldiers grouped together and covered themselves with their shields for protection. This defense was called "the tortoise." The men gathered into a square, and those at the edges linked their curved shields together to make a wall of wood. The men in the middle held their shields above their heads to make a roof. This kept them safe from enemy missiles.

mattock for building camp

ON A CAMPAIGN, Roman soldiers slept in leather tents in temporary marching camps, which they set up at the end of each day. The rest of the time, they lived in barracks in permanent forts made of wood or stone.

FRONTIER FORTS were dotted along the borders of the Empire. They were usually manned by auxiliaries recruited from the local area, so German auxiliaries defended the Empire against German invaders. Legionaries lived some way behind the frontier, providing a second line of defense. If the front line was attacked, guards in the watchtowers would light beacons to send the urgent news.

▽ *This is a typical Roman frontier fort.*

mile castle built every Roman mile (5,000 ft. or 1.5 km) along frontiers

a main gateway

stables

barracks

workshop

FORTS changed over time, but they were often rectangular and surrounded by a ditch. Early forts were protected by a wall of timber and turf. Later, they were built with stone. Two main roads crossed the camp, leading to four gates, one on each wall. The fort was a permanent home for the soldiers, so it had to be as comfortable as possible. The soldiers always had their own baths, and sometimes amphitheaters for gladiator contests.

THE HOSPITAL was an important building in every fort, as the soldiers were often sick and sometimes injured. Military doctors knew how to reset broken bones, and they operated to remove splinters or arrowheads from wounds.

defensive ditch

THE COMMANDER'S HOUSE, or *praetorium*, was a lavish building with heated rooms where the commander lived with his family and their slaves. The business of running the legion took place in the headquarters, or *principia*. It had a strong room for the legion's money, a shrine for the standards, and a platform for addressing the troops.

IN THEIR FREE TIME, soldiers could drink beer, gamble with dice, and organize wrestling matches, horse races, and tug-of-war contests. The commanding officers preferred hunting deer and wild boar with packs of dogs.

IN MAINLAND EUROPE there were wide rivers that also acted as frontier lines. The Romans built forts and watchtowers along the west bank of the Rhine and on the southern bank of the Danube. They used them to keep an eye on the fierce German tribes across the river.

☙ THE EMPEROR HADRIAN ordered that a wall be built across northern Britain to defend the frontier. The Romans called the people who lived north of the wall *Picti*, or painted ones, because they covered themselves in war paint.

▷ *The Emperor Hadrian ordered the building of a 73-mile (117-km) long wall, sections of which can still be seen today.*

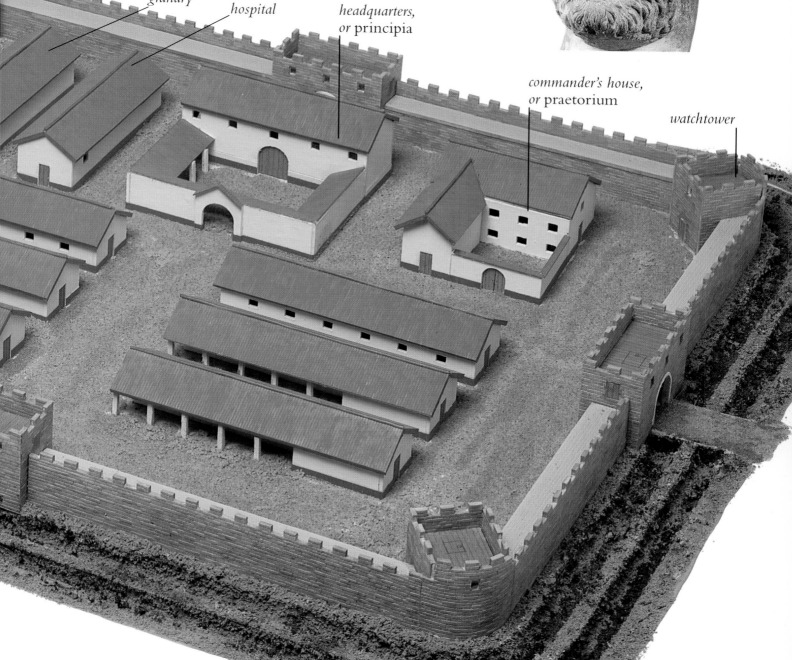

granary

hospital

headquarters, or principia

commander's house, or praetorium

watchtower

The Fall of Rome

In the A.D. 300's, the Roman Empire was weakened by a series of invasions. German tribes poured over the Rhine and Danube rivers. To meet the threat, the Roman Empire was split into two halves. There was an emperor in the west, sometimes ruling from Rome, and another in the east ruling from Constantinople (Istanbul) in Turkey.

✷ **ROME WAS CAPTURED** and plundered in A.D. 410 by Alaric, king of the Visigoths. The news of the fall of the city shocked the Roman world. Jerome, a monk in Palestine, wrote to a friend: "Terrifying news has come to us from the West. Rome has been taken by assault… My voice is still and sobs disturb my every utterance. The city has been conquered which had once controlled the entire world."

△ *Many tourists visit the remains of the Colosseum in Rome.*

THE GERMAN INVADERS set up their own kingdoms in western Europe. One group, the Franks, settled in Gaul and became the French. Other German peoples, the Saxons and Angles, settled in Britain and became the English. The invaders did not usually want to destroy the Roman Empire. As a result, many aspects of the Roman way of life were kept alive in western Europe.

▷ *The title "Caesar" was used by the emperors, from Augustus to Hadrian, and by other powerful rulers throughout history.*

◁ *The eagle, once the symbol of the Roman Empire, is now a symbol of the United States and appears on the one-dollar bill. For the Romans, the eagle was the king of birds and represented Jupiter, the king of the gods, and god of the sky.*

ROMAN POLITICS AND LAW have had a lasting influence. The United States has modeled its system of government on the Roman Republic and adopted the eagle as a national emblem. Throughout history, many rulers have looked to the power and inspiration of the emperors and the Roman Empire. In some countries, rulers adopted the title "Caesar": in Russia, it became "Tzar," and in Germany it became "Kaiser."

THE EASTERN EMPIRE survived for another thousand years. It was only in 1453 that the last eastern emperor died defending his capital, Constantinople, against the Muslim Turks.

By the 1500's, the Empire no longer existed, but its influence lived on in the lands surrounding the Mediterranean in the form of architecture, language, literature, and government.

ROMAN ARCHITECTURE still influences modern buildings. Public buildings, such as banks, libraries, churches, and museums, are often modeled on Roman temples, with tall, decorative columns.

THE LATIN LANGUAGE developed into French, Italian, Spanish, Portuguese, and Romanian. Latin was kept alive in church services and writings. It also became, with Greek, an international language for scientists, who classify plants, animals, and parts of the body using Latin names.

THE MONTHS OF THE YEAR are still known by their Roman names. March, for example, is named after the Roman god Mars, and August gets its name from Rome's first emperor, Augustus. The planets are also named after Roman gods.

cyclamen
cyclamen persicum

△ *Latin is used to classify plants and species of animals.*

NATIVE AMERICANS

Studying Native American Life

All human beings need food and shelter to survive. They also need things to look forward to that give their lives hope and meaning. Throughout history, different groups of people around the world have come up with their own ways of meeting these basic needs. Studying past **civilizations** can tell us how people used the resources around them to build shelters, how they farmed or found food, and how they met their spiritual needs and hopes for a better future.

△ *This man, from the Crow group in Montana, is decorating buffalo hides. Hides were used to make dwellings (see page 199).*

△ *The Shoshone of the Great Basin lived in fertile regions near the Teton Range, Wyoming.*

NATIVE AMERICANS were scattered over a vast country with a wide range of climates and **terrains**, from parched deserts in the Southwest to the frozen wastes of the North to the dense forests in the East. Those who lived in the Canadian Subarctic region had to deal with an even more extreme climate. We look at their lives, along with those of the people who lived even further north, in *Arctic Peoples*, another title in the Make it Work! History series.

TO HELP YOU study this vast area, with its wide range of different peoples, North America has been divided into seven climate regions. Each has a symbol which is used purely as a guide, when information relates to a group of people from a particular part of the country.

KEY TO THE SYMBOLS AND AREAS

 - the Plains

 - the Northeast

 - the Northwest

 - the Southwest

 - California

 - the Southeast

 - the Great Basin and Plateau

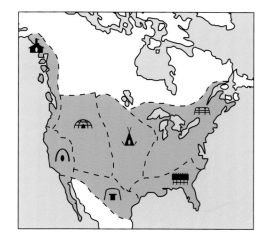

IN THIS BOOK we look at how Native Americans lived, from five hundred years ago, just before their traditional way of life was changed by the arrival of the European settlers, to the present day. We can build a picture of what this life was like from the tales told by explorers and traders. These people were among the first from other parts of the world to have any contact with Native Americans. We can also learn a great deal from the stories that have been passed down from generation to generation by the Native Americans themselves. The studies of **archaeologists** and **anthropologists** are another source of information (see page 240).

THE TRADITIONS AND LIFESTYLES of Native Americans are a vital and living part of US history. They are kept alive today by those who choose to live as their ancestors did. Many Native Americans have a strong sense of their roots, such as the Mashpees of Cape Cod.

▽ *These Plains people continue to live according to the traditions of their ancestors.*

△ *This Blackfoot chief is painting pictures showing experiences in his life (see pages 232-233).*

THE MAKE IT WORK! way of looking at history is to ask questions of the past and find answers by making replicas of the things people made. You do not have to make all the replicas in the book to understand their way of life. However, you should realize that some of the objects included are based on sacred or ceremonial traditions. Therefore, they deserve the same respect as you would give to objects that are special to your own culture or beliefs.

▽ *The Iroquois believed that these sacred masks gave the wearer the power to cure illnesses.*

Origins _____

There are many theories about how people arrived on the continent. Many native peoples believe they were created in North America. There are far too many versions of the story to explain here, but many of them can be found in libraries.

SOME SCIENTISTS believe that the first people came to the continent around 15,000 years ago from Siberia. They believe the people followed mammoth and giant bison over a bridge of ice or land that joined Siberia to Alaska. When the earth warmed and the ice melted, the bridge disappeared, leaving the continents separated by what is now the Bering Strait.

OTHER SCIENTISTS believe there is not enough evidence to support the Bering Strait theory. Some of these other scientists believe that the first people came to North America from Africa by boat. Whatever the real story may be, it is true that in 1500, when the first Europeans arrived on the continent, there were at least 600 nations living in North America. Today, there are more than 500, including Alaskan natives such as the Aleuts and the Inuit.

▷ *This map shows the location of some of the main **nations**. Many of these peoples are discussed in this book.*

PACIFIC NORTHWEST
(warm, wet summers; cool, wet winters)

Haida
Tlingit
Chinook
Nootka
Kwakiutl

CALIFORNIA
(hot and dry all year round)

Chumash
Miwok
Maidu
Karok
Pomo
Yahi

SOUTHWEST
(hot and dry all year round)

Pueblos
Apache
Navajo
Yuma
Hopi
Zuni

Pacific Northwest

Great Basin and Plateau

California

Southwest

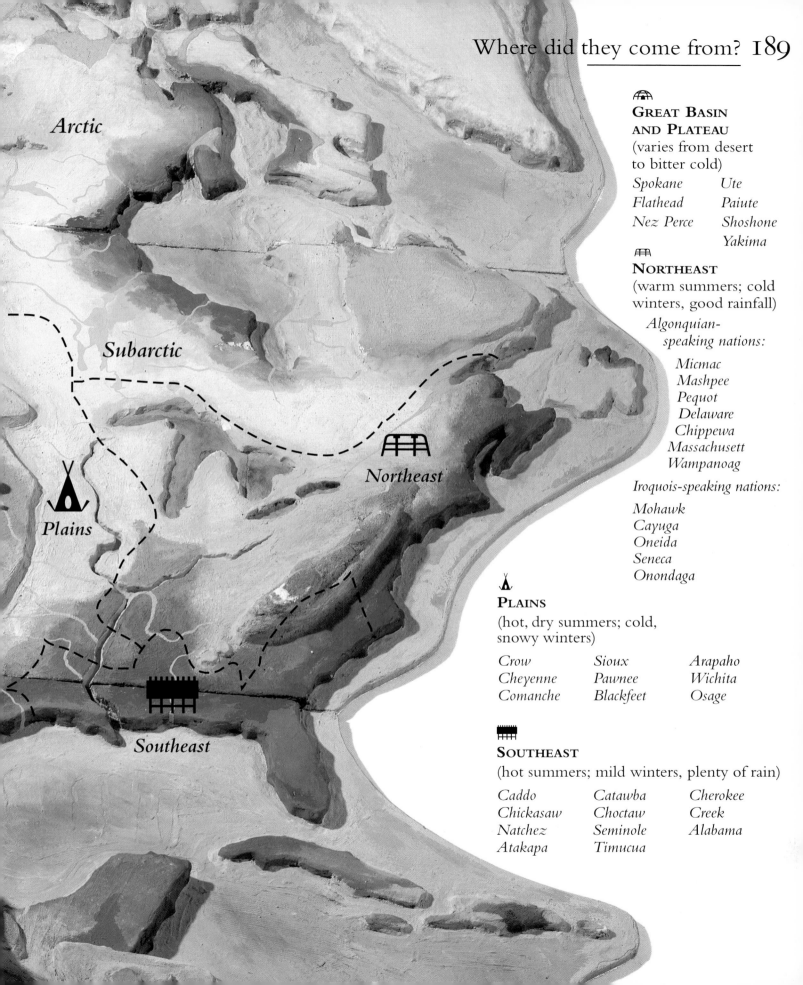

Arctic

Subarctic

Plains

Northeast

Southeast

GREAT BASIN AND PLATEAU
(varies from desert to bitter cold)

Spokane   Ute
Flathead   Paiute
Nez Perce   Shoshone
              Yakima

NORTHEAST
(warm summers; cold winters, good rainfall)

Algonquian-speaking nations:

Micmac
Mashpee
Pequot
Delaware
Chippewa
Massachusett
Wampanoag

Iroquois-speaking nations:

Mohawk
Cayuga
Oneida
Seneca
Onondaga

PLAINS
(hot, dry summers; cold, snowy winters)

Crow   Sioux   Arapaho
Cheyenne   Pawnee   Wichita
Comanche   Blackfeet   Osage

SOUTHEAST
(hot summers; mild winters, plenty of rain)

Caddo   Catawba   Cherokee
Chickasaw   Choctaw   Creek
Natchez   Seminole   Alabama
Atakapa   Timucua

Clothing

Although many people think of traditional Native American dress as fringed tunics, feather headdresses, and braided hair, this is not what everyone wore. Tunics were worn by some Plains groups. As with everything in Native American life, the clothes people wore depended on where and how they lived. Those in northern and eastern areas needed warm clothing. Many western and southern Native Americans wore little clothing, decorating their bodies instead with tattoos. Hunters made clothing from animal hides and fur, while gatherers and farmers used plant fibers.

△ *Wolf Robe, of the Southern Cheyenne, is wearing feathers from the golden eagle. This photograph was taken in 1909.*

♦ WARBONNETS were made from the tail feathers of the golden eagle. Warriors proved their bravery by collecting feathers from the fierce, powerful birds. They cut and colored them in different ways to let others know about their fighting skills (see page 228).

wearer wounded | *wearer wounded many times* | *wearer counted coup four times* | *wearer cut enemy's throat* | *wearer killed enemy*

♦ MAKE A SIOUX HEADDRESS

You will need: canvas or plain fabric, 12-15 feathers, tape, glue, colored ribbons, paint, paintbrush, scissors, hook-and-loop fasteners

1 Paint the tips of the feathers and wrap tape around the quills.

2 Cut a canvas strip long enough to fit around your head with some overlap and twice as wide as the headband will be. Turn in and glue the edges, then fold the strip in half lengthwise. Mark and paint a design on it, as shown.

3 Glue inside the folded strip, leaving small, evenly spaced pockets for the feathers. Glue a feather into each pocket. Decorate the headdress with colored streamers made from the ribbons.

BODY PAINT made from reddish brown mud, called ocher, mixed with animal fat was used by woodland groups to paint their bodies. The designs and colors showed that people belonged to a special group, or told of their deeds or dreams. Body paint had a practical use, too. The grease in the paint protected their skin from the sun, wind, cold, and stinging and biting insects.

TATTOOS were worn by people in the hot, sunny Southeast and in California. They wore few clothes, but used tattoos to decorate and express themselves. They used needles made from cactus spines or slivers of bone to prick patterns on their skin.

HAIRSTYLES were important ways to look different but still fit in with national traditions. Some groups smeared their hair with mud and sculpted it into elaborate shapes. Many warriors shaved their heads so they looked fierce and threatening. They sometimes tied a stiff tuft of animal hair, known as a **roach**, in the center.

TWEEZERS made from shells, wood, or bone were used by men to pluck the hair from their faces. They rarely grew beards or moustaches.

HATS were made by many tribes, using materials that came to hand. California Indians wove sun hats from reeds and decorated them with poppy flowers. In the Pacific Northwest, hats were woven from cedar bark. Woodland tribes wore headbands made from fur or hide, or turbanlike sashes woven from plant fibers.

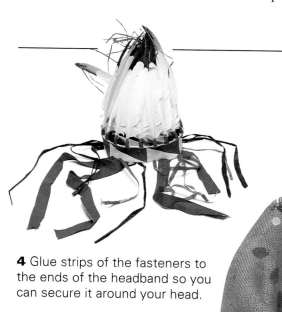

4 Glue strips of the fasteners to the ends of the headband so you can secure it around your head.

⚑ **THE MEN OF THE GREAT PLAINS** wore only a piece of soft **buckskin** passed between their legs and tied with a belt. In winter, when the weather was fiercely cold, they added fitted, thigh-length leggings and a knee-length tunic.

⚑ **WOMEN'S LEGGINGS** were held up with garters just below the knee. Dresses were often made of two deer skins sewn together, with the animals' legs making natural sleeves. In the chillier North, both men and women wore robes made of softened buffalo skin with the hair left on.

⚑ **CHILDREN** wore nothing in the summer and child-sized versions of adult clothes in winter. Tunics, leggings, and dresses were often decorated with quillwork or beaded embroidery.

△ *Ute warriors like this man (right) wore magnificent breastplates of bone, porcupine quills, and shells and decorated themselves with body paint.*

⚑ **MAKE A PLAINS OUTFIT**

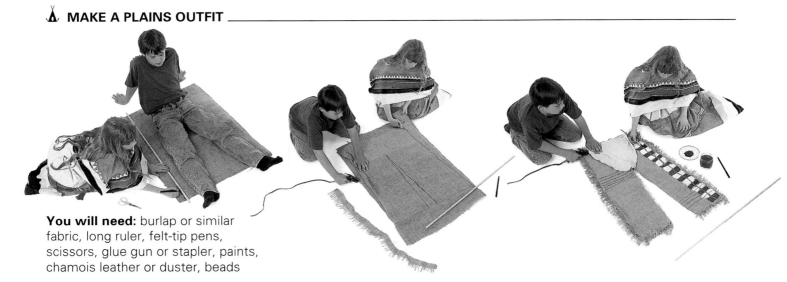

You will need: burlap or similar fabric, long ruler, felt-tip pens, scissors, glue gun or stapler, paints, chamois leather or duster, beads

1 To make the leggings, fold fabric in half to make a double thickness. Measure and mark the trouser shape, as shown, using a long ruler or a straight piece of wood.

2 Cut through the two thicknesses of fabric. Glue or staple the seams (or sew them), adding strips of frayed fabric to the outer seams to look like fringes.

3 Paint designs directly onto the fabric, then glue or sew on a triangular piece of chamois leather or scrap of leftover fabric. This represents the buckskin loincloth.

△ *Clothes with a lot of beadwork were very heavy and were usually worn just for special occasions.*

⚑ **ANIMAL SKINS** used for clothes had to be softened. This skilled work was done by women, who rubbed the skin with a mixture of animal brains, liver, ashes, and fat. They soaked it in water and pulled, stretched, or even chewed the leather until it became soft buckskin. Clothes made from skins were dry-cleaned by rubbing them in clay and chalk to absorb the dirt.

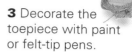

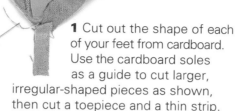

You will need: burlap or similar fabric, cardboard, felt-tip pens, paints, thin string, a darning needle, scissors

1 Cut out the shape of each of your feet from cardboard. Use the cardboard soles as a guide to cut larger, irregular-shaped pieces as shown, then cut a toepiece and a thin strip.

2 Fold, and use string to sew the fabric around the cardboard soles, folding in the wings. Use the strip to join the two pieces at the heel.

3 Decorate the toepiece with paint or felt-tip pens.

4 Sew the toepiece into position with string, as shown. Finish off your moccasins by stitching around the top edge, starting and finishing at the heel end. Then you can adjust the fit by tightening the string.

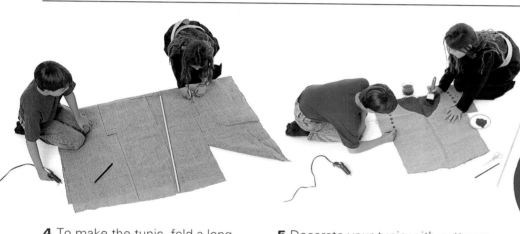

4 To make the tunic, fold a long piece of fabric to make a double thickness, with the fold at the top. Measure and mark the shape, as shown, then cut it out through both thicknesses of fabric. Cut a neck hole at the top. Glue, staple, or sew the seams, as before.

5 Decorate your tunic with patterns, using paints or felt-tip pens. Add fringes, beads, or feathers. You will find suggestions for designs and colors on pages 218-219.

6 To make a woman's outfit, make a long tunic (see photo on page 195).

⚐ **MOCCASINS** were made in various styles for different uses. Some were low cut and others came almost to the knee. Work shoes had hard **rawhide** soles, while shoes worn at home were soft-soled. Moccasins helped protect people's feet from sharp stones, spiky plants, poisonous snakes, and stinging insects.

▷ *Plains warriors carried spears and hide shields (see page 229) and wore elaborate headdresses for ceremonial occasions.*

JEWELRY AND ORNAMENTS were made from many different materials. Coastal peoples used shells, while those on the Plains used quills from birds' feathers and from porcupine spines colored with vegetable and mineral dyes. Northern groups had long been making copper necklaces. Once southern groups had learned how to work silver, they made beautiful ornaments with traditional designs.

GLASS AND CERAMIC BEADS brought by Europeans were very popular because cutting, drilling, and polishing stones and shells to make beads was hard work. The most important beads were **wampum**, made in the Northeast from ground, polished shells. They were used for decoration, keeping records, sending messages, making medicine, and as money.

buffalo-horn helmet

shell decoration

ceremonial headdress

decorated goat-hair blanket

deerskin apron

woolen tunic

Nez Perce

Chumash

Tlingit

Navajo

THE NEZ PERCE lived in high plateau country to the west of the Rocky Mountains. The weather was cold and no crops grew. People relied on gathering roots, berries, and nuts and on fishing and hunting. Nez Perce warriors wore ermine-tail and buffalo-horn helmets, and buckskin war shirts with porcupine-quill decoration and horsehair tassels.

THE TLINGIT, like other Native Americans in the Northwest, led comfortable lives. The winter months were a time of festivals and fun. Party outfits included blankets woven from goat hair and plant-fiber tunics. It rained often, so people wore waterproof hats, tightly woven from spruce roots. Their tunics were good rainwear, too, drying out more quickly than a soggy deerskin ever could.

THE CHUMASH lived near the California coast, in an area with plenty of food and a warm climate all year round. Women wore two deerskin apron-type garments around their waists. The back skirts were painted and decorated with shells, and the front aprons were fringed. Shoes were made of plant fiber. Women decorated their faces to show the family from which they came.

MOHAWK WARRIORS wore fringed animal-hide cloths around their waists, with leggings and moccasins. They had tattoos on their foreheads that declared their bravery in battle, and sometimes wore fan-shaped roaches made of animal hair. Their war clubs were carved from a wood so hard that it was known as ironwood.

feather decoration

bead necklace

hide cloth

leggings

fringed tunic

Sioux

Mohawk

Seminole

THE NAVAJO herded sheep, introduced by Spanish settlers, and therefore had access to wool. They wove blankets, often boldly striped and decorated with patterns unique to them. Women wore simple tunic dresses made from two pieces of blanket tied at the waist with a woven sash. Leggings, soft moccasins, and beads and buckles of silver completed their traditional outfits.

THE SEMINOLE was a group formed by the Creek people and others from different areas. They gradually came together in the Southeast after Europeans began to settle in North America. Their clothes were influenced by early European styles of dress, which they decorated with their own elaborate patchwork and beadwork.

Housing

The climate of the vast North American landmass varies between year-round snow and ice in the frozen North and scorching heat in the deserts of the Southwest. As the Native Americans settled into their homelands, they built houses that were suited to the climate and natural features of their particular region. They used any available materials.

A LEAN-TO was a temporary shelter built by Subarctic peoples from sticks, leaves, or bark.

A PLANK HOUSE was a winter home for the peoples of the Northwest. It was made from hand-split planks fixed onto a frame made from logs, and it was usually rectangular.

TEPEES were perfect homes for the mobile, buffalo-hunting Plains peoples. They were portable and were made of buffalo skins and wooden poles.

WICKIUPS were cone-shaped or domed houses built around frames made from wooden poles, often covered with grass or rush. They were the homes of many Great Basin people.

CLIFF DWELLINGS, or **pueblos**, were the homes of native groups in the Southwest, where humans have lived for at least 6,000 years and a settled farming culture thrived. Houses made of mud, rubble, and blocks of stone were called pueblos (meaning "villages") by the Spanish, who arrived in the sixteenth century.

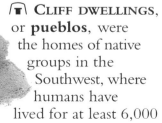

REED HOUSES were made from reed mats covering a wooden pole frame. Inside, there was often a central pit for a fire and a smoke hole in the roof. These conical houses were often found in the Southwest and in California.

IGLOOS are domed houses made from blocks of frozen snow. They were used as a temporary base during the seal–hunting season in the central Arctic region.

WIGWAMS were built by the Algonquians in the Great Lakes area. These homes were typically cone-shaped and consisted of a frame of poles lined with wood, bark, and grass matting.

LONGHOUSES were the homes of the peoples of the Northeast, who lived in fertile woodlands and prairies. They were built from timber and bark and housed up to 20 related families.

WIGWAMS in most parts of the Northeast were oval or round, with a dome-shaped top. They were made of wooden poles bent around to form arches and were covered with mats of reeds and bark.

EARTH LODGES were made by piling earth over a frame made from large, long-lasting beams that could be reused when a new home was built. They were built by the Navajo and by early farmers in the central Plains.

A CHICKEE was no more than a roof and floor on stilts. It was the summer home of Southeastern groups, who lived in villages ringed with secure barriers.

⚠ **SOME PEOPLES**, such as the Cheyenne and the Sioux, spent much of their lives on the move across the central Plains following the buffalo, which were their main source of food. Their tepees were pleasant, practical homes that were cool in summer, warm in winter, strong enough to stand up to fierce winds, and big enough for the family and all its belongings.

⚠ **TEPEES** were sometimes made from fourteen buffalo hides sewn together with buffalo sinews (the tough, stringy fibers that attach muscle to bone). Needles were carved from buffalo bone.

△ *These Comanche women, photographed in 1890, have pegged out buffalo skins so they can scrape them clean.*

⚠ **MAKE A TEPEE**

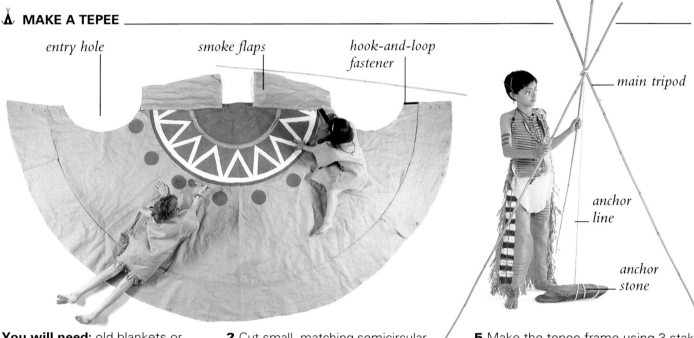

entry hole

smoke flaps

hook-and-loop fastener

main tripod

anchor line

anchor stone

You will need: old blankets or double sheets, thumbtack, string, scissors, garden stakes (8 feet long), stapler or needle and thread, white glue, rope or clothesline, paints, paintbrushes, hook-and-loop fasteners, short sticks, stones

1 Cut a piece of string 20 inches shorter than your stakes and use it like a compass to draw a semicircle on the fabric. Tack one end to the center of the long side of the fabric and tie a pencil to the other end. Swing the string around and mark an arc.

2 Cut small, matching semicircular openings for the entry hole, as shown. Sew or staple strips of hook-and-loop fasteners on either side of the hole for fastening the tepee over the stakes.

3 Cut out the smoke flaps as shown and staple or sew them in place. Make a small triangular pocket in the top inside corner of each flap (see step 7).

4 Paint the cover, adding about one part glue to one part paint to make it waterproof. Use the scissors to make holes for the tent pegs around the base.

5 Make the tepee frame using 3 stakes. Tie them together with the thicker ends at the top. Use a heavy object as a weight to secure the other end of the rope, as shown.

6 Wrap the cover carefully around the stake tripod and secure it by sticking the strips of fasteners together. People such as the Cheyenne and Crow used tepee pins to hold the covers of their tepees in place. You can make your own pins using short sticks. Make holes in both layers of the tepee cover, where it overlaps, and thread the pins through the holes as shown.

⚐ **THE MAIN TRIPOD** was tied together on the ground, then lifted upright using an anchor line made from rawhide. A family tepee was usually 16 feet high and just under 16 feet in diameter, which is about as big as a medium-sized room.

⚐ **SPECIAL PATTERNS AND COLORS** were used by each group to paint their tepees. People would adapt the national pattern for their own family or region. The number of dots, for instance, may represent the number of lakes in the area. The women did all the painting, using ground-up rock and colored soil mixed with buffalo blood.

7 Slide more poles inside the tepee cover to make the frame stronger. Secure the base, using short sticks as tent pegs. Push one end of a stake into each smoke flap pocket to prop the flaps open. Finally, cut out and pin on a door flap to fit over the entry hole.

⚐ **ON RAINY DAYS** a tepee's smoke flaps were closed and fastened with tepee pins.

⚐ **MEN AND WOMEN** had their own particular responsibilities. Women made and put up tepees, while men kept lookout. Two women would take about an hour to erect one tepee.

⚐ **BLACK ELK**, of the Sioux nation, said: 'Our tepees were round like the nests of birds and these were always set in a circle, the nation's hoop, a nest of many nests where the Great Spirit meant for us to hatch our children.'

smoke flaps

entry hole

tepee cover

tepee pin

INSIDE THE TEPEE people slept on piles of warm, furry buffalo skins. When they gathered around the fire, they had comfortable wooden backrests to lean against. Native Americans stored their food, medicine, and clothes in soft hide bags, embroidered with elaborate patterns. A typical Plains family had many horses, but few possessions other than the things they really needed.

EXTRA INSULATION against wind and cold was often provided by a decorative inner lining that trapped a pocket of warm air between it and the outside layer to keep the inside temperature comfortable.

THE FIREPLACE, sometimes raised on a slab of stone, was the main source of light and heat. The supply of firewood was never allowed to run low.

WARNING: DO NOT LIGHT FIRES IN A MODEL TEPEE

△ *This soft buffalo-hide tepee liner belonged to a Cheyenne family. Tepee liners were not hung all around the tent, but were attached at the points where the wind whistled through, positioned at waist height to protect people from drafts as they sat around the fire or lay in bed.*

VENTILATION was provided during warm summer weather by rolling up the sides of the tepee to let air in.

BACKRESTS were used only by the men of the family. The firm but springy supports were made of wooden slats lashed together with leather strips.

EVERYTHING HAD ITS OWN PLACE inside the tepee. The beds were placed on either side of the fire. The fire itself was set in front of the central anchor rope. Backrests were positioned against the sides, and a supply of firewood was kept just inside the door.

▲ **A STRICT CODE** of manners meant that a person could not just walk into a friend's tepee. There were rules to follow:

● If the door flap was open, visitors could enter, but if it was closed, they had to wait to be invited in.

● The male visitor went in first, moved around to the right, and waited for the host to offer him a seat on his left. Women could then enter, and they turned left.

● Men were allowed to sit cross-legged, but women were not.

● Guests invited to a meal had to bring their own spoons and bowls and eat everything their host provided for them.

● No one was allowed to walk between the fire and another person.

● When the host lit his pipe, it was the signal for the guests to go home.

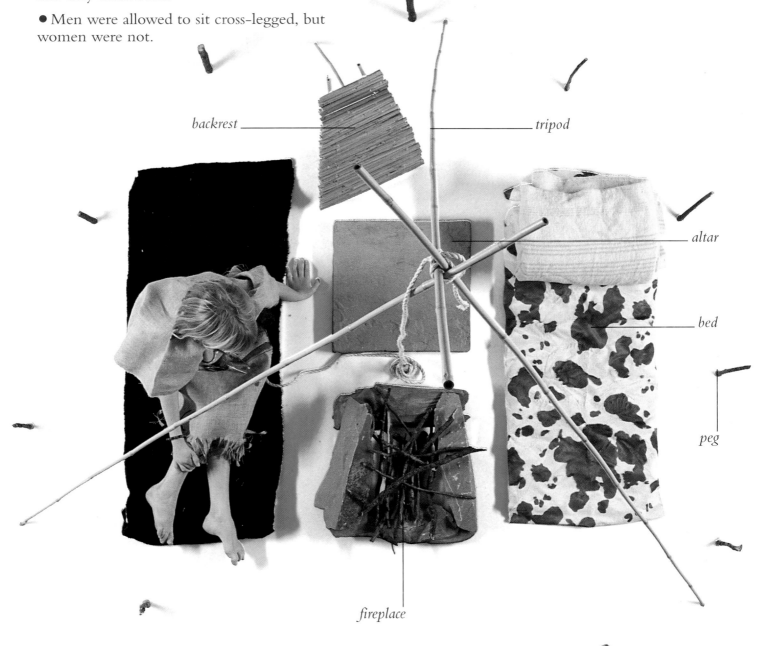

backrest

tripod

altar

bed

peg

fireplace

THE IROQUOIS settled on the East Coast, in what is now southern Ontario, Quebec, and New York State. They built villages and farmed the rich land, where there was plenty of firewood and clear, clean water from the many rivers and springs. They lived in close-knit groups, and their villages were collections of enormous longhouses surrounded by high, protective fences, or palisades, made of sharp stakes. But these villages were not really permanent. Early farming methods exhausted the land after about 20 years. When the crops would no longer grow, the people moved on and rebuilt in a more fertile place.

LONGHOUSES were as high as they were wide. The average size was 65 feet long, 20 feet high by 20 feet wide. One house was home to a group of related fireside families. Each family had its own space along the side of the house and shared a fire in the central corridor with the family opposite. There was a door at each end, but no windows. Smoke from the fires eventually found its way out through a series of ventilation holes in the roof, but the inside was very smoky. As a result, many longhouse people suffered from eye trouble and became blind as they grew old.

MAKE A LONGHOUSE

fire corridor   sleeping platform

You will need: 3 lengths of wood (2 thick, 1 thin), thick and thin twigs, plywood base (26 x 16 in.), wood filler, soil, glue, scraps of fabric or leather

1 Make sleeping platforms and a fire corridor by laying the strips of wood parallel to one another, with the thinner one in the middle.

2 Cut some thick twigs to the same length and, spacing them equally, glue them upright on the board.

3 Mix the filler with water to make a paste and spread it over the board and platforms. Sprinkle the soil over the wet filler so that it sticks.

4 Cut beams from thick twigs to make the roof frame. Stick pairs of beams together to make the roof shape, as shown, and glue them in place on top of each pair of upright posts. Make a framework of thin twigs over the walls and roof to form a support for the bark tiles.

5 Cut the fabric or leather roughly into squares. Glue them to the framework in overlapping layers, starting at the bottom so that there are no cracks for rain to seep in. Glue a lattice of thin twigs over the tiles.

6 Make a palisade from sharpened twigs. Stick them to the base board, sharp ends up and pointing outward, to form a defensive wall around the longhouse.

When Navajo people built their earth lodges, they hammered the frame posts into the ground next to each other to form a solid wall of timber. They made the doorway shoulder-width, so the home was easier to defend. The houses of the northeastern Wampanoags varied in shape and were covered with bark or mats .

You will need: base board (16 x 16 in.), thick and thin twigs, moss or leaves, soil, glue

1 Cut all the thick twigs to the same length and glue upright to the base board in a square. Leave a small gap in one side for the doorway.

2 Lay a lattice of thinner twigs over the top and cover it with moss or leaves. Pile soil over the frame to form a cone, leaving a clear pathway to the door.

bark tiles

upright beam

roof beam

framework of thin poles to hold tiles down in high winds

palisade to defend the longhouse village

🏠 **LONGHOUSE BUILDING MATERIALS** were mainly wood and bark. The outer frame was made from thick posts, firmly driven into the ground. Horizontal beams were lashed in place with strong bark fibers. The roof frame was made from thinner poles and the whole house was covered with overlapping tiles of ash or elm tree bark.

🏠 **THE PALISADE** was made from stakes that were spaced so that the distance between them was just the width of a person's shoulders. Villagers could come and go freely, but attacking warriors had to thread their way through with their arms pinned to their sides, making it very difficult for them to use their weapons.

Family Life

A village in the Plains was made up of groups of families, or **clans**, who often traced their relationship to one another through the women of the family. There could be 50 or more loosely related clans in one group, which occupied an area of land, or territory. The most important ties were not to the group but to the family: the mother, father, and children who shared a home and a fireside.

TEPEES were set up with their entrances facing east to keep out the winds that usually blew across the open Plains from the west. They were grouped according to family relationships.

▽ *Tepee villages were built on carefully chosen sites, close to a river or stream and sheltered from the wind wherever possible.*

strips of buffalo meat curing in the sun

door flap

buffalo chips for making a fire

tepee frame

LIFE ON THE MOVE meant a tough routine for those who hunted buffalo in the vast, dry, windy central Plains. They spent their lives packing up camp, dragging or carrying their possessions, and setting up camp all over again. But their efforts were repaid by a constant supply of food, clothing, and shelter from the buffalo.

VILLAGES were run by chiefs and elders, who were chosen by fellow villagers to offer advice, rather than to tell people what to do. Most people could do as they chose, as long as they worked for the general good, for villages shared their **livelihood**. Men hunted and fought, while women cleaned skins, made clothes, put up tepees, and cooked.

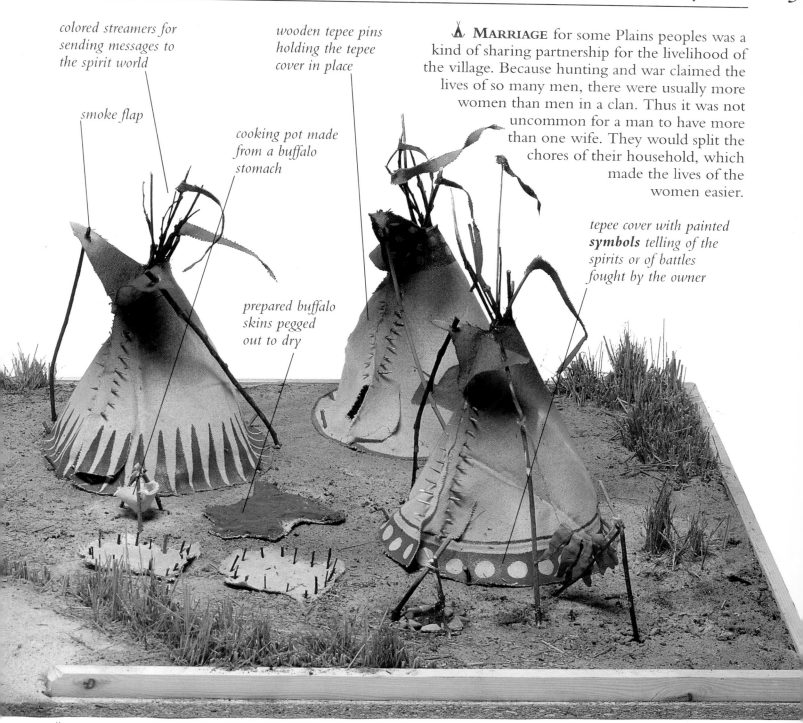

colored streamers for
sending messages to
the spirit world

smoke flap

wooden tepee pins
holding the tepee
cover in place

cooking pot made
from a buffalo
stomach

prepared buffalo
skins pegged
out to dry

MARRIAGE for some Plains peoples was a kind of sharing partnership for the livelihood of the village. Because hunting and war claimed the lives of so many men, there were usually more women than men in a clan. Thus it was not uncommon for a man to have more than one wife. They would split the chores of their household, which made the lives of the women easier.

tepee cover with painted
symbols telling of the
spirits or of battles
fought by the owner

CHILDREN were educated through playing with toy bows, tepees, and dolls and learning from their elders about the life they would lead as adults. They were always expected to behave in a way that would bring no danger or dishonor to their clan or group. They learned very quickly not to cry or make a fuss if an enemy was near.

WARRIORS were usually men, but some women also fought enemies and hunted buffalo. Men thought so highly of one Crow warrior, Woman Chief, that they were too scared to ask to marry her. She "married" four women so she would have someone to look after her tepee. If a man preferred to work at home, no one minded.

THE PEOPLES in the Pacific Northwest lived in fishing villages along the coast. There were nearly 50 groups there, leading well-ordered, comfortable lives. They were the richest peoples in the land, thanks to a flourishing trade in dried and smoked fish and finely woven basketware. These were the Native Americans most concerned with showing their social rank and wealth.

WOODEN HOUSES were strung out in villages along the coastline, with all the houses facing the sea. Each plank house was home to several related families, and the carved **totem poles** outside let everyone know the histories of the families living there.

△ Totem poles were made by skilled carvers of the Northwestern groups. Their main function was to record family crests and glorious moments of family history.

MAKE A PLANK HOUSE AND TOTEM POLE

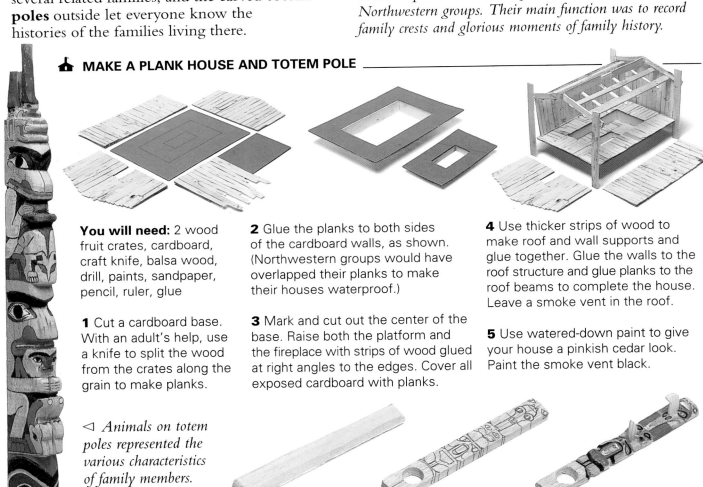

You will need: 2 wood fruit crates, cardboard, craft knife, balsa wood, drill, paints, sandpaper, pencil, ruler, glue

1 Cut a cardboard base. With an adult's help, use a knife to split the wood from the crates along the grain to make planks.

◁ Animals on totem poles represented the various characteristics of family members.

2 Glue the planks to both sides of the cardboard walls, as shown. (Northwestern groups would have overlapped their planks to make their houses waterproof.)

3 Mark and cut out the center of the base. Raise both the platform and the fireplace with strips of wood glued at right angles to the edges. Cover all exposed cardboard with planks.

4 Use thicker strips of wood to make roof and wall supports and glue together. Glue the walls to the roof structure and glue planks to the roof beams to complete the house. Leave a smoke vent in the roof.

5 Use watered-down paint to give your house a pinkish cedar look. Paint the smoke vent black.

6 To make a totem pole, cut a piece of balsa wood a little taller than your house. Sand it to make a flattened cylinder shape and drill a hole for the doorway as shown.

7 Draw your design and carve the lines with a craft knife. Glue on extra pieces for wings or beaks. Sand and paint your totem pole and glue it to the front of your plank house.

♠ **CEDAR WOOD** was easy to carve and hollow out to make canoes. The stringy bark gave fiber for making baskets, ropes, and clothes. Northwestern groups reasoned that these trees must be on Earth to help humans.

♠ **RAINFALL** is high in the Pacific Northwest, and the winters are cold. Plank houses were made of overlapping cedar planks so that the rain ran off. They had no windows, just a hole in the roof that could be closed with a wooden shutter.

♠ **A PLANK HOUSE** was home for up to six families, related through the women. Their shared living space was about 160 square feet, with a sunken area in the center where children played and women cooked. A sleeping platform around the edge was divided into family spaces, with the most important family at the back and the lowliest near the drafty door.

♠ **A POTLATCH** was organized by a Northwestern family to celebrate a special event, such as a wedding. They put on a lavish feast and gave their guests many valuable gifts, including canoes, slaves, furs, and blankets. The more gifts a host gave, the higher his or her status rose. The guests who received the most then had to throw an even greater potlatch. Among the Northwestern peoples, being wealthy meant being more important. People used potlatches to show how rich they were, and to settle old rivalries. Through potlatching, they could force their rivals to give away everything they owned.

totem pole

smoke hole in roof

Food

Native Americans lived on a healthy diet of meat or fish, grain, nuts, fruit, and other food plants. Most of them had learned how to preserve meat and fish by drying or smoking, so there were always emergency supplies if the hunters came back empty-handed.

BUFFALO HUNTING was exhausting and lonely. It took up most of the day, but it was necessary for survival. Tracking and killing large animals on foot was dangerous. To succeed, men had to be in tune with nature and understand the animals they hunted. They sometimes dressed in buffalo skins and moved among the herd. Hunters only took what they needed and never killed animals just for the sake of it.

△ *Ishi, of the California Yahi, photographed in 1914 making a salmon harpoon, or leister.*

ANIMALS that provided food were treated with great respect. A ceremony was held for the first salmon caught in each run. It was taken to a special altar, welcomed with speeches, and cooked with great care. Some Native Americans believed that there were people living in the sea who took the form of salmon each year. If they were not treated properly, they might never come again.

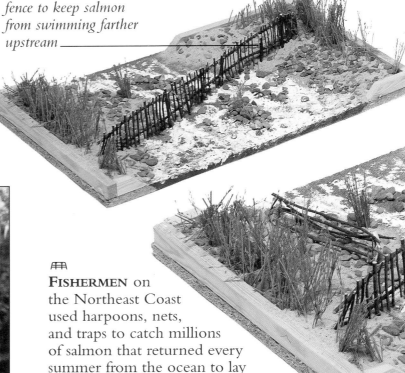

fence to keep salmon from swimming farther upstream

FISHERMEN on the Northeast Coast used harpoons, nets, and traps to catch millions of salmon that returned every summer from the ocean to lay eggs in the rivers where they were born. There was also an ocean full of fish, seals, and whales, and plenty of shellfish and birds' eggs along the shore.

MAKE A SALMON TRAP

You will need: dried grasses, paint, plywood base (10 x 18 in.), stones, twigs, sand, craft knife, glue

1 Paint a river on the board. Make sand banks on both sides, dotted with dried grasses and pebbles.

2 Build a fence across the river. Glue the crosspieces to the supports.

(Native Americans who fished would have pushed the supports into the ground and tied the sticks with sinews.)

The fence stops the salmon from swimming farther upstream. They will never turn back, so they struggle and leap against the fence, while more fish swim up behind them.

3 Make trapping gates in the same way as the fence. Bend twigs to make the rounded ends of the tunnel-shaped pens. Add to the fence.

Men with spears would have waded into the killing pen. Any fish not harpooned at once were swept back by the current into the trapping gates and collected in the pens.

PREPARING AND PRESERVING FISH was done by the women. The rich fish oil was highly prized and used as grease for cooking and for lamps. It was traded along "grease trails" down the coast and over the mountains.

▷ *Fish traps were made to much the same design all over the Northeast and Subarctic.*

killing pen

trapping gate

tunnel-shaped pen

SOUTHEASTERN HUNTERS caught small animals in traps. They used blowpipes and poison darts to hunt deer. Some could knock birds from the sky with **bolas** made from stones tied to a line of sinew, which they whirled around their heads and then let fly.

THE THREE MAIN FOOD CROPS grown by Native Americans were corn, beans, and squash. Farmers used tools made of wood or bone. Men turned the earth and women planted the seeds.

RUBBING STICKS TOGETHER to make a fire took so long that fires were often left smoldering all day. Many hunters traveled with a slow-burning rope so they had a quick way of lighting a fire when they set up camp.

RICH SOIL meant good crops, and farmers believed in putting something back into the earth in thanks for what came out. The Iroquois, for example, put herring into the ground before they sowed corn. The nutrients in the fish made the soil much richer.

A TYPICAL IROQUOIS MEAL included roasted meat, raw salad, baked pumpkin, and corn dumplings. Families ate just once a day, before noon. Meals were eaten in silence, standing or squatting on the ground. Men ate first, and women and children ate what was left. Children were told that if they did not thank their parents for each meal, they would be punished with a stomachache.

MAKE HOPI BOILED CORN CAKES

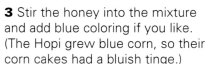

You will need: 30 corn husks (the outer part of a corncob), 1 cup of cornmeal, half a cup of honey, blue food coloring (optional)

1 With an adult's help, boil the corn husks until they are soft. Drain them and let them cool.

2 Put cornmeal in a bowl and, while stirring, gradually add a cup of boiling water, until mixture is like thick custard.

3 Stir the honey into the mixture and add blue coloring if you like. (The Hopi grew blue corn, so their corn cakes had a bluish tinge.)

4 Open out the corn husks and drop 2 spoonfuls of corn mixture into the center of about 20 of them. Fold them neatly into parcels. Shred the remaining husks and use the shreds to tie up the parcels.

5 Ask an adult to help you bring water to the boil in a large saucepan, then carefully put in the corn cake parcels.

6 Boil the parcels for 15 to 20 minutes, then take them out with a slotted spoon. Let them cool before you unwrap and eat them.

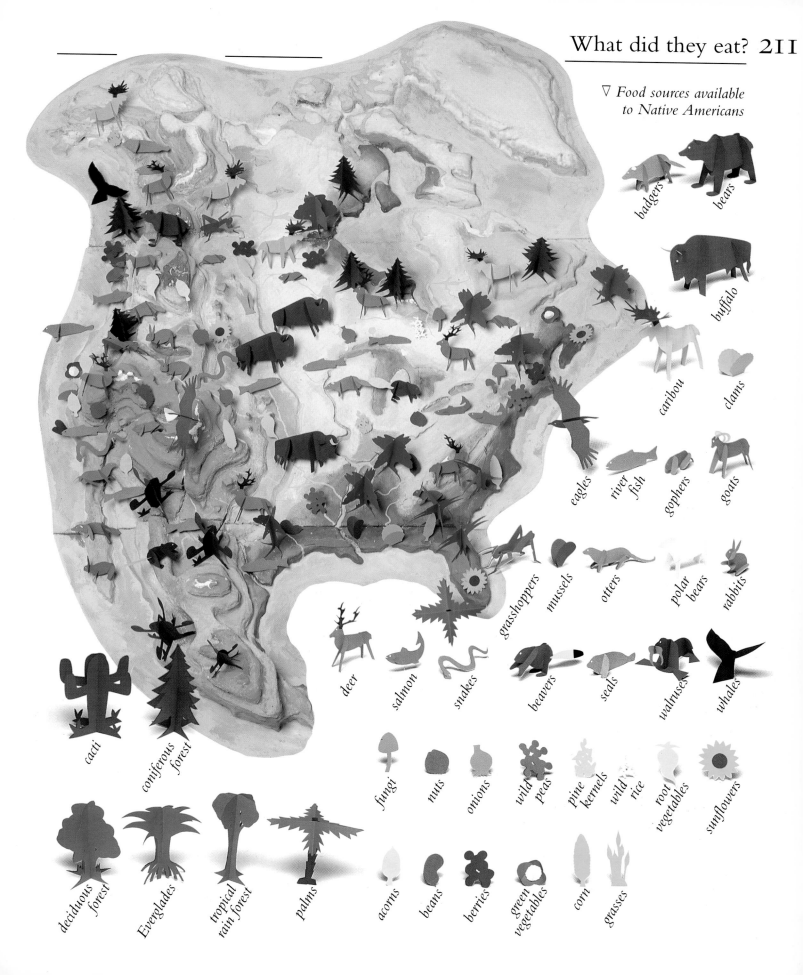

▽ *Food sources available to Native Americans*

badgers

bears

buffalo

caribou

clams

eagles

river fish

gophers

goats

grasshoppers

mussels

otters

polar bears

rabbits

deer

salmon

snakes

beavers

seals

walruses

whales

cacti

coniferous forest

fungi

nuts

onions

wild peas

pine kernels

wild rice

root vegetables

sunflowers

deciduous forest

Everglades

tropical rain forest

palms

acorns

beans

berries

green vegetables

corn

grasses

Sports and Leisure

Most Native American games were a preparation for life, and many were ceremonial. Men played vigorous team games to help prepare themselves for war and hunting games to sharpen their skills. Women played games of skill and chance, using their everyday work tools. Both men and women also liked to sing as they placed bets in games of chance. They made music to summon up good spirits and good luck.

△ *Lacrosse* players were allowed two sticks each.

MAKE A LACROSSE STICK

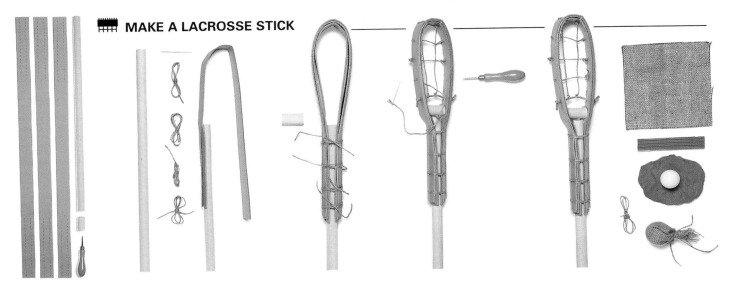

You will need: broomstick or thick dowel, strong cardboard, ping-pong ball, string, glue, awl, saw, square of burlap, modeling clay

1 Ask an adult to help you cut three strips of cardboard and to cut the handle and spacer bar from the dowel. Bend one strip of cardboard around and carefully glue both ends to the handle, as shown.

2 Repeat this with the other two strips, until you have a loop made of three thicknesses of cardboard. (The Native Americans would have used strips of hide.) Use string to tie the loop securely in place.

3 Push in the spacer bar at the top of the handle and glue it into place. Use the awl very carefully to make holes around the loop.

4 Thread string through the holes to make the net, as shown. Knot the ends on the outside of the loop to hold the net in place.

5 To make the ball, flatten the clay and wrap it tightly around the ping-pong ball. Cover it with the square of fabric and tie tightly with string. (Native Americans used a ball of animal hair covered with hide.)

GAMBLING GAMES were very popular with women, who sometimes played for very high stakes, such as offering to become a slave to the other player. Games were more often played for furs, skins, household goods, moccasins, or horses.

POST BALL was played just for fun by both men and women. They set up a post in the village square and the object was to hit the post with a ball. The women could use their hands, but the men could use only sticks.

▽ *picking up the ball*

◁ *throwing the ball*

△ *tackling, or checking, to get the ball from another player's net*

WAR'S LITTLE BROTHER was a fearsome game. It is still played today, in a much more controlled form known as lacrosse. In the past, up to 100 people could play on each team. The playing field had no boundaries and the goals could be over 100 yards wide. Players had to hurl a ball through the goalposts, and the game was won by the first team to score 12 goals. It often lasted for hours. There were no rules of fair play, so it was often a bloody battle with many casualties. Players were pushed, beaten with sticks, often badly injured, and sometimes killed.

△ *players jumping to catch the ball in their nets*

THE AWL GAME was a game of chance. The board was marked out on a blanket. Each player pinned an awl (a tool used for piercing hides) through the blanket in various places. They moved their awls around the blanket in opposite directions.

FOUR STICKS were thrown at the central stone to decide each move. One carried a special mark. If a stick fell flat side up, it counted for one move. If the mark came up, it meant an extra throw. The board showed dry and flowing rivers. Dry rivers were safe, but players who fell in flowing rivers or on an opponent's position had to go back to the start.

MUSIC AND DANCE were central to the Native American way of life and everybody took part. People believed that music was the language of the spirits. Mothers sang lullabies to their children, warriors sang to call upon their guardian spirits, hunters made magic animal music, and farmers chanted to their crops. There were ceremonial songs for births, marriages, deaths, and funerals.

▷ *These Ute musicians and dancers in the Great Basin and Plateau area were photographed in 1900.*

RATTLES, RASPS, AND DRUMS were used to create rhythms. Turtle shells, coconuts, gourds, and buffalo horns were natural percussion instruments. People made other instruments from wood or hide. A gourd rattle's sound could be improved by putting pebbles or beans inside, along with a few of the original seeds to help the rattle keep its spiritual powers.

rattle

🏠 MAKE A RATTLE

You will need: dried beans or peas, a tennis ball, a dowel (10 in. long), glue, paper, paint, thick string, colored raffia

1 Make holes on either side of the tennis ball, put the beans inside, and push the dowel through, as shown.

2 Tear the paper into pieces and glue them onto the ball in a smooth papier-mâché layer. When the glue has dried, wind the string around the handle and ball, gluing it in place as you go. Leave a gap around the middle of the ball.

3 Decorate the rattle by painting a pattern on the plain part of the ball and adding a raffia tail.

🔺 MAKE A DRUM AND DRUMSTICK

You will need: a flower pot, glue, canvas, thin string, paints, felt-tip pens, two thin sticks or dowels, modeling clay, string, raffia

1 Cut a curved piece of fabric to fit around the pot and glue it on. Cut another piece to fit over the top and to reach well down the sides.

2 Braid or twist the string to make a decorative cord. Stretch the fabric over the pot and use the cord to tie it firmly in place just below the rim.

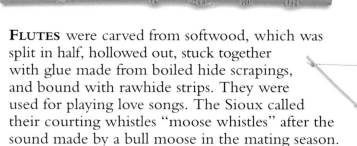

flute

FLUTES were carved from softwood, which was split in half, hollowed out, stuck together with glue made from boiled hide scrapings, and bound with rawhide strips. They were used for playing love songs. The Sioux called their courting whistles "moose whistles" after the sound made by a bull moose in the mating season.

WHISTLES made music for war. Warriors rode into battle blowing whistles made from eagle bones. Eagles symbolized courage.

SONGS were not complicated. They often had a simple tune, usually going down the scale from high notes to low notes. Songs and chants were owned by the person who made them up. If the singer had enjoyed a long and happy life, the right to sing the song would be passed on to the family or even sold for a high price.

△ *A group in California called the Maidu made a simple musical bow. The player plucked the single string, changing the pitch of the note by opening and closing his or her mouth.*

THROBBING DRUMS were like a heartbeat to these peoples. Their sounds were sacred, particularly that of the water drum, which could only be played by those thought worthy, such as distinguished warriors.

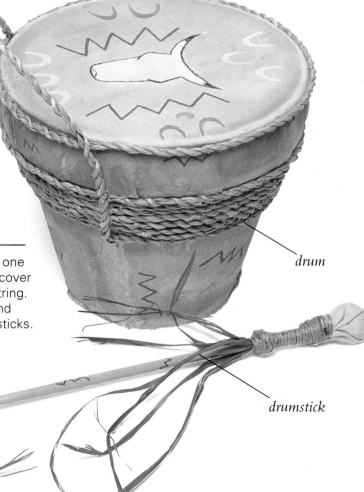

drum

drumstick

4 Stick balls of clay to one end of each stick and cover with fabric tied with string. Decorate with raffia and paint patterns on the sticks.

3 Finish off with a loop of cord for a handle. Paint the drum to make the cloth look like buffalo hide. Wetting the fabric with paint will shrink it and improve the tone of the drum. Use felt-tip pens to decorate the drum.

Artwork

In some cultures, art represents real things. For Native Americans, art was more than that. It was a way of expressing their hopes and fears, of thanking the creator for gifts, and of pleasing the creator with prayers and promises. Because of this, their art was symbolic. It used symbols and signs to represent their ideas, beliefs, dreams, and visions. When artists drew an animal or a person, they were trying to show the inner spirit, not the outer appearance.

△ *This California Karok basket maker was photographed in 1896. She is using the twining method, rather than the coiling technique shown below.*

⬛ **BASKETS** were made by almost all Native Americans, but those of the Southwest and California were particularly skillful weavers. They used baskets for everything from cradles, storage chests, and sieves to bird and fish traps, backpacks, hats, and mats. Some were so tightly woven that they were waterproof and could even be used for brewing beer. Materials used included rushes, bear grass, yucca leaves, and willow, which were steamed until the fibers were supple. Symbolic designs were woven into the baskets using fibers that were colored with mineral or vegetable dyes.

⬤ MAKE A BASKET

You will need: thick twine or plaited string, raffia, darning needle

1 Thread the needle with a length of raffia. You will need several lengths to make the basket.

2 Begin the basket base by coiling the twine or plaited string tightly. Work outward from the center. Sew each layer to the last one as you build up the coils.

3 Once you have a flat base, about five coils wide, begin to build up the sides of the basket. Finish off by sewing down the end of the twine securely.

▷ *These Pueblo pots were used for storage, cooking, and eating.*

POT-MAKING was a skill that probably came from the Mexico area, where there was plenty of clay in the soil. In some places, such as parts of California, pots were not made at all because clay was hard to find and baskets served every possible need.

🔲 **FIRING POTS** to turn soft mud into hard pottery was done by baking them at a high temperature for a long time. They were buried in a mound of dried animal dung, which burned more evenly than wood.

🔲 **MAKE A CLAY POT**

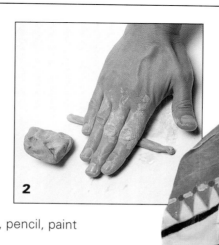

You will need: self-hardening clay, pencil, paint

1 Flatten and pinch out a clay base as shown.

2 Roll the clay into thin sausages, and begin to build up the sides of the pot by coiling the clay around. Make the pot wider as it grows taller, then narrower at the neck. (Southwestern peoples used coiling for making pots, and they used the same technique for baskets.)

3 Smooth the outside of the pot, let it dry, and then draw and paint your design. (Native Americans stamped symbolic patterns on soft clay or scraped designs on hardened clay. They colored pots white, brown, red, and yellow, using pigments from the earth.)

TEXTILES have been woven in North America for two thousand years. Very early cloth was not woven on a loom. The threads were made by spinning fibers from plants and animal hair. Then they were woven together by knitting, crocheting, plaiting, and twining in many different ways.

THE DYES AND PAINTS used by Native Americans were made from minerals and plants. Minerals are found in different colored soils. Iron in soil gives a range of reds, yellows, and browns. Soil with copper makes greens and blues. Graphite makes black; and clay, limestone, and gypsum make white. Color can also be taken from plants, berries, roots, moss, and bark. Boiling or soaking the materials with the plant changes their color.

DESIGNS AND COLORS had different meanings for different groups, and even for individual artists. Sometimes the artist had a dream that showed him or her what designs and colors to use. Although it is difficult to say exactly what particular colors meant, there were some general uses:

Blue	Female, moon, sky, water, thunder, sadness
Black	Male, cold, night, disease, death, underworld
Green	Earth, summer, rain, plants
Red	War, day, blood, wounds, sunset
White	Winter, death, snow
Yellow	Day, dawn, sunshine

DYEING FABRIC

turmeric makes bright yellow

onion skin makes yellowish brown

blueberries make mauve

avocado skin makes pink

You will need: white cotton fabric, piece of muslin, string, ingredients for color (see left), cutting board, knife, old pan, wooden spoon, pitcher or bowl, strainer

1 Choose the colors you want to dye your fabric and prepare the ingredients. Place them on the muslin and tie into a bundle with the string.

2 Put the fabric and muslin bundle into the pan. Cover with water and ask an adult to help you boil it.

3 When the fabric has changed color, let the dye cool and strain it into the pitcher so you can reuse it.

4 Let the fabric dry naturally. Remember that the color will fade and run if you wash it.

▷ *Chilkat dance blankets were worn by Tlingit people for ceremonies (see page 220). They were decorated with stylized symbols representing animals.*

tail and wing
shape of a bird

bear's legs
and paws

head of a
brown bear

*human face drawn
in the shape of
a bird's body*

frog's head

bird's feet

FRINGES appeared in the decoration of almost all their clothes and artwork. A fringe was the symbol for rain, which was said to be a blessing because it made plants grow, but also a curse because it could make life so damp and uncomfortable.

SHAPES AND SYMBOLS that people used for decoration varied from one area to another:

Southeast

Southwest

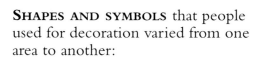

Northeast

Northwest

California

Plains

CURVES AND SPIRALS were popular in the Southeast, where bird and animal shapes were often used.

PARALLEL LINES as well as curves featured in the cultures of the Southwest.

THE FLOWING LINES of plant and flower shapes were used by people in the Northeast.

BIRDS, FISH, AND HUMAN FACES featured in the Northwest, often within a curved shape.

TRIANGLES, RECTANGLES, AND SQUARES were used in many designs in California, especially for basketwork.

GEOMETRIC SHAPES, particularly triangles, were popular on the Plains.

SIMPLE LOOMS with a fixed warp (the vertical threads) were used in ancient times in the Southwest. Later, people in this area developed the true loom. It had a pair of horizontal sticks separating every other thread of the warp. The weft (the horizontal threads) could then be pushed through from side to side with a shuttle, making weaving much easier and quicker.

THE CHILKAT, a branch of the Tlingit nation, were expert weavers. In their homelands, there were no flocks of fleecy sheep and no wild cotton, just mountains and cedar trees. People wove with the hair of wild mountain goats and shredded fibers from the soft inner bark of cedar trees. A blanket took up to a year to make.

MAKE A SIMPLE WEAVING FRAME

You will need: strips of wood (8 in. and 14 in.), glue, pencil, ruler, small nails, hammer, large yarn needle or bodkin, colored yarn

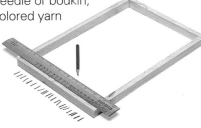

1 Glue and nail the strips of wood to make the frame, as shown. Measure and mark positions for the nails at each end. Make them evenly spaced, about $\frac{1}{5}$ in. apart. Ask an adult to help you hammer the nails in.

2 To make the warp, tie a piece of yarn to the first nail at one corner. Stretch it back and forth across the frame, looping it around the nails. Tie it off on the last nail.

3 To make the weft, thread a length of colored yarn through the needle and wind it around as shown.

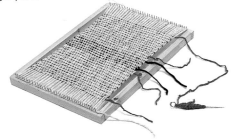

4 Tie the loose end of the yarn to the outside warp thread, then weave the needle in and out from side to side.

5 When you want to change color, tie the new yarn to the outside warp thread as before.

6 When you have filled the frame, tie the end of your last weft row to the outside warp thread and carefully lift your finished piece off the nails. Tie together the two loops at each corner.

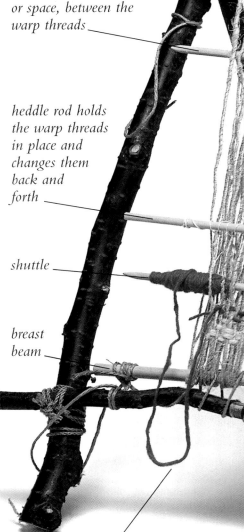

shed rod makes the shed, or space, between the warp threads

heddle rod holds the warp threads in place and changes them back and forth

shuttle

breast beam

weft or horizontal thread

◉ **THE SPIDERWOMAN** was a spirit who wove webs to catch rain clouds and had taught the first people on Earth how to weave. Weavers in the Southwest used the symbol of the spiderwoman in their designs as a way of thanking her for the knowledge that she had passed on to them.

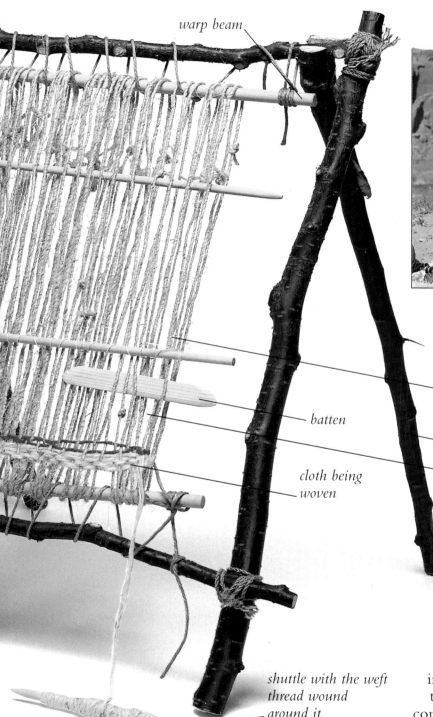

warp beam

warp or vertical thread

batten

weaving frame

cloth being woven

shed, or space where the shuttle passes through

shuttle with the weft thread wound around it

△ *The present-day Navajo weave using the traditional methods and designs.*

◉ **THE NAVAJO** are perhaps best known for their beautifully woven blankets with strong, geometric designs. The ideas for the designs, it is said, came directly from the weaver's inner spirit. The women who made them boasted that their blankets were so closely woven, they could hold water. They always made a tiny mistake in the weaving, as they believed if they were ever to make one perfect thing, their lives would be complete and their time on Earth would be over.

Transportation

Walking was the main way of getting around on land until the Europeans brought horses to North America. Native Americans had developed backpacks and baskets to help them carry things more easily. When they traveled by water, they found that every lake, river, or sea presented different problems, so each kind of water had its own type of boat.

BUFFALO-HIDE CANOES were round river craft made of hide stretched over a wooden frame. They were made by people on the edge of the Plains, where there were few trees for building boats.

SEAWORTHY BOATS were built by Native Americans living along the Northwest Coast. Large, strong, straight cedar trees grew there, and they were cut down, dug out, and shaped to suit deep ocean waters and the shallows off the coast. Large dugouts, with high, curved ends to keep inshore waves from splashing aboard, were used for trading runs up and down the coast. For fishing and whaling trips in the open sea, people built bigger, stronger boats with straighter sides.

TRADING was the main reason for traveling. Apart from the Plains nations, which followed herds of buffalo, people usually stayed close to the territory in which they were born. Some did move between summer and winter villages, some traveled to wage war on neighboring groups, and some journeyed to attend gatherings and ceremonies.

platform from which hunters could spear fish

high bow to keep waves out

carved or painted decoration, often representing animals, to show the owner's importance

CANOE-MAKING TOOLS included stone and bone axes, adzes, gouges, and wedges that were used to hollow out cedar logs. To soften the wood for final shaping, the logs were sometimes filled with water, and hot stones or a carefully controlled fire would be used to burn away the inside.

△ Seagoing canoes were dug out from a single tree. Some could carry up to 60 men.

PLANK BOATS were built for sea journeys by the Chumash of Southern California. They used hand-split planks, making little holes in them so they could lash them together with leather thongs or plant fibers. They waterproofed them with tar.

REED RAFTS were light, easy-to-carry, canoe-shaped boats used by Californian groups. They were made from reeds tied together in bundles.

wooden seat or thwart

wooden paddle

interior painted with tar to make it waterproof

THE PRICE OF GOODS traded by Native Americans went up and down according to supply and demand. When something is plentiful, it is worth less, and when there is little available, the price goes up. These values applied when there were few horses and many buffalo:

8 buffalo robes = 1 ordinary horse
5 buffalo robes = 1 bear-claw necklace
1 buffalo robe = 36 iron arrowheads

GOODS FOR TRADING varied from nation to nation, but included some of the following items:

Baskets, acorns, seaweed, dried fish, shells

Dried fish and fish oil, salt, boats and dugouts, copper and silver jewelry

Hides, horses, eagle feathers

Blankets, wool, dyes, jewelry

Shells, wampum, furs, copper and copper tools, pearls

Tobacco, shells, pearls

BOATS OF DIFFERENT SHAPES were built for different conditions. Native Americans living by lakes and rivers needed easy-to-steer, lightweight canoes that could be taken out of the water and carried when it became too dangerous or shallow. Small canoes were perfect for shooting over waterfalls, but larger boats were needed for carrying goods for trading. A boat with a low bow and stern is good in calm waters. A high bow and stern give protection from rough waters but slow the boat down because of greater wind resistance.

gunwale   *decorative stitching*

wooden paddle

🪶 **BIRCH TREES** were plentiful in the Northeast and the Great Lakes area. These tall, thin, straight trees are wrapped in up to nine layers of bark that comes off in sheets when carefully peeled. The outer skin is thick and white, the inner skins thinner, browner, and softer.

🪶 **CANOE BARK** was peeled from a cut tree in the spring, when the outer layer is at its thickest. It was used, brown side out and white side in, to cover a frame of cedarwood. The bark sheets were sewn together with spruce roots. The seams were then made waterproof with a covering of gummy sap from the pine tree, heated until it became a thick, gooey syrup.

🪶 **PADDLES** were shaped from wood, anchors made from stones, bails from shells, and ropes from plant fiber or strips of hide. Native Americans saw no need for sails on their boats. They did not particularly want to go where the wind blew them, so paddles were all they needed for their short fishing and trading trips.

🪶 **MAKE A BIRCH BARK CANOE**

You will need: thick and thin balsa wood strips, bulldog clips, craft knife, pencil, needle, thread, paints, glue

1 Take the thick strip of balsa (about 16 in. long), mark out the gunwale (the top part) of the canoe as shown, and cut it out carefully, using a craft knife.

2 Soak the thin strips of balsa in hot water for half an hour. Lay the gunwale over the strips and fold them upward to make the sides of the canoe. Lift the gunwale into position and glue it to the top of the sides, using clips to hold it in place.

3 When dry, cut off any balsa sticking out above the gunwale. Glue on a thin finishing strip and sew it in place as shown.

4 Sew thin strips of balsa wood together to make ends of the canoe.

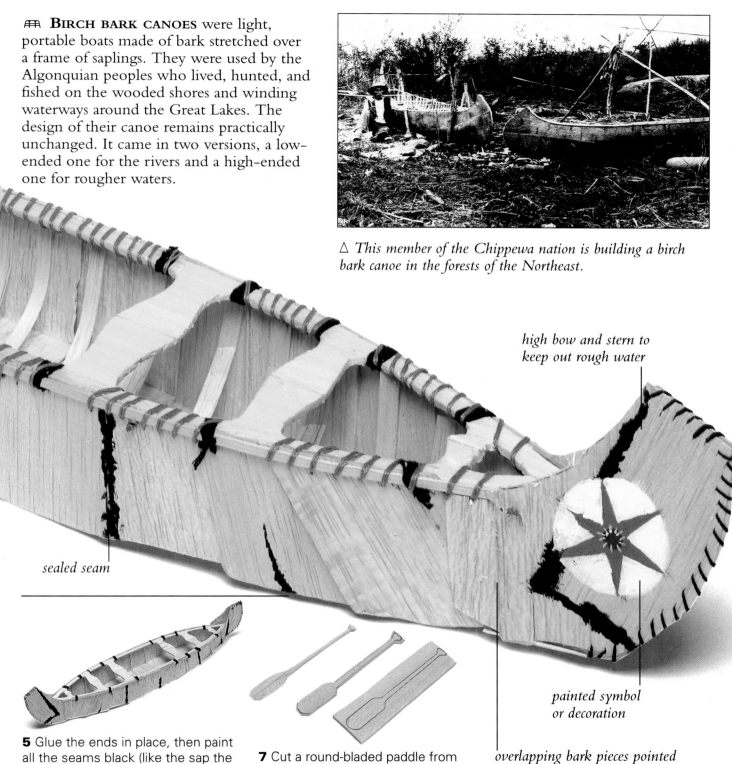

🏠 **BIRCH BARK CANOES** were light, portable boats made of bark stretched over a frame of saplings. They were used by the Algonquian peoples who lived, hunted, and fished on the wooded shores and winding waterways around the Great Lakes. The design of their canoe remains practically unchanged. It came in two versions, a low-ended one for the rivers and a high-ended one for rougher waters.

△ *This member of the Chippewa nation is building a birch bark canoe in the forests of the Northeast.*

high bow and stern to keep out rough water

sealed seam

painted symbol or decoration

5 Glue the ends in place, then paint all the seams black (like the sap the Algonquians used for waterproofing).

6 Put thin reinforcing strips inside the canoe as shown. Decorate the canoe with stitching and motifs.

7 Cut a round-bladed paddle from the thick sheet of balsa wood, as shown. These paddles were designed for shooting rapids, because a rounded end is less likely to be damaged by stones and rocks.

overlapping bark pieces pointed toward the stern to help the water flow easily around the canoe

⚐ BEFORE THE HORSE was brought to North America about 400 years ago, all land journeys were made on foot. Anything that needed to be carried was hauled by women, or by dogs pulling a **travois** made from two tepee poles attached to a harness. Native Americans following a buffalo herd on foot covered only about six miles a day. They had few possessions, and they kept their tepees small so they were easy to carry.

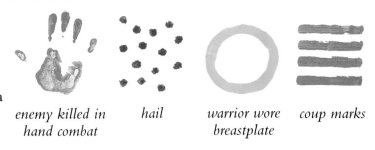

enemy killed in hand combat   hail   warrior wore breastplate   coup marks

△ *Plains warriors decorated their horses with painted symbols.*

⚐ MAKE A TRAVOIS

You will need: twigs, string, plain fabric, paints, paintbrush, glue, model horse

1 Use two long twigs and two short crosspieces to make the basic shape, as shown. Tie them securely.

2 Cut thin strips of fabric and weave them to make a carrying platform. Glue to the frame. (Plains people tied a travois with strips of buffalo hide.)

3 Wind string around the length of the poles and glue it. (On the Plains, strips of hide were used for this, to stop the horse's skin from chafing.)

⚐ AFTER THE HORSE was brought to the Americas by Spanish settlers, life for Plains nations was transformed. They used horses to move swiftly in battle, to outrun buffalo, and to pull the travois. A camp could now move 30 miles in one day. Tepees became bigger and more spacious. Women no longer had to carry heavy loads, and they had more time for leisure and for making things. People owned more and could transport things more easily.

⚐ A SIOUX SONG tells of the respect and honor with which Plains warriors treated their horses:
'My horse be swift in flight
Even like a bird:
My horse be swift in flight.
Bear me now in safety
Far from the enemy's arrows
And you shall be rewarded
With streamers and ribbons red.'

4 Bend and glue thin twigs to form a cage on the platform. Cut and paint a piece of fabric for the horse blanket. Paint symbols on the horse. Tie the poles and blanket to its back.

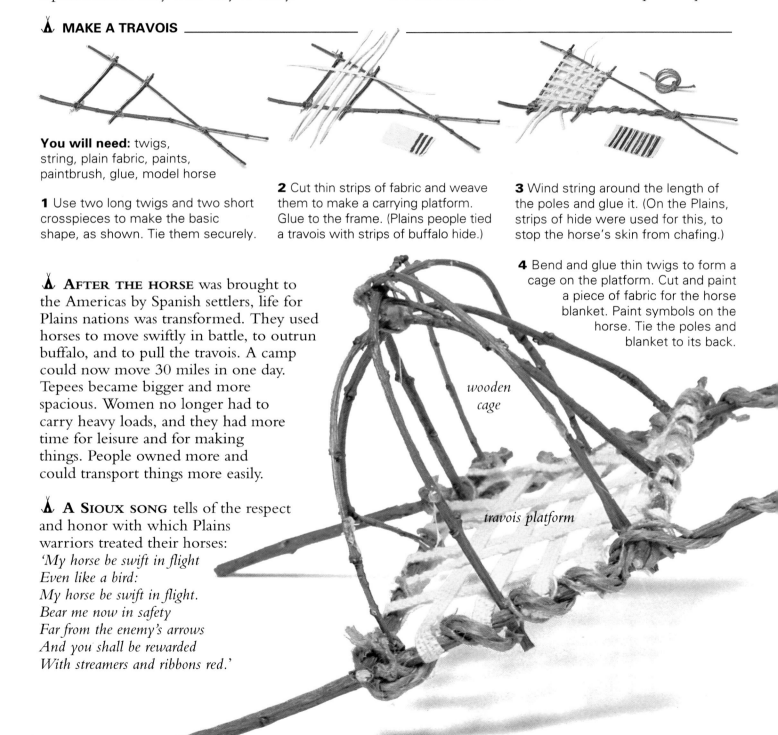

wooden cage

travois platform

△ *Young children often rode on a travois. Sometimes a wooden cage was put over the platform to keep passengers and possessions from falling off.*

△ BABIES were carried on cradle boards by their mothers. They were tightly wrapped up and strapped to the boards with leather thongs, so that they could not wriggle around and could be kept warm and safe.

△ SADDLES AND BRIDLES were made from buffalo hide and hair. A braided buffalo–hair rope or a thin strip of rawhide looped around the horse's lower jaw was all Plains riders needed to control their horses. While out hunting or fighting they rode bareback or used a simple hide saddle stuffed with buffalo hair. Women had wooden saddles padded with hide. Stirrups were made from wood, steamed into shape, and covered in rawhide. Wealthy horse owners often had their **tack** decorated with paint and beads.

△ TRAVOIS were made by women. The women took pride in their craftswork; they were thought to be bad wives if their hide straps were cut unevenly or, worse still, had hair on them.

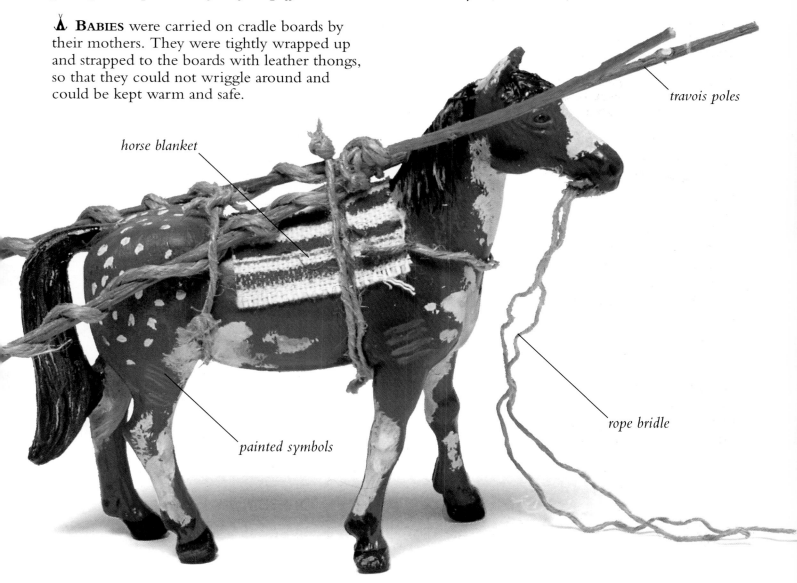

travois poles

horse blanket

painted symbols

rope bridle

Hunting and Warfare

Native American hunters needed to be brave, confident, and skillful. If they were successful, they were rewarded with glory and praise. For Native Americans, the respect given to successful hunters was perhaps the most important thing in life. Before the European invasion, arguments over hunting grounds and raids for horses were some of the reasons for setting out on the warpath. Some nations viewed warfare as a chance to appear heroic. However, many sought peace rather than war.

△ *This Plains warrior was an Arapaho chief in 1870.*

war club

NATIVE AMERICAN warriors crept up on the enemy quickly and quietly, attacked fiercely, then turned and ran for it. There was no shame in retreat.

coup stick

⚔ **BRAVERY** was measured by how close warriors got to their enemy. Riding in close to touch the enemy with a coup was called counting coup. It was seen as more courageous than killing at 50 yards with a bow and arrow.

⚔ **A BOW WITH ARROWS** was the most widely used weapon. The Sioux made bows from ash wood, with a bow string made of two twisted sinews. A war bow could be fired more quickly than a gun and be deadly accurate from over 100 yards away.

⚔ **MAKE A BOW AND ARROW** _____

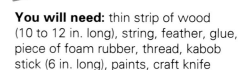

You will need: thin strip of wood (10 to 12 in. long), string, feather, glue, piece of foam rubber, thread, kabob stick (6 in. long), paints, craft knife

1 Mark the bow as shown, and shape and nick the ends as shown. Use the craft knife carefully.

2 Make a loop in the string, thread it into the nick at one end, and tie it to the other end, bending the bow a little as shown.

3 Wrap and glue two lengths of string around the bow to make a handgrip as shown.

4 Make flights for the arrow by splitting the spine of the feather and cutting out three small sections as shown above.

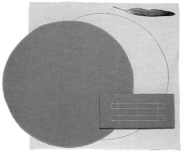
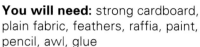
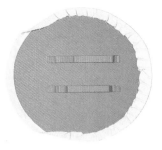

You will need: strong cardboard, plain fabric, feathers, raffia, paint, pencil, awl, glue

1 Cut a cardboard circle (diameter 14 in.) and a slightly larger fabric circle. Glue the fabric to the cardboard, sticking it down around the edge, as shown. Cut two cardboard strips as handles and glue to the back of the shield.

2 Draw a design on the front of the shield and paint it. Make small holes in the shield with the awl, thread raffia through them, and tie on feathers as decoration.

🔺 **RAWHIDE SHIELDS** were painted with signs and kept wrapped up before battle so the power would not leak away.

war ax

spear

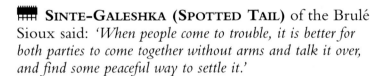

🀫 **TOMAHAWKS** were curved, light, axes used in hand-to-hand combat. They could also be thrown with fearsome force and accuracy.

🀫 **SINTE-GALESHKA (SPOTTED TAIL)** of the Brulé Sioux said: *'When people come to trouble, it is better for both parties to come together without arms and talk it over, and find some peaceful way to settle it.'*

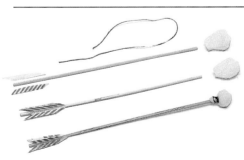

6 Paint and decorate both the bow and the arrow. Plains warriors painted pictures of their enemies on their arrows, so the arrows would know where to go. You can dip the arrow tips into water-soluble paint and fire them at a target.

5 Glue the flights onto the kabob stick as shown. Cut the arrow to half the length of the bow. Stick a small ball of foam rubber onto the cut end of the arrow and secure it with thread.

NEVER FIRE AN ARROW AT ANYONE. EVEN A TOY ARROW CAN CAUSE AN INJURY.

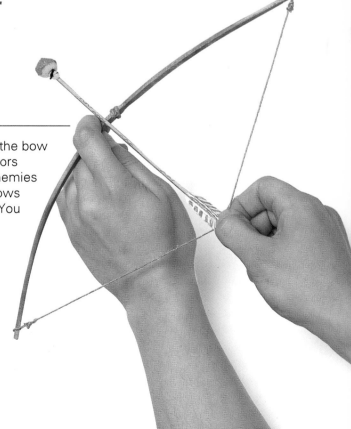
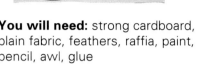

Communication

As recently as 200 years ago, there were over 300 languages spoken in North America. None of these had any links to languages that were spoken in Europe, Asia, or Africa. Families belonging to the same nation did not necessarily speak the same language, and people who shared a language were often spread over a wide area, because of trade and mobile ways of life. So Native Americans developed sign language to help them communicate with their neighbors. It allowed them to express emotions, as well as warnings and signals.

SIGN LANGUAGE used by Native Americans was made up of a mixture of mime and signaling, based on actions and shapes of things rather than on sounds. When Plains people visited Europe in the last century, they found they could communicate easily and naturally with deaf people.

EARLY EUROPEAN EXPLORERS and settlers tried to write down the sounds of Native American words, but some just could not be conveyed using our alphabet. Some Native American words became familiar place names:

Place	Pronunciation	Meaning
Alabama	alba-amo	plant reapers
Dakota	dak-hota	the friendly ones
Canada	kanata	cabin
Illinois	ili-ni-wak	men
Idaho	ee-dah-how	behold! the sun coming down the mountain
Iowa	aayahooweewa	sleepy
Kentucky	ken-tah-teh	land of tomorrow
Minnesota	minne-sota	cloudy water
Texas	tiesha	friend

⚐ PLAINS SIGN LANGUAGE

Native American— stroke hand twice

Cheyenne—chop at left index finger

Comanche—imitate motion of snake

Crow—hold fist to forehead, palm down

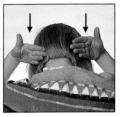
Osage—move hands down back of head

Pawnee—make V sign and extend hand

Nez Perce—move finger under nose

Sioux—drag hand across neck

alone—move right hand to the right

buffalo

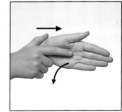
cannot—move finger along palm and down

horse

bad—make fist, then open downward

moon

opposite

Caught the Enemy

Eagle Horse

He Dog

Kills by the Camp

Spotted Face

Stabber

△ *Native American names were meaningful. People were often named after an animal or a special event in their lives (see page 236). These* **pictographs** *of names were used as signatures by the Sioux.*

SMOKE SIGNALS were sent by hunters and warriors in the flat, open Plains country, on clear days when no wind blew. By flapping a blanket across the column of smoke from a fire, they made combinations of long and short puffs to tell of the presence of buffalo or the approach of enemies. The system was far from reliable.

▷ *A Sioux girl and a Nez Perce boy would have been able to speak to one another using sign language.*

◁ *In the early nineteenth century, Sequoya developed a writing system for the Cherokee language. His alphabet contained 85 characters, and each one represented a syllable, or unit, from which a word is made ("syl-la-ble" has three units).*

LANGUAGE WAS SPOKEN, not written. For centuries, Native Americans passed down many stories and traditions by word of mouth. Since they did not put their thoughts on paper, they developed fantastic memories and were good at telling stories and making speeches. They used their spoken languages in beautiful, moving ways.

THE MAIN REASON that we know today about the rich spoken tradition of the Native Americans is because of the powerful speeches that were made by their chiefs and leaders in **post-contact** times. Many speeches were about their sadness at losing their lands and at the white people's wasteful ways with nature.

CHIEF SEATTLE made a speech when the city of Seattle was founded on the lands of the Duwamish in 1855. He said: *'There was a time when our people covered the whole land as the waves of the wind-ruffled sea cover its shell-paved floor... Every hillside, every valley, every plain and grove has been hallowed by some sad or happy event in days long vanished. Even the rocks, which seem to be dumb and dead as they swelter in the sun along the silent shore, thrill with memories of events connected with the lives of my people, and the very dust upon which you now stand... is rich with the blood of our ancestors.'*

SEQUOYA'S CHEROKEE ALPHABET was the only written form of Native American language. Sequoyah (1760–1843) dreamed of giving his people the power of the written word that the Europeans used so well. It was a great success. Every Cherokee man, woman, and child saw how useful reading and writing could be. They began producing their own newspapers, both in Cherokee and in English.

Pictographs were often painted on hide or carved into wood and then colored. Some Northeastern people used this technique to make calendar sticks.

PICTOGRAPHS AND IDEOGRAMS were used in **precontact** times to leave messages and records of historical facts. Pictographs were simple drawings used to represent people, animals, objects, or events that had taken place. Ideograms were symbols that stood for abstract ideas, such as love, longing, hatred, or sadness.

WINTER COUNTS recorded the passing years by focusing on particularly important events that everybody in the group remembered. These might include an outbreak of illness or the sighting of a spectacular comet. Plains peoples painted their winter counts on buffalo hides.

MAKE YOUR OWN WINTER COUNT

You will need: paints, paintbrush, pencil, plain fabric (about 24 x 24 in.)

1 Cut the fabric to the shape of a buffalo hide, as shown. Paint it off-white, to look like hide.

2 Make up your own symbols to remind you of important events. Choose one for each week to sum up the main event of that week, such as playing a sport, getting measles, or having a birthday.

3 Paint your symbols on the canvas, starting at the center of a spiral as shown.

Pictographs used by the Dakota Sioux:

smallpox epidemic

shower of meteors

village attacked and inhabitants killed

peace with a rival nation

successful horse raid

new settlement

Religion

The unseen spirit world was very real to Native Americans. They believed that the natural world and the spirit world were joined together on Earth. Everything in their lives—the rising of the sun in the morning, people's success at hunting, and the health of their children—was controlled by major and minor gods and spirits. They recognized the power of these spirits in everything they did and said.

THREE WORLDS made up the universe, according to Southeastern nations. They believed that an Upper World, a Lower World, and This World were separate but linked. This World, in which humans, plants, and most animals lived, was a round island resting on water. It hung from the sky on four cords attached at the north, south, west, and east. The Upper World was pure, perfect, and predictable; the Lower World was full of chaos and change. This World was balanced between the two. Spirits moved freely between the Worlds, and people had the privilege of helping the spirits keep the Worlds in balance.

MAKE A SPIRIT MASK

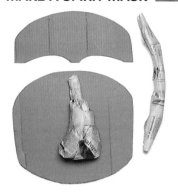

You will need: cardboard, masking tape, newspapers, papier-mâché, paint, raffia, elastic, glue, hook-and-loop fasteners

1 Cut basic shapes for the mask and forehead from cardboard. Tape on a paper nose and eyebrows.

2 Tape the forehead to the mask, using crumpled paper to fill it and build the forehead out. Make eye sockets from rings of folded paper. Cut cardboard ears and tape into place.

3 Paste strips of paper over the shapes. Allow to dry.

4 Paint the mask white, then add your design in color. Glue on raffia for the hair.

5 Use cardboard, crumpled paper, and papier-mâché to build different mouth shapes. Attach them to the basic mask with fasteners.

The Kwakiutl made masks of the spirit Echo with a different mouth for each creature they believed he could imitate.

basic mask

the spirit of Echo himself

an eagle or a raven

a bear

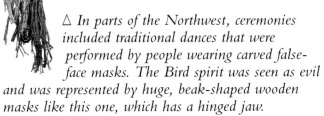

△ *In parts of the Northwest, ceremonies included traditional dances that were performed by people wearing carved false-face masks. The Bird spirit was seen as evil and was represented by huge, beak-shaped wooden masks like this one, which has a hinged jaw.*

STORIES OF HOW THE WORLD BEGAN were told by most Native Americans. Pueblos believed creation was the work of the Spider Grandmother. Some Northwestern nations believed it was the Raven, while others believed that the world was made by a number of assorted spirits. Their neighbors in the Plateau region saw the world as a clever joke played by their Coyote god. Southeastern people gave the credit to the Master of Breath who lived on high.

VISION QUESTS were an attempt to get personal power from the spirits, instead of relying on the medicine men and women, or **shaman**. Young people went off alone, fasting, sometimes hurting themselves on purpose, and keeping awake until they saw visions. The visions gave them a key to getting the spirits' help for the rest of their lives.

⚖ **BLACK ELK** said this about his visions: *'I saw more than I can tell, and I understood more than I saw; for I was seeing in a sacred manner the shapes of all things in the spirit.'*

▦ **FALSE-FACE MASKS** were made by medicine men and women for the Iroquois. They believed that illness was caused by unkind spirits with horrible faces and no bodies who lived in the forest spreading sickness. The cure was to confuse the spirits, so they cut mask shapes from living trees and gave them gruesome faces. Then the shaman danced while wearing the masks until the bewildered spirits left the area.

RITES OF PASSAGE are **rituals** that mark the important stages in a person's life. For example, many people mark the birth of a child with a naming ceremony, a marriage with a wedding ceremony, and a death with a funeral. For most early civilizations, the most important ceremony of all was the celebration of puberty, which is the time when a child becomes an adult. For Native Americans, this meant that young people no longer needed to be protected and could contribute fully to their group.

◮ A BABY WAS NAMED a few days after it was born. A respected warrior would be paid, usually in horses, to name the baby. The child's given name often reflected some glorious action in the warrior's past, but it would be changed when the child made a mark for itself and earned its own name.

△ *The Southwestern Hopi wore **kachina** masks when they performed certain festive dances.*

MAKE A KACHINA DOLL

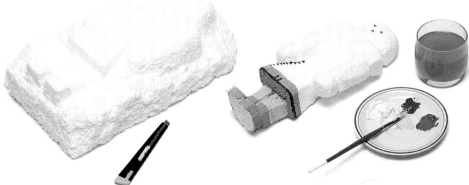

You will need: polystyrene foam (12 x 3 x 1 in.), acrylic paints, yarn, fine sandpaper, craft knife, raffia

1 Draw an outline on the foam.

2 Carve out the shape carefully with a craft knife, as shown. When the basic shape is cut, use sandpaper to smooth and round off the edges.

3 Paint a face and clothes on your doll, and add your own designs. Decorate waist and wrists with raffia and colored yarn.

BECOMING AN ADULT was tough. Boys as young as 10 would have to prove that they were made of strong stuff. Yuma boys had to run 10 to 15 miles a day for four days, with no sleep or food. Girls had to lie still, face down, on a bed of warm sand for four days while friends and relatives made long speeches.

MARRIAGE was mostly a free choice. In the Pueblo nation, the bridegroom moved in with his wife's family, but he could be sent home to his own family if things did not work out. Husbands and wives were expected to be faithful while their marriages lasted. A bridegroom was expected to weave his bride's wedding clothes.

Tawa, who was associated with the sun

Sio Calako, a giant spirit

Eototo, chief of the kachinas

⚟ **THE KACHINAS** brought help from the spirits, who were everywhere and in everything, controlling every part of Pueblo life. The spirit world and the real world could not be separated. People wore kachina masks in their ceremonies, to represent the spirits. Children were given kachina dolls to help them understand the spirit world and identify kachinas.

AT THE END of their lives, Native Americans generally accepted death with little fuss, however it came. As it drew near, people sang their personal death song, which they had rehearsed throughout their lives. The dead were usually cremated or buried in simple, shallow graves or on scaffolds, so they eventually blended back into the earth. Most people believed in a happy afterlife, in a place where the sun shone, crops ripened, and hunting grounds teemed with animals.

SMOKING THE PIPE OF PRAYER was one of the most important rites. People smoked a mixture of tobacco and sweet-smelling herbs in a ceremonial pipe. They believed that the smoke was the very breath of prayer, and the pipe itself was seen as a sacred pathway to the spirit world.

Natural Science

Native Americans respected nature and so did not take from it without giving something back. The many nations hunted and fished carefully so as not to upset nature's balance. They cut down few live trees, and they took only what they needed to survive.

NATIVE AMERICANS UNDERSTOOD NATURE and had a special relationship with it. They watched the seasons come and go. People observed the movements of the stars and planets, the life cycles of plants and trees, and the habits and breeding seasons of the animals they hunted. They believed that these things happened as a result of the work of the spirit world.

🔺 MAKE A SAND PAINTING

You will need: sand (fine sand is easier to use than builder's sand), water-based powder paints in a variety of colors, bowl, stirring stick, thick cardboard, pencil, craft knife, glue

1 Mix paint and a little water into a thick paste in the bowl. Add a handful of sand and stir.

2 Spoon the mixture onto a piece of cardboard and leave in a warm place until completely dry. Repeat for all colors.

3 Make a sand painting tray. Measure and cut the cardboard (10 x 15 in. base). Make the side pieces by cutting three identical strips of cardboard and gluing them together.

4 Work out the space between the base and surround by measuring the thickness of the sides. Wedge each side into place.

5 Fill your tray with uncolored sand, about a quarter of an inch deep. Taking a pinch of one of your colored sands, trickle it carefully onto the base.

HEALING THE SICK was one of the main tasks of the shaman, or medicine man or woman. Healing was done with herbs and with a lot of ritual, which in itself can often help a sick person to feel better. The Native Americans discovered the healing properties of many plants, including willow bark, which contains salicylic acid, the main ingredient of today's aspirin.

◁ *The Navajo used sand paintings as their main way of treating sick people.*

A CHEROKEE STORY told that people upset the spirits of the animals because they killed them for food and crowded them out of their habitats. The animals took their revenge on humans by creating disease and sickness. But the spirits of the plants, who were people's friends, decided to help out. Each single plant, from the tallest trees down to the tiniest creeping mosses, agreed to produce a remedy that would fight and cure one of the diseases.

6 Gradually build up the different colors in your design. It is important to plan the design and colors before you begin. The design shown here is based on a Navajo sand painting used to cure a sick baby. It would have been painted on the hogan floor spread with a smooth layer of uncolored sand.

SAND PAINTINGS were made by medicine men or women. A sick person sat on the ground while a colored sand picture was created around them. After the ceremony, when the shaman had prayed and chanted, people took a pinch of the colored sand. This young woman is making a sand painting similar to the original sacred ones.

Looking Back

Finding out how people lived in the past needs careful detective work, especially when they left no written records of their lives.

THE FIRST STEP is to gather evidence. To investigate Native American life, we can listen to the stories and memories of their descendants, passed down from generation to generation. We can take account of travelers' tales from the earliest European explorers, who wrote about and drew what they saw. We can also look at the findings of archaeologists, who study the objects that people have left behind, and of anthropologists, who study how people lived their daily lives.

THE SECOND STEP is to use the evidence we have found to draw conclusions about how Native Americans lived many hundreds of years ago. This task may be complicated by the fact that different experts sometimes reach different conclusions. Their pictures of the past do not always match up, and every generation looks at history from a slightly different angle. The past is always much more complicated than we think.

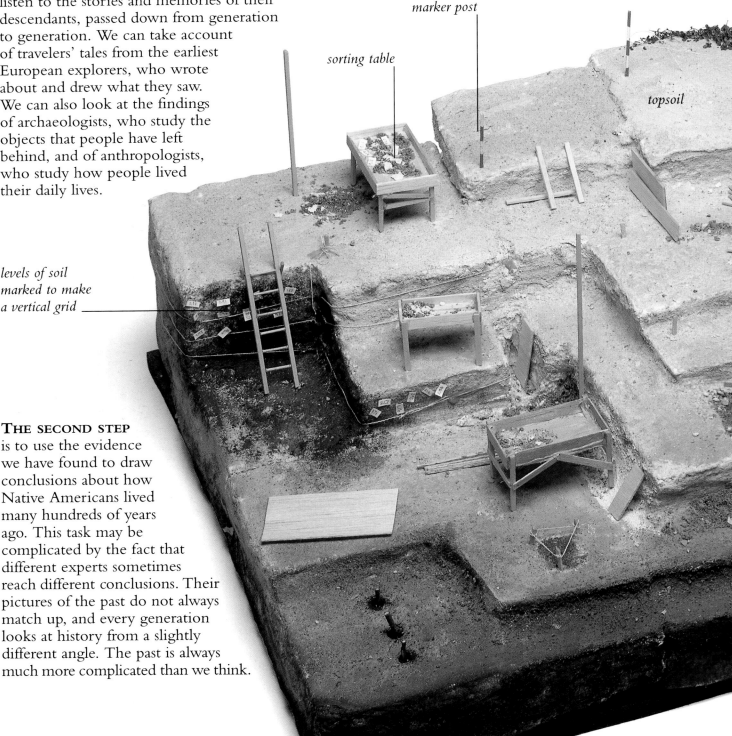

▽ *This model is based on the archaeological dig at the Koster site in western Illinois. The site is named after the farmers on whose land the first finds were made in 1969. Since then, experts have dug through evidence of 15 settlements. The oldest, at about 3 feet below the present level, dates from 9,000 years ago.*

marker post

sorting table

topsoil

levels of soil marked to make a vertical grid

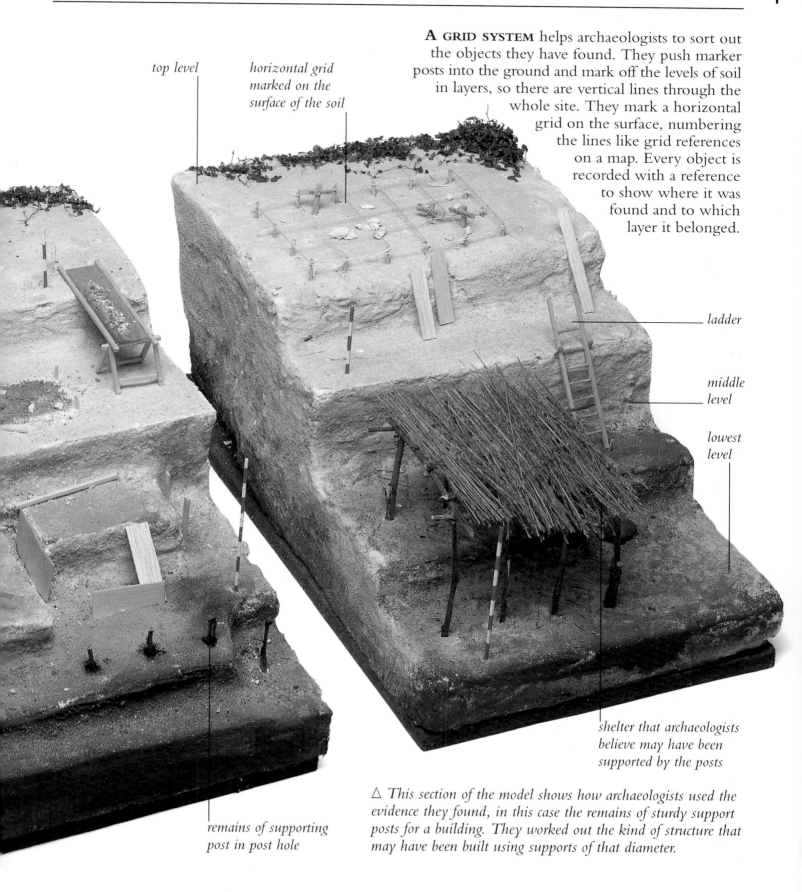

A GRID SYSTEM helps archaeologists to sort out the objects they have found. They push marker posts into the ground and mark off the levels of soil in layers, so there are vertical lines through the whole site. They mark a horizontal grid on the surface, numbering the lines like grid references on a map. Every object is recorded with a reference to show where it was found and to which layer it belonged.

top level

horizontal grid marked on the surface of the soil

ladder

middle level

lowest level

shelter that archaeologists believe may have been supported by the posts

remains of supporting post in post hole

△ This section of the model shows how archaeologists used the evidence they found, in this case the remains of sturdy support posts for a building. They worked out the kind of structure that may have been built using supports of that diameter.

Post-contact Times

Native American history spans about 15,000 years. During this time a number of different cultures have come and gone. But the greatest upheaval that Native Americans have ever faced was the coming of the Europeans, starting with Christopher Columbus in 1492. The Spanish, the Dutch, the French, and the English arrived in waves. They landed in the East and gradually pushed the Native Americans farther and farther west. These new settlers came with guns and they believed the rich, fertile land was theirs for the taking, so they took it.

△ *Chief Red Horse, of the Sioux, drew a series of pictographs representing the Battle of Little Bighorn. This pictograph shows the climax of the battle.*

THE NATIONAL POLICY STATEMENT made by the American government toward Native Americans in 1787 was full of promises that were soon broken. It said:
'The utmost good faith shall always be observed toward the Indians; their lands and property shall never be taken from them without their consent.'

THE NEW SETTLERS, whose ancestors had arrived from Europe, took territorial control from the Native Americans in the East and gradually acquired land in the West. Between 1776 and 1854, the Native Americans were forced back until all their land was lost. By 1912, 48 of the United States had been formed.

◁ *This map shows the stages by which the new settlers took territory over from the Native Americans. Each shaded area shows the land that had been acquired by the date shown.*

△ *Custer hoped to improve his reputation with a victory over the Sioux. His troops, however, were defeated, and the General was killed.*

GEORGE CUSTER was an American General who led his troops into many battles with the Plains peoples over their land and traditional hunting grounds. He grew to respect Native Americans. In 1874, General Custer published a book about his life called *My Life on the Plains*. In it he wrote: *'When the soil which he has claimed and hunted over for so long a time is demanded by this... insatiable monster (modern civilization) there is no appeal; he must yield, or it will roll mercilessly over him, destroying as it advances. Destiny seems to have so willed it, and the world nods its approval.'*

TWO YEARS LATER, in 1876, General Custer and one third of his cavalry regiment were killed in the Battle of Little Bighorn. The soldiers fought against the Sioux nation under its chief, Crazy Horse. This was the Native Americans' greatest victory against the advancing enemies, but in the end it changed nothing.

▷ *The Zuni still produce intricate jewelry from precious stones and silver. This picture was taken in the Southwest in 1970.*

THE LAST OF THE NATIVE AMERICAN WARS was at Wounded Knee in South Dakota in March 1890, when American troops opened fire on a band of Sioux men, women, and children, killing 200 of them. In reality, more Native Americans died of diseases brought by the Europeans, against which they had no defense, than in the wars. In 1890, the last of the Native Americans were driven onto reservations, where land was set aside for their use, but was run by the American government.

TODAY MOST NATIVE AMERICANS live on reservations in the central and western parts of the United States and Canada. At first, reservation life was a nightmare, with traditions and religions banned and children sent away to school to learn European ways. But Native Americans are now much more in control of their own lives. They hand on knowledge of their rich and varied traditions, and reach out to everyone with their unique record of achievements as a nation. Their understanding of the environment and nature's delicate balance is of great importance to people all over the world today.

Glossary

afterlife The ancient Egyptians believed that after death they would live on in a perfect world, if they traveled safely through the Underworld.

Ainu A group of people who once lived in northern Honshu and who now live in Hokkaido. They have a different appearance and culture from other Japanese people.

Algonquian nations A group of Northeastern nations who spoke the Algonquian language. There were about 50 different versions of this language.

amphitheater An oval-shaped Roman building without a roof. It was used for public shows, such as fights between gladiators and wild animals.

amphora A tall pottery vase with two handles used for transporting and storing wine, olive oil, vinegar, and fish sauce.

amulet A piece of jewelry worn as a magical charm to protect the wearer against evil or illness.

anatomy The study of the way the parts of the body fit together.

anthropologist A person who studies the origins, development, and behavior of people.

anthropology The study of the culture, language, origins, and behavior of people.

aqueduct An artificial channel, made of stone and concrete, used for carrying water from one area to another.

archaeologist A person who searches for and studies the remains of buildings and artifacts from the past.

archaeology The study of the remains of buildings and artifacts left behind by people who lived in the past.

artifact An object made by people.

atrium The entrance hall of a Roman house.

augur A Roman religious official whose job was to find out whether the gods approved or disapproved of a course of action. The augur did this by watching the flight and behavior of birds. Many important decisions were made after consulting the sacred flock of chickens.

auxiliary Soldiers drawn from the noncitizen population of the Roman Empire. They were paid less than citizen soldiers. On retirement, they could become Roman citizens.

Bakufu The Japanese government set up by the samurai in the times when they had political control.

barbarian A word used by the Greeks and Romans to describe foreigners.

barter A system of trade where goods are exchanged instead of using money.

bola A rope with weights such as stones attached to it. A bola was a Native American hunting weapon whirled around to knock birds from the sky or thrown to bring down prey by entangling its legs.

Book of the Dead An Egyptian scroll made from papyrus reeds that was buried with the dead. It contained instructions that would ensure a safe passage through the Underworld.

bow drill A drill made from a flint or metal-tipped stick. A bow string is wrapped around the stick and pulled back and forth. This makes the stick turn, so that the sharp end drills.

buckskin Animal hide scraped and softened until it looks and feels like the soft, supple skin of a male deer.

Buddhism A religion based on the teachings of Buddha (Gautama Siddhartha) in India in the 500's B.C. Buddhists believe that they can reach a perfect state called enlightenment through meditation.

Bunraku A form of Japanese theater using puppets that are about half the size of a person.

calligraphy The art of fine handwriting. The characters are written from top to bottom and from right to left across Japanese paper. This paper was often made by hand.

canoe A thin, lightweight open boat with pointed ends and no keel. Canoes are pushed through the water by paddles.

canopic jars When an Egyptian body was embalmed, the internal organs were removed and stored in these to protect them from spells.

cartouche A royal name written in Egyptian hieroglyphs and surrounded by an oval border.

centurion A middle-ranking Roman officer in charge of a "century" of soldiers (80).

ceramics Objects made from pottery or porcelain. Japan is famous for its ceramic ware, such as *raku*, and some pieces are considered national treasures.

chickee A dwelling on stilts with no walls.

Chi-Rho (pronounced Ky-roh) A sign used by early Christians to show their faith. It combines the Greek letters X (Chi) and P (Rho), the first two letters of the word Christ.

chronicle A record of events, described in the order in which they happened.

circus An oval track for chariot races. The most famous was the Circus Maximus in Rome.

citizen A citizen of the Roman Empire was a full member of the Roman state.

civilization A developed and organized group of people or nation. The Romans believed that civilization was marked by town life, laws, reading and writing, and religious ceremonies.

clan A large family group or group of related families. For hundreds of years, Japan suffered from a series of clan wars, until single rule was imposed in 1603.

class structure The way in which people in some societies are ranked according to certain attributes, such as wealth or ability.

client A person who owed loyalty to a wealthier Roman, who was his or her patron.

cloisonné A type of decoration made by filling an outline of metal with colored enamel or with glass.

Confucianism A system of belief founded by Confucius (K'ung-fu-tzu) in China in the 400's B.C. Confucianism encompasses a range of rules of behavior. These include putting loyalty to one's country and lord above one's family and obeying authority without question.

consul The most important Roman government official. Two consuls were elected each year.

Coptic Church The Christian Church of Egypt, established in the fourth century A.D.

counting coup (say coo) A Native American way of judging a warrior's bravery. The warrior had to come face to face with the enemy and touch him or her with a coup stick. A coup is a sudden act or attack.

crook A hooked staff which looks very similar to that used by a shepherd. It was one of the pharaoh's symbols of office (along with the flail and scepter), and it represented kingship.

culture The activities, ideas, and beliefs of a group of people that form the basis of their shared way of life.

daimyo A powerful Japanese landowner who was also sometimes a military leader.

delta A place at the mouth of a river where the river splits into smaller channels, forming a triangular shape.

demotic A form of ancient Egyptian writing which replaced hieratic script around the seventh century B.C.

early imperial period The period of Roman history from 27 B.C. to A.D. 284. For most of this time, the Empire was ruled by the emperor.

Edo period The period of Japanese history from 1600 to 1868, named after the city of Edo (Tokyo). It is also called the Tokugawa period.

embalming Treating a dead body using spices and ointments to preserve it as a mummy.

emperor The ruler of the Roman Empire. The rule of the emperors was known as imperial rule.

enlightenment A perfect mental and physical state that Buddhists try to reach by meditating.

equestrian A member of a class of wealthy Roman citizens. Each equestrian owned a personal fortune of at least 400,000 sestertii.

Etruscans The people who lived in northwest Italy in ancient times. The Etruscans were an important influence on the Romans.

faience A glasslike substance made by heating powdered quartz or sand. The ancient Egyptians used faience to make colorful jewelry.

fasces A bundle of rods, tied around an ax. An Etruscan symbol of power, adopted by the Romans.

flail A tool used for threshing grain, which was one of the pharaoh's symbols of office. The flail represented the fertility of ancient Egypt.

flax A plant that is used to make linen cloth.

forum The central marketplace and public meeting area in every Roman town.

freedmen and freedwomen Roman slaves who bought or were given their freedom. However, they did not have as many rights as free-born citizens.

fresco A type of wall painting in which paint is applied to damp plaster.

geisha A Japanese woman trained to entertain, mostly wealthy businessmen and officials, through music, dance, and witty conversation.

general election An occasion when the people of a country can vote to be represented in the government. They can choose from a selection of candidates from several different political parties.

geometry The branch of mathematics that deals with lines, angles, curves, and spaces. It is an important part of architecture.

gladiator A Roman man or woman who fought in the arena against another gladiator or an animal. Gladiators were mostly slaves, although those that were successful were able to buy their freedom.

Go A Japanese game involving a board marked with a grid and two sets of counters. The object is to cover more space on the board with your counters than your opponent does.

groma A tool used by Roman surveyors to plot straight lines, right-angles, and grids.

hanko A Japanese cylindrical seal with a character carved at one end that is dipped in ink and used to "sign" documents.

haruspice A religious official whose job was to predict the future or to find out the wishes of the gods. He did this by inspecting the inner organs of sacrificed animals. He also interpreted lightning and unusual events in nature, such as earthquakes.

Heian period The period of Japanese history from 790 to 1185, named after the city of Heian, which the Emperor Kammu made his capital.

henna A reddish hair dye made from a plant that was thought to ward off danger.

hieratic A simple form of hieroglyphs used for everyday business, letters, and stories.

hieroglyphs An early Egyptian form of writing which uses picture symbols to represent objects, ideas, and sounds. In ancient Egyptian writing there were about 700 symbols, mainly used for religious inscriptions and monuments.

historian A person who studies and writes about history.

hogan A hexagonal or octagonal Navajo house made from a log framework plastered with mud.

Ice Age Throughout history there have been a number of Ice Ages, when the world's climate became very cold and parts of Northern Europe, Asia, and America were completely covered in ice. The last Ice Age, which was fairly mild, lasted about 40,000 years and ended about 11,000 years ago.

ideogram A written sign that represents an idea such as love or hate.

igloo A dome-shaped house built from blocks of hard snow or ice.

ikebana The art of flower arranging. It was originally part of Buddhist and Shinto rituals.

insula A block of housing in a Roman town.

Iroquois nations A group of Northeastern Native American nations who spoke the Iroquois language. These groups were known in post-contact times as the Five Nations.

irrigation Supplying land with water so that crops can grow.

Isis An important Egyptian goddess worshiped by some Romans. She was seen by her followers as the queen of the whole universe. Isis also had specific roles as a goddess of wheat and barley, childbirth, and seafarers.

judo A Japanese martial art in which the contestants try to throw or wrestle each other to the ground.

Kabuki A form of Japanese theater in which actors in elaborate costumes and makeup perform using dramatic gestures.

kachina Native American spirits of nature represented by a religious or ceremonial mask or by a doll-like figure.

Kamakura period The period of Japanese history from 1185 to 1333. It is named after the place in eastern Japan where the shogun Yoritomo established his military government.

kami Spirits worshiped in the Shinto religion. Kami can live in objects, animals, and people.

karate A martial art that involves fighting with the fists and feet.

ken A measurement used in house building. One *ken* is about six feet.

kendo A Japanese martial art in which opponents fight using bamboo staffs. Kendo developed from sword fighting and means "way of the sword."

kiln An oven used for baking or "firing" pottery to make it hard and waterproof.

kimono A loose-fitting garment tied with a sash that is traditionally worn by Japanese men and women.

kohl A black powder made from lead ore (known as galena) which was used as makeup for the eyes.

lacquer A natural varnish from the lacquer tree used to harden and decorate objects.

lacrosse A team sport that originated among Native Americans. It was played using sticks with rawhide nets at the end, and a ball made from hair and hide.

late imperial period The period of Roman history from A.D. 284 to 476. For most of this period, the Roman Empire was divided into two halves. It also became a Christian empire during this period.

Latin The language spoken by the Romans and the other peoples of Latium, an area in central Italy. The ancient people of Latium were called "Latins."

legionary A Roman citizen who served as an infantry soldier in a legion.

livelihood The way in which a person or group supports itself.

loom A machine used for weaving.

magistrate An elected official who governed the Roman state. Under the Republic, the most powerful were the two consuls. There were also the praetors, who were in charge of justice, and the quaestors, who looked after state money.

martial arts Various kinds of armed and unarmed combat that developed in the East. Japanese forms, such as judo, karate, kendo, and sumo, developed from the fighting skills of the samurai warriors.

meditation Spending time thinking deeply and trying not to be influenced by things around you.

Mithras A god of light, worshiped in secret by people, especially soldiers, throughout the Roman Empire.

moccasins Native American shoes or boots made out of animal hide.

mosaic A picture made from hundreds of tiny pieces of pottery, stone, or glass tiles inlaid in cement.

mummy The dead body of a person or animal which has been preserved by embalming.

Muromachi and Momoyama period The period of Japanese history from 1392 to 1600. During this time, there were many wars between the different daimyo. Eventually, Japan was brought together under one ruler, Toyotomi Hideyoshi, in 1582.

natron A type of salt used by Egyptians to dry out bodies before they were embalmed.

necropolis An Egyptian cemetery or burial ground, often near a large city. Anubis was the Egyptian god of the necropolis, as well as the god of embalming and of death.

New World The New World was made up of the continents of the western hemisphere, that is North and South America, the nearby islands, and Australia. It was known as "New" because these were the last parts of the world to be discovered by European explorers.

Noh A form of Japanese theater that uses dance, mime, and masks.

nomadic A nomadic life is one which is spent wandering, with no fixed home.

obelisk A tall stone pillar with four flat sides and a pyramid-shaped top used as a monument.

ochre A red, powdery form of iron oxide that the ancient Egyptians mixed with fat and used as makeup for lips and cheeks.

Old World The continents of the eastern hemisphere: Europe, Asia, and Africa. These were the parts of the world from which explorers set sail on voyages of discovery to areas that they called the New World (see separate entry).

origami The Japanese art of folding paper into interesting or beautiful shapes.

page A boy who becomes a member of a household in order to serve the master and to receive training in return.

papyrus A tall reedlike plant which grew along the banks of the Nile. The ancient Egyptians used it to make a form of paper, as well as sandals, baskets, ropes and even boats.

pater familias The father and head of an ancient Roman family.

pharaoh A king of ancient Egypt. The word "pharaoh" means "great house."

pictograph A sign that is written down to represent a person or an object.

political To do with the government of a country and its policy-making.

post-contact The time in Native American history after they had come face to face with explorers and settlers from Europe, Asia, and Africa.

potlatch A Northwestern Native American ceremonial feast, during which many gifts are given to the guests to demonstrate the host's wealth and generosity.

precontact The long period of time before Native Americans had any contact with people from other continents.

province A large area of the Roman Empire ruled by its own governor.

provincial A native of one of the provinces of the Roman Empire. Provincials had fewer rights than citizens, but were much better off than slaves.

pueblo A village of terraced mud houses.

pyramid A large Egyptian burial tomb with four sloping triangular sides which was built for a pharaoh.

rasp A tool with a rough surface used to scrape and file.

rawhide Stiff animal hide that has been cleaned but is untreated.

ritual A ceremonial way of doing something, such as celebrating an important event.

roach A stiff tuft of animal hair tied on top of the head, worn for decoration.

Roman Empire The different lands and peoples ruled by the Romans. "The Empire" also means the period when Rome was ruled by emperors, rather than by elected officials.

Roman Republic A period when Rome and the Empire were ruled by elected officials.

sake A type of Japanese wine made from rice.

samurai A Japanese warrior whose duty was to serve his lord, or daimyo. The samurai were the highest–ranking people in society.

sarcophagus A stone box containing a coffin.

scarab A magic symbol in the shape of a dung beetle. It was one of the most powerful symbols because it represented the sun and rebirth.

scribe A person who wrote and read for a living. Scribes often traveled around on behalf of the government, recording information on the progress of building projects and the harvest.

senator A member of the senate, a council of leading nobles who advised the consuls and the emperor. In the Empire, senators commanded the armies and governed provinces. To be a senator, you had to be elected as a member of the magistrates, and have a huge personal fortune of at least a million sestertii.

senet An ancient Egyptian board game.

shaduf A device used for raising water from a channel in order to irrigate the land.

shaman A Native American man or woman who was believed to have a close relationship with the spirit world. Native Americans believed shaman could explain the workings of the gods to them and make their prayers heard.

shamisen A lutelike instrument that arrived in Japan in the 1500's. It is used in Bunraku and Kabuki theater.

Shinto A Japanese religion based on the worship of nature and the spirits of ancestors.

shogun A military ruler of Japan. From the 1100's until 1868, shoguns had more power over the country than the emperor.

shogunate The government established by the shogun of Old Japan.

shrine A place where holy objects, such as statues of gods, were placed and worshiped. Many Romans had shrines in their homes.

silt Sand, clay, or other soil that is left behind by flowing water.

society People living together in an ordered and organized community.

soy sauce A sauce made from fermented soybeans and used to season food.

standard bearer Someone who carries a pole with a flag or placard on the top. Standards were used in Roman religious processions, and as rallying points for soldiers in battle.

Stone Age The period when people used stone tools and weapons. It was during this time, in about 5000 B.C., that the first settlers arrived in the Nile Valley of Egypt.

strigil A curved metal tool used at the Roman baths for scraping oil and dirt off skin.

stylus A penlike instrument used for writing on wax tablets.

sumo A type of wrestling that originated as a harvest thanksgiving ritual in the Shinto religion. Sumo is the oldest sport in Japan.

sushi A Japanese dish made from raw fish, vegetables, and vinegared rice.

symbol A visible sign that represents an invisible idea. For example, the cross is a symbol of Christianity; a lionskin headdress is a Native American symbol of bravery.

tablinum A Roman reception room.

tack Equipment, such as bridles and saddles, used for riding horses.

tepee A portable, cone-shaped dwelling of animal skin or bark set over a wooden framework.

terrain The physical characteristics of an area, such as its mountains, rivers, and vegetation.

tofu A type of food made from soybean milk that sets into a curd.

toga A single woolen sheet worn wrapped around the body by male Roman citizens.

tomahawk A Native American war club with a rounded end. The word was later used to describe war axes, introduced by Europeans.

totem pole A Native American post that was carved from wood and painted with symbols (usually animals) to represent family members and ancestors.

travois A Native American trailing sled, pulled along by dogs or, later, by horses and used for carrying possessions and people.

triclinium A Roman dining room with three couches in an open square for guests to lie upon.

Underworld A dangerous land that the Egyptians believed they would have to pass through after death, before they reached the land where they would spend the afterlife.

vinegared rice A sweet, sticky rice used in making sushi. To make it, rice vinegar, sugar, and salt are mixed with warm cooked rice.

wampum Small, white, cylindrical beads made from polished shells and used by Native Americans as money or expensive jewelry.

wickiup A cone-shaped Native American house made from grasses and rushes over a wooden frame.

wigwam A dome- or cone-shaped Native American home made from wooden poles covered with reed or bark mats.

Zen Buddhism A form of Buddhism involving meditation and self-examination that came to Japan in the Kamakura period. Zen Buddhism is passed directly from teacher to pupil, rather than relying on religious writings.

Index